Lorraine,

Hope yo~

Carol

Vision Narratives
of Women in Prison

Vision Narratives
of Women in Prison

Carol Burke

The University of Tennessee Press
KNOXVILLE

The paper in this book meets the minimum requirements
of the American National Standard for Permanence
of Paper for Printed Library Materials.
∞
The binding materials have been chosen for strength
and durability.

Library of Congress Cataloging in Publication Data

Burke, Carol.
    Vision narratives of women in prison / Carol Burke. — 1st ed.
        p.   cm.
    Includes bibliographical references and index.
    ISBN 0-87049-727-8 (cloth: alk. paper)
    1. Women prisoners — United States — Social life and customs.
2. Women prisoners — United States — Folklore.   I. Title.
HV9466.B85   1992
365'.43'092273 — dc20   91-3516   CIP

For Grace Burke and for
Kate and Elizabeth Christensen

Contents

Acknowledgments   ix

Preface   xi

1. **From Home to Prison:**
   A Personal Narrative   1

2. **Women in Prison**   12

3. **Signs**   29
   Second Sightings   31
   Messages from Home   35
   Premonitions   41

4. **Return of the Dead**   47
   Revenants   47
   Oppressive Forces   54
   Prison Ghosts   63

5. **Gods and Demons**   68
   Visions of Heaven and Hell   76
   Divine Cures   82
   Angel Helpers   87

6. **Gifted Women**   92
   Luscious   93
   Wilma Bond   103
   Violet Star   110
   Verna Brown   119

7. **Visions in the Context of Life Stories**   130
   Betty Jones   131
   Eraina Roberts   141

Afterword   157

Appendix 1
Criminological Debate
on the Subject of Women in Prison   161

Appendix 2
Narratives   165

Glossary   177

Notes   179

Bibliography   185

Index   191

Acknowledgments

I wish to thank the women who generously shared their stories with me, and the prison staff members who worked around the many institutional rules to make our interviews possible, especially Sharon Johnson and Barbara Scanlon in Maryland and Gary Scott in Indiana. I first wrote on women in prison as a graduate student at the University of Maryland, with Gladys Fry. Bruce Jackson's constructive comments helped transform a fledgling manuscript into a book. I am also grateful to the Mellon Foundation for its support while I completed revisions. My greatest debt is to Jerome Christensen.

Preface

Male inmates in the state and federal prisons of the United States have, we know, countered the repressive measures taken to separate and silence them by means of ingenious methods of communication: by exchanging confidences through cell heating ducts, inventing coded languages, and sending illegal notes across the prison yard through a chain of prison messengers. They have fashioned an underground solidarity by recollecting, inventing, and transmitting rebellious stories, ribald songs, and subversive jokes. The studies conducted in male prisons by Inez Cardoza-Freeman, John Coggeshall, and Bruce Jackson recover and analyze this proscribed communication in all its intricacy and exuberance.

The experience of women in prison is a different one. It cannot be inferred either as mere supplement or simple inversion of the male accounts. As the experience differs, so does the lore with which these imprisoned women make sense of their experience. Yet because the penal machine has historically been more successful in silencing women than men, the stories that women have to tell are more difficult to retrieve. They are audible, nonetheless, whispering through the silence that immures them. Women prisoners exchange narratives of supernatural and supernormal experiences privately one to the other. In helpless solitude they rehearse these narratives over and over to themselves, invoking powers, dread and benign, that temporarily eclipse the power the state exerts over their lives.

This book is a collection of visionary accounts of women in prison, which aims to give voice to a group of radically disenfranchised and marginalized women. The discussion accompanying these narratives makes no claim to sociological representativeness nor theoretical generality. It is an obstetric vehicle for the delivery of these personal narratives from carceral darkness into the bright world of public discourse, so as to disclose their oblique but powerful relations with one another and with the penitentiary culture that surrounds them.

These narratives are not at all what I expected to document when I set out on my first interviews of women prisoners ten years ago. Inspired by Bruce Jackson's pioneering work on prison folklore, I began weekly interviews at the Indiana Women's Prison in search of a body of performed "feminine" lore. Although I found women who had brought folk poetry (toasts[1] as well as "raps and rhymes") with them from the street, rarely did I hear of them performing these for other inmates. And most had learned such patterned verse from their fathers, grandfathers, husbands, and boyfriends. To say that the folklore I had intended to collect existed only in fragmentary form in the women's prison is not to say that this closed female community lacked folk material. On the contrary, once I abandoned a prejudice for performed lore in which one entertains the group with jokes, stories, raps, and toasts and looked closely at the personal narrative, I was richly rewarded.

The shift in my expectations roughly corresponds to a change in perspective in folklore studies. In the past, folklorists valued the personal experience narrative as ethnographic context for the more highly rendered formal tales of their informants; in the last twenty years they have increasingly insisted on the integrity of the personal narrative as a rich verbal construction in its own right.[2] More and more folklorists have abandoned a static view of folklore as a collection of frozen artifacts and fixed texts in favor of a dynamic one that admits the rich possibility of innovation and restores the teller to the tale, while at the same time challenging previously held definitions of tradition bearers, performance, and audience. Scholars like William Clements, Richard Dorson, and Gladys Fry have even pointed to the personal narrative as the predecessor of the legend, saga, and joke.

Answering to the challenge of feminist critiques, such folklorists as Linda Dégh, Margaret Brady, Claire Farrer, and Susan Kalcik have shown a new willingness to listen to women and to legitimate the personal narratives they tell. With that legitimation comes a willingness to value lore that may have no previous life in tradition, lore which may be performed only for the collector.[3] Even though the accounts presented here were not performed for the folk community, they are neither unique nor idiosyncratic. Exchanged as secrets between inmates in pairs or small groups, these "private," though not solitary, performances share themes and motifs.

This collection sets its subjects' personal narratives within the prison community which frames (generates and regulates) them. By presenting only narratives collected in two women's prisons (Indiana Women's Prison and the Maryland Correctional Institution for Women) I do not mean to suggest that the visions they describe are only experienced in prison or that they are experiences unique to that subgroup of the population who end up in our state penitentiaries. Many of the narrators represented here recollect visions experienced before incarceration. And since I began this research, a number of women who have never set foot in prison or jail have recounted similar stories to me. What I do maintain, though, is the special importance these visions have to a woman serving time. In an institution built on total surveillance, all activities from bathing to talking with a friend are performed under the eye of authority and subject to institutional regime. Visions and dreams are the only private acts possible for an inmate.

This collection is framed by two personal narratives of my own. In the first (chapter 1), I reflect on my passage from documenting the family folklore of rural Indiana to recording the stories of prison inmates. In the second (the Afterword), I discuss a disturbing return to the Maryland Correctional Institution for Women three years after I had concluded my fieldwork. Chapter 2, the book's more formal introduction, describes the prison and the women who inhabit it as the subjects of my fieldwork. Chapters 3, 4, and 5 outline the types of narratives I collected: those detailing visions that carry with them a message (of what has happened, of what is happening in another place at the moment of the vision, or of what will happen in the future); those involving the return of the dead; and those chronicling the appearance of frightening devils and merciful Christs. Chapter 6 comments on four women who regard themselves and whom other inmates view as spiritually gifted. They experience many visions and interpret the visions of others. Chapter 7 presents the case studies of two women whose lives of impoverishment and catastrophe accommodate visions in fundamental ways.

Vision Narratives
of Women in Prison

1. From Home to Prison: A Personal Narrative

In north central Indiana the fields run on like extended metaphors. Farmers, comfortable in their religion and Ford pickups, gather for coffee and conversation at "the Elevator." These hard-working people are proud of their Germanic past, proud to be 48th in the list of states receiving federal aid, proud of their Mister Basketballs and Miss Golden Girls, proud of Purdue University, where even during the sixties you could send your son and know he'd come back to the farm.

In 1975, fresh out of graduate school, I moved from New York to Indiana with my husband, who had accepted a teaching position at Purdue, and for the next four years I interviewed families who lived on the surrounding farms and in nearby villages. In senior centers, in offices, in livingrooms I gathered reminiscences from men and women who worked this rich black soil.[1] Reclaimed from bogs, this land once supported diverse crops and livestock. Now most of the cattle, the wheat, and the oats are gone; the traveler who passes through on I-65 can see at one time all the variety there is to see — thousands of acres devoted to the efficient, profitable production of soybeans and corn. The weather is still the farmer's most benevolent friend as well as his cruelest foe; but the weather now has formidable rivals for preeminence: the lobbies of Congress, the laboratories of universities, and the exchanges in Chicago and New York. No matter how much they have conserved, no matter how much they own, no farmers in this part of the state can hope any longer to live solely off the land.

In their stories, these farmers recalled a time when they were, of necessity, closer to the land: when the weather was forecast by the signs, when there was no insurance for crops. Residents of Wolcott, Remington, Reynolds, Chalmers, Brookston, and Monon shared with me stories of little money and much work, of school pranks, of chivarees, and of dates on bobsleds.

Nostalgic, they reconstructed a past rich with sentiment and suffering that somehow both justified and diminished their present prosperity. Their narratives celebrated times of scarcity when they'd burned corncobs because they could afford no coal, when they'd saved rather than borrowed, when they'd gathered together in threshing rings of twenty men to do the job that today requires two people and a $100,000 machine.

At first, their tales were reassuring: I knew I was in the land of genuine folk and authentic lore, replete with legends, tall tales and accounts of pranks, remedies, superstitions, and cures. But after a couple years of hearing comfortable tales in comfortable livingrooms, I seemed to sense a disjunction between these stories and the land itself, which to me appeared frighteningly open, too wide for a frame. I sought in their narratives some image, I guess, to coincide with my own of the danger or the fear of living in such geographic openness.

I remember driving on a narrow two-lane road after a morning collecting holiday traditions from a grandmother who still drove the tractor in the fields. The snow had been falling lightly all morning, but by the time I headed back to Lafayette it had thickened to what the farmers called a "white out." With no way to distinguish the blustery sky from the wavy white fields, no way to find the thin line of pavement once limiting it all, blinded by the white, I steered only by feel as my right tires slipped on and off the tarmac. But for such a precarious anchor to the land I could have been riding through sky.

And the springs could be as fierce as the winters. One spring a tornado chased me home. The oppressively heavy air silenced the streets of Wolcott; doors were shut, windows secured. The sky turned a strange mustard green as I headed down a deserted interstate, past the newly plowed fields—some deeply ridged, others disked smooth and ready for planting, but all rich and enticing to the violent swirling storm. The farmers said that the churning up of the soil in preparation for planting spawned these savage winds till they'd spin a great cord that would sweep the ground clean.

On this May afternoon I got back to Lafayette in time to pick up my ten-month-old daughter from the sitter's across the street. The sky cast a pale mauve; the air stood still as if anticipating its bruise. As I climbed the porch stairs of our white clapboard house, its siding strangely pinkish, I heard the loud tornado alarm warning all of us with basements to take refuge. Throughout the city everyone sought shelter: some in their carpeted, paneled basement rec rooms and others, like my daughter and me, on lawn furniture in the damp for over an hour awaiting the all-clear alarm when we'd surface into the fresher, cooler air.

As they emerged from their seclusion and their fear, my neighbors would compare notes on fallen limbs, loosened shingles, and past storms: "You should have seen the damage to the 7–11 on Sagamore Parkway last year." "I remember what it looked like in Elkhart after the Palm Sunday tornado; nothing could compare to that!" After such storms the next day's paper would inevitably detail the massive destruction of a trailer park. The front page would carry a picture of the rubble—roofs ripped like paper from their frames, pickups upside down. Trailers always seemed to be the lightning rods where tornados invested their passion. Always, though, amid the accounts of disaster were the stories of uncanny privilege: the shed lifted one hundred yards down the road without as much as a hammer out of place, or the doghouse deposited in the middle of the street, its dish still brimming with Purina chunks—evidence of grace in what was otherwise arbitrary violence.

But my informants spoke seldom of this violence, granting me no glimpse into the eye of the tornado, of either its beauty or its horror. They doted on the past, excusing its misbehavior and its ugly moods. Even after four years, I was still the outsider from the present, greeted kindly but cautiously, entertained with family folklore as fresh as the new quilts made by the local craft guild.

What I saw only later was that the guardedness they showed me was one they also adopted toward each other. So fearful of local criticism was one rural high school that it kept books by black authors off the shelves and instructed librarians to draw clothing on the scantily clad models in magazine and newspaper underware ads, as if blacks and sexuality were equally alien to the community. What startled me about this latter practice was not the obvious prudity but the extra labor it took to draw little magic-marker blouses and skirts rather than simply to obscure the whole ad.

Not ashamed enough to destroy the white robes and hoods, costumes of fear, some still kept in attics, they nevertheless hesitated to speak about those secret rites. The rage silent in their tales resounded one warm summer night in 1978 when several gathered in a parking lot behind the town hall to burn the science books of their children and grandchildren, books that taught evolution. The rage blazed in a fiery cross on the front lawn of a teacher who'd assigned *The Diary of Anne Frank* to her sophomore English class.

The folklore I collected from these people lacked this strain of rage fueled by fears, at once richly violent and unpredictable. Whether it lay on the other side of language, articulated only in fraternal rites that take place in the dark, or whether it remained simply one of those truths forever concealed from outsiders, I could not tell. Whether these residents ever talked of such events in local bars and coffee shops, I never learned.

Suspecting first that I would never get beyond the warm reminiscence and fond recollection of family life to focus more sharply on the lives and beliefs of these people and secondly that what I was seeking might, in fact, be of my own invention, I eagerly took advantage of the opportunity to begin fieldwork with a different group of people: inmates of the Indiana Women's Prison. Such a switch reinvigorated my quest for the exotic, the extraordinary, and the dangerous. North of picturesque Bean Blossom and Bedford (Dorson Country), south of the infernal fires issuing from the refineries of Gary, Indianapolis is the middle ground in a middle state in the middle west—the golden mean of America and first state capital to be constructed at the perfect geographic center of a state. Mapmakers simply sank their compass into the state's center, and Indianapolis was invented.

Indiana Women's Prison was the first separate prison for women in the country. Once on the outskirts of Indianapolis, now in a poor white neighborhood on the east side of the city, the walled, wooded block is a relic of the nineteenth century. Since its opening in 1873, the Women's Prison has housed women convicted of the most violent crimes—multiple murders, armed robbery, manslaughter—and has been a way station for those chronic alcoholics and drug addicts who periodically come to the prison to dry out. Within its walls have been the psychotic, the retarded, the habitual criminal, and the shoplifter.

In my transition from farmhouse to prison I discovered a new ease on the part of the women I interviewed, an eagerness to tell their stories. Many of them needed no questions to prime their memories. I allowed them to chart the direction of their narratives, and they told life stories with such fluency that they appeared to have been rehearsed. These autobiographical narratives fell into two types. First, there was the story of the life of crime. The narrators of these stories spent a great deal of time recounting their childhood, characterizing themselves as high-strung babies and irascible children, more interested in spending their days running with the boys and hanging out with the warehouse derelicts than in attending school or engaging in what they refer to as "girls' play." Theirs was the often comical picaresque tale of the rascal making her way through like more by her wits than her industry.

The tellers of these life histories were sometimes regarded as "the old girls," women who had been in and out of institutions since childhood. Their narratives, a series of episodes—adventures and misadventures—had little plot. What tied these episodes together was the often witty, sometimes wise, voice of one who had endured and who would, in her own feisty way, continue to do so.

Sixty-two-year-old Anna May was such a woman.[2] At the time I began my fieldwork she was serving a ninety-six-day sentence for disorderly conduct. Although she'd spent several short stints in county jails and the state prison (the first at eighteen when, drunk and angry, she "busted up" the front hood of her lover's Chevy), what was most interesting were her stories of life out of prison and her days as a member of the "Moon Light Hawaiians," a country and western band who dressed in white crepe outfits with orange and purple lace and performed throughout Ohio and Indiana. Anna May told me that on the night she and fellow band member Roy Aikens decided to leave the group, he cut his name on the top of her breast. "Well, I just let him do it—blood and all! I just let him do it." The story of Anna May's life was a litany of violent episodes; in some she was the aggressor, in others the unfortunate victim: "I been had three men and got the fourth one now I'm not married to, and all my guitars they've torn up."

Completely without self-pity, Anna May was a witty and warm narrator who related a zany life story with little introspection and no self analysis. Delighting as much as I in the crazy details of her life, she told me of the hard work she'd done as a girl helping her sickly Aunt Mabel and crippled Uncle Russell at the filling station. Recovering from the removal of one lung, Aunt Mabel kept the ribs the surgeon had removed in a jar near her bed. As a kid, Uncle Russell had broken his hip in a fall from a second story window: "His mother tried to grab him by his clothes, but when she saw it was gonna drag her out the window, she let him loose." Always matter-of-factly and often humorously, she told of a bizarre world in which even the closest relationships were marked by lurid violence and strange chance: children fell out of windows, women slept next to jars of missing ribs, men carved their names in women's flesh.

A variation of this picaresque narrative was told by young women in their late teens and twenties. Theirs was the story of adolescent depression (sometimes the result of a family crisis) leading to a rebellion against the control of parents and the authority of the law. The protagonists of these stories, the young Huck Finns, often ran away from an abusive, sometimes alcoholic, father in search of adventure, and they traveled down the streets of their cities encountering hustlers, pimps, dealers, and conmen ready to initiate them into a fast and exciting world, a world of intense action where someone was always "getting it over" on someone else. These were women who manipulated the men in their lives by their cleverness and their sex. There was always a "john" they could hustle; there was always someone they could con. They often took pride in their exploits and the skill they had acquired in the criminal "trade."

Take Pat, for example—a tall, slender, freckled blonde who married at sixteen to get away from home:

> He was a real nice guy. I only lived with him for six days, and then I left him. See, there was this other guy I really liked. I lived with my husband for six days, and then I left and went with this other dude. Hey, we went out partying and having a good time!

But after a few days, Pat returned to her new husband who sought her mother's help in keeping the sixteen-year-old at home. Pat's mother called the police.

> They took me down to detention. I said, "Hey, you can't hold me; I know you can't hold me for this." They held me for an hour or so, long enough to throw me in a cell, and then they let me go. They had to. But my mom was gonna try, since I wasn't gonna live with my husband. She said, "Well, then we're just gonna send her to reform school. We just have to send this child to reform school 'cause there's no help for her." See, I couldn't of just left home. I figured I'd be caught sooner or later. I was a juvenile, and it'd be inevitable that I'd be sent to some school or somewhere. But if I'm married, then I could be released from their

custody and couldn't nobody say nothing. I thought this was a better angle for me to work because I would be protecting myself. No, I didn't want to just take off and maybe be caught and go to reform school for a runaway.

After that Pat worked as a go-go dancer, turning tricks on the side, posed for nude portraits on black velvet, turned new girls out in northern Kentucky, and worked for a pimp until she soon discovered that she preferred to work on her own, traveling across the country stopping at "respectable houses" where the product was quality sex at high prices. Pat named her own schedule ("two weeks on and two weeks off") and never wanted for·work because she was not only young and pretty but specialized in kinky sex:

> I prefer to turn strictly freaks because that's where the money is. You can take men that just want straight sex—they know what to spend. They spend a limited amount. The only way they're gonna spend any more is if they're in love with you. But now freaks, they know that they're weird, and they know that they have to pay extra. You can usually charge them whatever you want to. Once they tell you what they want, they feel committed to pay you whatever you ask.

For an undertaker's assistant in Akron she'd soak in an icy bath till she got real cold. For others she'd play the parts of little girl or mother. Pat spoke fondly of her young clients:

> I always like the little guys, too. A lot of them would lie; you could tell they were lying. They'd say they were eighteen in order to get in, but they were sixteen or seventeen. But I always felt like I was helping them, showing them what they were supposed to be doing. They would have one little, crumpled twenty dollar bill they'd saved. They'd immediately want to start kissing and all this, but I'd say, "We're gonna sit down," and I'd talk to them like my child, "You're giving me a hard time. Don't do that 'cause I ain't gonna give you no hard time." They'd always listen and be OK.

It was only after my afternoon with Pat that I began to see these prison narratives as responses to the world of nostalgic and repressive domestic harmony evoked and lived by my rural informants. It was a world that bred outsiders. As I had left it, so, with greater reason and far graver consequences, had she. Pat could not stand home, and in order to be free of it she married, but when she fled that domestic relationship, husband and mother colluded to imprison her, if not in either of their homes, then in the state "home" of corrections.

The countrymen's suspicion of outsiders was a futile defense against the inevitable realization that the price of staying inside the home was an alienation so severe that it imposed on some women the single choice of continued violence to oneself or explosive violence to others. Over and over women told me of abuse in the home and of their conflicting responses of anger and fear—subjects of the second major category of life stories I collected. The life stories of these women were the gothic inversion of conventional lore; they recounted not the good wife at her hearth but a heroine paralyzed by fear before the monster in the home. Theirs was often a private terror, knowing that they could expect periodic and certain mistreatment if they remained in their marriages but dreading even greater abuse directed towards them and their children if they tried to leave. The plots of these tales had uncanny uniformity; their tellers were amazingly similar: imprisoned at home, released by the murder of a husband or lover, and then imprisoned by the state. Most were women with no previous convictions whose crime was the cataclysmic act in their lives, the first and perhaps last independent action they would ever take. These women did not think of themselves as criminals or outcasts, but as victims: victimized by parents, husbands and lovers, and the legal system. They had once tried to escape the confinement of home through marriage, sometimes because of early pregnancy, sometimes just to be free of parents. But in marriage, they found no freedom, just a greater and often more brutal constraint:

> Several things might trigger my husband's violence. I'll give you an example. We could never leave a light on or water running. That was cause for real anger. The kids and I were always very cautious. When we left a room, the light had to be turned off. There were never two lights on in a room. We never used any more electricity than had to be. Our bills were lower than anybody else's anywhere, I know. We were many times charged the minimum, and this is with a family! That's probably unheard of.
>
> Anyway, my son went into my daughter's room once and was watching TV. This was Tommy, my youngest, watched TV in my daughter's room and went to sleep with it on. This would normally initiate a good slapping around, into your room, restriction, a lot of hollering. It might

last for days—just over going to sleep with the TV on. But David, my older son, saw that Tommy had gone to sleep with the TV on so he went in and turned it off and was waking Tommy so that he could go to his own room and go to bed. Tommy, because he was sleeping, made a fuss. My husband heard it, went in and grabbed David, threw him down the hall into his own room, took out his belt (he wore a heavy belt), and just started beating. He beat David, and beat David with the belt doubled. David only had on a pajama bottom, and the belt came un-doubled. He was just beating him; he was out of control. He was beating him with the buckle end. He just kept beating him, and beat-ing him, and beating him. I was trying at this time to stop it, trying to grab the belt, trying to stop my husband. I don't know if I made him more angry, I don't know if I could have stopped him even with more interference in what he was doing. He just kept beating David until he was wore out. David was black and blue all over from the belt buckle. His skin was open. He just swelled up all over. It went on and on. He beat until he couldn't beat any more. Then my husband went into his room, lay down and rested. I stayed with my son as long as I could. I couldn't stay out very long once my husband went to bed. [Fowler]

These desperate women attempted to stop the brutality with gun, poison, or hired killer.

From one perspective, their crimes may be considered the revolt of the repressed, but whatever "liberation" they accomplished was, osten-sibly, at least, ephemeral. The act against society was summarily pun-ished by society. Despite their violent divorce from the past, these women had merely exchanged the arbitrary brutality of home for the systematic discipline of the indifferent penal machine. No strangers to confinement, they did well in prison. They married it, and with some success. After all, they had more rights in prison than they ever did in their homes.

By the end of my first year of weekly visits to the women's prison in which I would interview two inmates a day, I dreaded interviews of this type. The cast of characters in each family drama was always the same: older, brutal husband/father, teenage wife, children beaten if they were boys, sexually abused if they were girls.

But finally, it was one meeting with Officer Verna Brown that made sense of it all. Early one April morning I checked in at the prison gate house and was escorted up to the sewing room where twelve prisoners mended the khaki uniforms of the male prisoners from other state prisons. Every time I entered the sewing room I reflected on the irony of women, even in prison, tasked with men's mending.

Veteran of twenty-two years, motherly guard and reputed clair-voyant, Verna Brown ran the sewing room. Most of the staff regarded her as eccentric; most inmates saw her as caring about those she governed and possessing an uncanny knowledge of things to come. Despite their belief or disbelief in her psychic ability, no one viewed her as harmful. Even the skeptics heeded her predictions, "just in case she might be right."

I had chatted informally with Officer Brown and even conducted three more formal interviews in which she told me of a divine calling that instructed her to come to the women's prison and about her knowl-edge of spirits, which assisted her in a ministry that aimed to ease the suffering of those under her charge and to maintain order in the in-stitution. The easing of pain and the maintenance of order may seem contrary missions, but Verna Brown overcame the contradiction be-tween the impulse to nurture and the necessity to control through her contact with a spirit world which aided her in both roles. Although unable to transform a harsh, inhumane place into a home, she chose to view her role as guide rather than jailer.

As maternal spiritual guide to those under her control, whom she viewed as wayward or disturbed children in need of nurturing and discipline, Brown took her instruction from a powerful spirit, her In-dian guide. Although she had previously mentioned this spirit guide, she had refused to answer any of my questions about this mysterious figure. For several weeks he had instructed her to remain silent about his identity, but at the conclusion of our conversation the preceding week she had promised to discuss him on my next visit.

She was true to her word and told me that her Indian guide warned her of dangers to come both to herself and to others and instructed her in the making of secret cures and small packets to ward off evil. Although he had appeared physically to her, his presence was more often discernable by touch; she would feel his fur against her skin as she walked through a doorway. A benevolent force, this warrior re-assured and protected; his warnings and instructions enabled Brown to control and to nurture those in her charge. This threshold figure mediated Brown's two worlds: the wing of prisoners she governed and the superimposed spirit world whose forces governed her.

As the Indian spirit guided Brown, so her story taught me. As I left that small supply room off the sewing room and headed back to the gate house, I thought what an institutional couple Brown and her spirit guide made: strong protective father who keeps his family secure and nurturing mother whose expressions of kindness and concern were rare among officers, who seemed to fear that any expression of sympathy would make them appear unprofessional to their superiors and vulnerable to prisoners. Learning to be a folklorist was, for me at least, discovering that, although spirits may only appear in stories, stories often appear like spirits—guiding us beyond ourselves, healing the splits in our selves and our natural lives that in the long run make no more sense than the supernatural.

I had fled the homes of north central Indiana two years earlier in search of the strange and the turbulent and had discovered much that was odd and violent in the lives of my new informants. But what I had not counted on finding in prison was the domestic. Not only did an officer, in her peculiar way, reconstitute the family in prison, but older inmates routinely "adopted" younger prisoners and served as their "prison mothers," offering sound advise, comforting them, and keeping them out of trouble. Occasionally, "studs" (masculine partners in prison lesbian couples) played father and uncle. Sometimes stern but never abusive, they reprimanded their daughters: "Watch your tongue." "Don't talk to your mother that way."

I realized, too, what should have been obvious to me all along: that these women were the daughters of those Indiana residents whose family traditions I had spent four years gathering. In seeing the homeliness in the prison, I could look back and see the prison of the home, a home which had seemed natural but was, in fact, as artificial as the fields.

2. Women in Prison

The one thing there is plenty of in prison is time, time to recollect events of the past and time to construct a picture of one's life which answers the question: why am I here? The answer is never a simple one. Most retrospective accounts by inmates place the moment of crime in the context of a life of struggle and hardship. But a past of misfortune and depravity or one of crime and punishment may also contain moments of revelation in the forms of visions and dreams that communicate a truth that is not the truth of law courts. By recalling these extraordinary moments, the teller acknowledges a power that appears, at least, superior to the state. Finding such accounts in rich supply in the women's prison, I began to focus my collecting on these moments of supernatural revelation. For over a year I made weekly visits to the Indiana Women's Prison and then continued my research at the Maryland Correctional Institution for Women.

The Indiana Women's Prison, the oldest women's prison in the country, maintains a stately presence in an Indianapolis neighborhood of small bungalows closely situated and in need of repair. Once you are inside its tall brick walls, the prison's green lawns and hundred-year-old shade trees convey to the casual observer what its nineteenth-century designers intended: the impression of an orderly efficient school. The buildings surrounding the well-kept green are even today still referred to as "cottages."

The Maryland Correctional Institution for Women, or MCIW as it is called by the Maryland Division of Correction, was built in 1939 on a ten-acre tract of land near Jessup, equidistant from Baltimore and Washington. With such close neighbors as the larger male prison, the Maryland House of Correction, as well as the Maryland Correctional Institution/Jessup, Brockbridge Correctional Facility, Patuxent, and the Clifton T. Perkins Institution for the Criminally Insane, the Maryland Correctional Institution for Women belongs to a little ghetto of prisons. Other than the pre-release unit in Baltimore which houses thirty-two women and county jails which hold women awaiting trial and sentencing and those offenders with sentences of less than ninety days, MCIW is the home of women serving time in Maryland, those on minimum, medium, and maximum security: the woman incarcerated for a $200 bad check, the drug dealer, the murderer.

Once the wardens of each prison had granted me permission to conduct interviews, I scheduled these interviews through the Director of Education in Indiana and the Coordinator of Volunteers in Maryland. These staff members would typically call an officer in a housing unit or a workroom and arrange for my meeting with a prisoner. When I had access to a prison phone at the Indiana Women's Prison I negotiated these arrangements with officers myself. In Maryland I conducted my interviews in a counselor's vacant office in the administration building, "up front" in the prison's only air-conditioned building.

In Indiana my movements were less restricted. I occupied whatever quiet space was available (a storeroom, an empty library or workroom, the nurse's office on her day off, or a guard's office on the segregation wing), and I walked unescorted from one building to another. That is not to say that I had free movement within the institution. Like inmates and staff I was required to inform an officer at one checkpoint where I intended to go, and then she, in turn, would inform another officer to expect my arrival.

I have no reason to believe that anyone monitored my interviews at either prison, but at the Maryland Correctional Institution for Woman I was definitely kept under closer supervision than I was in Indiana. Although I met the Maryland prisoners in a closed office, large windows made our presence visible to staff and inmates. Inmates came to me; I was not allowed to visit them in their rooms or workplaces unless accompanied by a staff member. On route, they usually passed through two guard stations. Those classified as "maximum security" walked across the prison yard shackled and escorted by a guard.

When women came to meet with me they sometimes knew of my presence in the prison; often they did not. With an initial list of between ten and fifteen "volunteers" recommended by staff members or the warden, I began my series of private interviews. I soon collected from the inmates themselves names of non–honor-status women, and after a few months I was allowed to interview women the institution refers to as "on segregation," women whom the inmates call "on lock," people we commonly refer to as "in solitary confinement."

My interviews were as short as one hour and as long as two, and I met in follow-up sessions with nearly half of the women I interviewed. As I was interested in meeting with women who knew the prison well, I rarely interviewed new admittees or those sentenced to less than a year. Typically, I interviewed a woman with a sentence of over five years who had already served at least a year of that time. These were either women who had been convicted of such serious crimes as first and second degree murder, manslaughter, drug dealing, armed robbery or women who, because of records with extensive criminal histories, had received lengthy sentences for less serious crimes. One woman I interviewed had a previous record that included sixty-eight arrests for prostitution. Another had been convicted and sentenced on three previous occasions for writing bad checks. On her fourth, the judge sentenced her to twenty years in prison for bad checks totaling over ten thousand dollars. Although I spoke with few women actually serving time for shoplifting, disorderly conduct, and prostitution, many, particularly those with histories of drug abuse, acknowledged having committed such crimes. And though women often recounted experiences of jail and reform school, I interviewed no juveniles unless they had been tried as adults (as sometimes happens when their crime is murder), and no women in custody awaiting trial or sentencing. In all, I interviewed over one hundred and twenty inmates.

An initial interview would generally focus on the following questions:

Would you describe your earliest memory?
Please describe your parents; were they nurturing parents or not?
What was your early schooling like? Junior high? High school?
When did you become sexually active?
Tell me about your current family. Do you have children?
What was the first illegal act you committed?
When were you first incarcerated?
How did you end up here?
Describe your first few months here.
What is the hardest thing you have to deal with in prison?

If you could give one piece of advice to a young woman just
coming here with a lot of time, what would you tell her?
Have you ever experienced anything mysterious or unexplainable, something that seemed to violate the rules of reality?

About a third of the women I interviewed were so eager to tell their
"life story" that I quickly abandoned my list of questions and listened
intently to what appeared to be narratives they had told before. When
I did follow my list of questions I found that responses to some questions were uniquely individual; responses to others were amazingly
uniform. Most women I interviewed, for example, had the same advice
to offer the new inmate: "Stick to yourself; that's the best way to do
your time." and "Keep busy; do your time so it doesn't do you." Nearly
three-quarters of those interviewed described a tyrannical father and
a passive mother and detailed much abuse in the home. Several told
of their efforts as children to stop their fathers from beating their
mothers. Such a terrifying scene was important, for it taught them a
harsh lesson: that they were powerless, often becoming victims, themselves, in the face of violence. A few ended discussion of their relations
with their fathers by telling of violently turning on their fathers in a
moment of revenge when they, as teenagers, worked up the courage
to return his abuse with verbal abuse of their own, or by striking,
stabbing, or shooting.

Others portrayed a father at once horrified and intrigued by his
daughter's nascent sexuality: the father who insisted on checking the un-
derpants of his nine-year-old daughter every time she returned home
from playing with friends and the father who, when he learned that his
thirteen-year-old had had a sexual encounter with a thirteen-year-old
boy, took her to the police station for interrogation. I heard many stories
of incest and even more descriptions of the verbally abusive fathers who
regularly called their young daughters "whores" and "bitches."

Nearly half of the women I interviewed described themselves as
tomboys, preferring the fast active life of running with the boys to the
quieter play close to home that the girls around them enjoyed. These
women almost always had brothers before whom they felt the need
to demonstrate their strength and their cleverness. Hyperactive, unable
to sit still, they often got into trouble both at home and in school.

Represented here are an equal number of black and white women, as well as one full-blooded American Indian (and two others with Native American grandparents). I quote Catholics, Protestants, Jews, and Black Muslims, as well as occultists and other noncomformists. The fact that the five women I quote most frequently are black and over thirty raises certain questions. Were these women simply more willing to talk at length about these phenomena? Had they had more opportunity to practice and polish their narratives so that they stood out from the rest? Did their cultural backgrounds validate them as the teller of personal experience narratives more than the white women? Or was this simply chance, due to the fact that, in the end, nearly 60 percent of the total number of prisoners I interviewed were black?

Any generalizations about these exceptional narrators are extremely difficult to make. These women are all "black," but they certainly do not share a common culture: one was raised a Jew, another a Baptist; two grew up in the rural South; the other three were city kids; one is an employee of a prison, the others convicts. Of those imprisoned, one wandered the streets as a child, another committed crimes as a young adult, and the other two have no previous convictions. And even their skin color ranges from dark to light. Four of these five women have worked as cooks, but where does that take us?

I distrust sociological explanations—too often reductive and tautological—of most cultural phenomena. Because it is difficult to rigidly identify what groups these women "represent" and because I am looking at a very small group of women, ethnicity becomes a somewhat tendentious category to apply. To force generalizations would produce nothing more enlightening than facile observations.

Identifying the class of these women (or any group of women, for that matter) is an equally difficult task. Do we assign them class based on their husbands' status? Their fathers'? According to income? When a woman earns a substantial income over several years for running dope from Florida to Maryland, do we classify her as middle class? And when she earns seventy cents for a day's labor in prison, do we call her working class? Making such discriminations in ways both accurate and nuanced is not easy.

In the beginning of my research I was surprised by the willingness of all these women to talk candidly with a stranger, but after meeting with many women in vacant classrooms, storerooms, and free offices,

I learned what a rare thing it is for a woman in prison to talk un-observed. That alone was sufficient inducement for them to come. And as a result, I was able to meet often for several sessions with women of diverse ages whose backgrounds cut across all social, ethnic, and cultural lines—urban and rural, black and white, lower and middle class.

Like any fieldworker investigating the lore of any group of people, I soon found those remarkable individuals, lively narrators with large repertoires who enliven the work of collecting and who seem to speak for the group. "Luscious" was one such woman. Despite repeated in-carcerations and long periods in solitary confinement, this chubby, five-foot-tall black woman who held her worn clothes together with safety pins projected a fiery defiance which prison had failed to ex-tinguish. Affectionate, mysterious, and witty, she charmed many (in-cluding this collector) with her spunk and her keen sense of those around her.

Of all the women I interviewed, Luscious elicited the most infor-mation from me, pausing at times in the interview to ask personal questions and to venture her impressions of me. Conscious of her manipulation, I ceded some control of the interview session to her, inviting her at times to talk about whatever she wanted. Her daily life was so infused with psychic messages that even Luscious's digressions fascinated me. The dull suspicion that over time hardens into the features of most who live and work in prisons (their "prison stare") had not masked her exuberance. Luscious never solicited pity; rather, she celebrated her success as "seer" and maternal guide.

Typically, the more recent the vision, the more enigmatic Luscious was in confiding its contents. Endowed with a keen sense of the dra-matic, Luscious occasionally withheld part of a vision narrative till a future conversation. Several times during the six months I met with her she left me with the promise to disclose the following week what was too mysterious to speak at that time. What was striking was not only the variety of her vision narratives but also the sphere of their in-fluence. For most women, visions provided knowledge about them-selves and their families. For Luscious, they communicated hidden knowledge about all around her: fellow inmates, prison staff, even me. By our third meeting I had become a figure in one of her visions—not me exactly, but people I had supposedly sent.

She recounted a vision in which she claimed that a man and a woman had been sent to her by me. They were seeking some knowledge, something she had learned in previous visions but was unwilling to disclose. I learned later that the secret these visionary people sought was the solution to a highly publicized murder case, a solution that Luscious had received in previous multiple visions. By associating her vision with a postcard from me and a fortune inscribed on a small piece of paper she carried with her, Luscious decoded its meaning.

I see many things. I've seen you. Not actually seen you — you sent two people to me, a man and a woman. The man had on a black — I believe a all-wool or cashmere coat, very fine, very well-dressed. And he had sharp features: very acute, stand-out features, not authoritative but used to getting his way. The woman was very timid, the timid type, and she had fox [perhaps *faux*] pearls around her neck. She had a nervous idiosyncrasy: she kept twirling the pearls around. She had a beautiful diamond ring on her finger and a beautiful dress on. It was a light maroon with flowers, and it was very sheer, I think maybe silk or chiffon. Her hair was real shiny in a ball like a knot on the back of her head. She was very nervous. They asked me something, and I knew what they wanted, but I didn't tell them.

Burke: What did they ask you?

Luscious: Oh, I don't want to say.

Burke: Why not?

Luscious: [*laughs*]: I don't know. That man, he says, "Miss Walker, come back; I need you to tell me something." I said, "In time." That's when it vaporized. Then your card came under the door and I says, "Oh, my God!"

Burke: Was it something about me?

Luscious: You were the one who sent the people.

Burke: But did they ask you something about me?

Luscious: No.

Burke: About you?

Luscious: No. They knew that I knew. Don't ask me how; they just knew that I knew.

And I looked down [at the envelope] and there was no address, no return name, and I said, "It's her." And when I opened it up I said, "Miss Allen [an officer on duty], read this."

And she read your letter, and just in my hand I had this little piece of paper with a saying on it that one of the girls had gave to me, and I opened this up. It says, "The written message will bring you profit."

Prior to your letter I says, "Well Ringo, so much for your profit. She says, "Keep it anyway." I says, "I don't believe this stuff." And she says, "Keep it anyway, Luscious, I don't want it."

"Why you gonna give me something you don't want?"

"I don't know, Luscious, just keep the damn thing."

And then I kept it and kept it. I slept with it, and one night I looked at it again and read it and says, "What does this mean?" I couldn't put it together. I had that little message when your letter came in, and I know what these people want. They know that I know. [Luscious]

The preceding account demonstrates how the sympathetic listener becomes a participant in the imaginative life of these women and how the collector is unavoidably a co-conspirator in a private, secret activity. Speaking unobserved in prison has been defined as a subversive act since the "reformed" penitentiaries of the early nineteenth century were built to operate as machines of silent precision (Dobash, Dobash, and Gutteridge, ch. 3). The role of collector as invisible listener, as scribe who records but does not influence the material being gathered, has been challenged and must go on being challenged. The collector as audience performs a specific role, a collaborative one helping to initiate, elaborate, and conclude the performance of telling.

In my interviews with these women I found them more willing to tell longer, more detailed narratives in a second or third session than they were on our first encounter. I was surprised that no one ever returned eager to disclaim what she had disclosed in a previous meeting; instead, she generally returned more willing to talk. On three occasions, however, women whom I wanted to interview a second time refused to come down from their cells. These may, in fact, have been instances of second thoughts, or the women may not have been feeling well, or they may have been angry with a guard and refused to acknowledge any request, or the message that I wished to see them may not have been delivered (this was a common complaint against officers voiced by teachers and counselors); I have no way of knowing.

Four of the women I interviewed used their accounts of visions (and in one case, "raps and rhymes") to secure my promise of future meetings. They would say, "Something strange happened this week, but I can't tell you about it now. I'll tell you next week." All four were true to their word, but one woman refused my request to tape the session even though each of four interviews concluded with her agreement to the recording at our next meeting. Such negotiation between narrator and collector is important to acknowledge. Folklorists may consider themselves as uninterfering, invisible listeners safe behind their microphones, but their informants never make that mistake.

The fact that I am a woman and mother who expressed sympathy for these women's accounts of prison hardships and respect (rather than disbelief) for their tales of divine intervention encouraged their trust. My easiest period of collecting was concurrent with a pregnancy. As I swelled, so did the friendliness of my informants. But the fact that I am white and in my thirties sometimes made it difficult for me to win the trust of young black women. To be the subject of one of Luscious's visions made me feel that I had been accepted into the community, but to be the inquiring force whose messengers tried to extract from her some important information she was unwilling to disclose assured me that I was not. In spite of the nickname I acquired ("Legs") during my fieldwork at the Maryland Correctional Institution for Women and the two propositions from lesbian inmates, I never forgot that I was an outsider and not a member of this community; and the women who kindly agreed to these interviews never forgot it either. After all, in Maryland we met in the only air-conditioned wing of the prison, and when the temperature reached 100°, with the humidity not far behind, it was clear to all that though we spent our days imprisoned by the same fifteen-foot-high fence, my experience of prison and theirs were very different.

My incorporation into Luscious's visions and later into her drawings (figures inspired by visions) indicates her controlled arrangement of real people and daily events in a fantastic world, one she sustains and supervises. In such a way, even apparently unrelated events like receiving a saying and the arrival of a postcard are retrospectively reinterpreted as corroborating evidence which authenticates the visionary communication. Like other accounts of visions that conclude with the letter received or the phone call made, Luscious's vision suggests that we may read both the message received through the vision and the message communicated in a letter as links with a world from which prison bars these women. The significant difference between the two is that the letter, card, or phone call is subject to surveillance by the officials; visions are not.

In the exchanging of vision narratives, women in prison avoid the scrutiny of an unsympathetic guard. The individual cell, rather than the rec room or work room is the usual setting for the disclosure of premonitions. Despite the fact that these exchanges are not as public as some performances in prison, they nevertheless form a lively part of prison social life. The narrative above indicates, too, how socially complex these experiences are. One woman gives a written message forecasting good luck to another. That message only makes sense when interpreted in terms of a vision and postcard which follow. Although the prison staff read and deliver the postcard, they remain ignorant of the way written communication fits into the magical world of secret knowledge. To forecast the future, to see events at home as they happen, to warn and to console are powers not sanctioned by the institution. Although hidden from offical scrutiny they pose no threat to prison discipline as long as they are private. Only when women persuade others of the force of their visions do they challenge prison authority (as do the women in the chapter entitled "Gifted Women"). That is why a woman like Luscious is referred to as "dangerous," "mind controlling," and "manipulating." That is precisely why a woman like Luscious is such an interesting informant.

In seeing herself as one who experiences visions, the prisoner stands apart from the identity prescribed for her by the institution.[1] She assumes two identities: the nameless but numbered prisoner subject to prison discipline, and the recipient of paranormal communications or supernatural visions. Some of the women I interviewed described this fracturing of their identity into public and private selves as something they experienced as children; others traced its beginning to their crimes and their trials.

A woman comes to a state prison from a county jail where she has spent anywhere from a few months to a year awaiting trial and sentencing (unless she is one of the lucky ones who get out on bail). Her crime and trial, often more dreamlike than real, seem like events that have happened to someone else. One woman recalls her reactions to her trial on charges of first-degree murder as those of disbelief and levity:

> I had a jury trial, and my lawyer let me pick 'em [members of the jury]: "Whoever you want, Marie, you can have." I was like, "Well, this persons looks nice. And he's good-lookin', so I'll have him, too." I didn't know. I just picked all the good-lookin' men and one little old lady. . . .

I got life in prison. I was stunned. When I was in court, I didn't take it as serious as I should have. Shit, the things they were talkin' about, I didn't understand. They were usin' words longer than my arm. I was ignorant; I wasn't stupid. I went to school and knew how to read and write, but big words like that, I never heard of. I just sat there. I would look at the jury. When the witnesses would testify, I couldn't believe they were sayin' this shit. I would just sit there; it was all lies. It was like I wasn't really there. I was like, "Tell me when it's over." But it was like it wasn't really happenin'. I just sat there.

Before the trial I told what happened to the police and to my lawyer so many times that it was like readin' it off of a piece of paper. I was numb. At my trial I just said what happened, and I got down and just sat there. When they came and said, "We find you guilty of first-degree murder and life imprisonment," I just sat there. I didn't believe 'em. It was like this is a dream and I'm gonna wake up and be in bed. [Berger]

A woman coming to prison for the first time, especially one sentenced to several years, often reports a similar sense of the alienation at her trial. Forced to forfeit control of her own story, a story she often believes would have vindicated her actions, she finds herself compelled to assume the role of audience. Lawyers for the prosecution and the defense reconstruct and deconstruct narratives of a past which often seems to this woman more fictive than real.

When the judge pronounces her sentence she experiences further disbelief—the crime and its consequences are like events in a dream:

But the worst part was when the judge gave me time, and my husband and daughter and my son was standing there, and they put these handcuffs on me. That was like something died inside of me. It was just like day turned to darkness. That was like a shadow crashed over me. And I was in—I guess I was in such a state the first couple days—it was all like a nightmare!

I couldn't believe that this had happened. I'm trying to figure out just what happened here; it's always like it's a dream, like I haven't woke up to face reality yet. I know it's real, but it's just like this is a dream. I'm like in the twilight zone here. [Bond]

The rumors a woman hears about the horrors of the women's prison, sometimes from such supposedly reliable sources as her lawyer, increase her anxiety. She expects that she will be forced to wear a uniform and have her head shaved, and fears that she may be beaten or raped. Usually upon coming to the women's prison a woman is fearful of everyone and frightened of being more alone than she has ever been. She no longer belongs to her family. She no longer belongs to her group on the streets. She is not even allowed the association that jail provided. She characteristically accepts, and occasionally welcomes, institutional regimen as a final form of security. A castoff of society, she now belongs to prison.

The first stage in the passage into prison is "orientation" or "quarantine," both a place (a floor of one of the buildings) and a time (two weeks to two months) when a woman is isolated. Following quarantine she is assigned a room and joins the rest of the prison population, where she is given a classification. If she is a good prisoner in the eyes of the officers who observe her, that classification will gradually be upgraded over time until she earns all the privileges possible for an inmate.

This system, coupled with the prison disciplinary court, defines the kind of sentence a woman will serve, whether she will be in isolation or allowed to associate with the rest of the population—whether she will do "good time" or "hard time." Isolation is the primary means of enforcing discipline. Violation of the elaborate set of rules—talking to a woman at another table, lending her clothes, not cleaning her room, passing a note to another prisoner, giving a gift to a fellow inmate, talking in the television room, and on and on—may result in a "write-up" (what some prisons call "tickets" and others "adjustments") and a hearing before the prison court. For these infractions and hundreds like them a woman can be more narrowly confined, locked in solitary for a week, a month, a year. Isolation is not only a means of discipline; it is the fundamental principle of social organization in the penal institution. Isolation makes the prison run, insures effective supervision and control. The officers maintain the day-to-day separation of one prisoner from another by mediating all relationships. Friendships between women serving time are discouraged, and the loner is judged the best prisoner and rewarded for keeping her distance from the women around her.

In this sense, the prison system is more successful with women than with men. Feeling a greater threat from physical violence, men form groups for protection. The only real subversion of isolation in the women's prison takes two forms: the familial bond between an older and younger prisoner and homosexual intimacy. Women compensate for the loss of children, parents, and lovers by discovering in prison "play mothers," "play fathers," "play daughters," and lesbian lovers. Although authorities officially discourage prison families, officers tend to ignore them; in some cases such bonds actually assist the maintenance of order by keeping younger, rebellious prisoners in line. With more vigilance, authorities seek to prohibit alliances between "studs" and "fems." Even the slightest physical contact (e.g., tying a friend's shoe) between suspected lesbians can result in harsh punishment. Actual love-making, though, generally escapes surveillance and is subject not only to proscription but suspicion and a kind of prurient interest on the part of the authorities.

The authorities systematically enforce isolation by proscribing all communication that does not have explicit official sanction. Speech for these women is a scarce and valued commodity, a privilege rationed to them in restricted areas at specific times. One of the few defenses the prisoners have against this isolation is to deepen it, to withdraw into themselves where they can carry on an internal monologue. They continually sift through the past, the plot of their lives, and rehearse the defense that was never made nor ever could have been made at their trials. The narratives I have collected are versions of these monologues, addresses to the society whose security they threatened, whose laws they violated, and whose courts they were incarcerated by.

Although clearly labeled criminals by society, these women maintain a conspicuous silence about the details of their crimes. Male prison lore celebrates criminal exploits. Female narratives, if they mention crimes at all, cast them as the desperate recourse of victims: the battered wife who kills her husband, the addict who retreats from a brutal life into drugs, and the check-writer who responds to every family crisis with a forged signature. Even those convicted of the most brutal offenses describe their crimes as anomalies that have no place in their tales of victimization. Only by understanding their crimes within a visionary framework, as acts more visited upon them than perpretrated by them, do they justify their passivity and explain their crimes as necessary evils.

Although reluctant to talk about their crimes (acts made public by the legal system), women in prison enthusiastically relate their visions, events in which they play the parts of passive observers. Told by young and old, violent and nonviolent offenders, these accounts report consoling visions of dead relatives, of Jesus, of a cross in the sky, of celestial lights, as well as visions of the devil and other menacing figures. They affirm the appearance of the spirits of inmates who have died on the grounds and whom their narrators have aided into the next world through their conjuring and prayer.

Many women in prison also express a belief in their ability to see into the future. Some claim, for example, that in a premonition, they saw the women's prison and knew that they would eventually come there. By attributing their actions to an outside power, they relinquish responsibility for their fates—both the crimes they commit and the imprisonment that follows. They are comforted by the conviction that a designing power communicates what is right to them personally, not socially, throught the legal system. That belief transforms isolation into a calling rather than a punishment, sets the believer apart as the recipient of privileges dispensed not according to the caprice of human overseers but according to the plan of a benevolent or terrible deity.

Belief or disbelief in spirits does not bear on the value of these spirits to the women any more than belief in the complete factual accuracy of prison tales of struggle, crimes, and incarceration affects their power and significance. Neither sociological data nor lawful truths, their stories are narratives which individually and in the composite express an imaginative world as much a datum as prison brick and as true as a court transcript. Whether drunk, prostitute, murderer, or guard, women in prison share an obsessive concern with authorities in their lives—parents, husbands, pimps, judges—authorities whom they have not been able to fully outwit or murder but whom they are able to imprison in the ceaseless weave of the story which has become their life.

Narratives of supranormal occurrences have historically been interpreted by some as a mark of spirituality and by others as evidence of demoniacal possession or psychosis. Enthusiasts have recorded these narratives, believing that they confirmed the existence of extrasensory perception, clairvoyance, or second sight; skeptics have dismissed them as evidence of delusions, hallucinations, or simply the over-reading of coincidence. But viewed from the perspective of a woman in prison, these accounts affirm a sense of a force other than the state at work in her life, one which bestows on her a sense of specialness and authority.[2]

I have elected to refer to the experiences depicted in these narratives as visions.[3] Despite its imprecision, the term "vision" embraces accounts of spiritual, psychic, and delusional phenomena. Only one-third of the women I interviewed named their experiences, and those who did called them "visions." By employing the term "vision" I do not mean to limit my focus to accounts of visual phenomena; I prefer, instead, to maintain an elastic definition that encompasses unusual events perceived with any of the senses: the touch of a dead person, the call of a child far away, or the odious smell of demons. In the term "vision" I also include the nonsensory "feeling" that something has happened in another place or is about to happen.

Many of these visions suggest a dream landscape, but only in a few cases have I included dream narratives and only then because of their striking similarity to other narratives within a chapter. Each dream narrative is clearly identified as such. At times during my interviews I imagined I was listening to accounts of dreams, but at the end of these narratives when I asked these women if they were awake or sleeping when this episode took place, each insisted that she was fully conscious.

Another characteristic of many of these narratives is their brevity; they are simple accounts told without elaboration, emphasizing plot rather than description. And when they detail contact with spirits, it is usually not sought. When such contact occurs, though, it is generally welcome because it brings important messages of consolation and warning. In contrast are two other kinds of visions: those oppressive, suffocating forces that visit women typically during the early days of incarceration and those mystical experiences consciously initiated by fasting and sleep deprivation. In the latter case, a woman actively solicits visionary experiences through meditation or conjuring.

In a number of these narratives women describe an encounter with an apparition, a figure which Green and McCreery define as "a figure of a person who isn't really there superimposed on the normal environment. The surroundings of the person who perceives the apparition do not change" (1). In perceptual terms, there is a change in the figure but not in the ground of the spectator's field of vision. One woman sees the ghost of her grandmother enter the room. Another sees an inmate who has died on the prison grounds walk around the corner of one of the buildings. Only a few visions in this collection might be labeled, according to Green and McCreery, "hallucinations or waking dreams," for they describe states in which the perceiver loses awareness of her normal environment (Green and McCreery 2). Her entire field of perception is temporarily replaced by a different one. One woman recalled that as a child she was walking down a street in Baltimore and looked up at a woman on a balcony. Not only did the woman miraculously appear, but the street the narrator was on became a street in New Orleans. Both figure and ground altered in her vision.

Generally, in these visions the figure is familiar to the perceiver, though occasionally, as in the previous account, he or she is not. Typically, the apparitions encountered in these visions avoid being touched and are silent. Their message is one inferred in retrospect rather than imparted directly. Whether we as skeptical researchers view these apparitions as "nothing more than ideas . . . , the recollected images of the mind" (Hibbert 22), we cannot fail to see their importance to the women who have contributed their stories to this collection. For them, these visions are evidence of a spirit world communicating with the living. They are believers who heed the messages of apparitions and who are comforted or disturbed by what they "see."

As religious experiences, these visions are direct, unmediated encounters with the sacred, and many women find in them the spiritual direction they need to survive in prison. Visions identify the individual in an institution that seeks to obliterate any distinguishing trait. Elizabeth Petroff's impressive study of medieval visionary women and Margaret Brady's provocative analysis of Mormon women examine the ways in which women in other oppressive patriarchies adapt and win for themselves authority as a result of their visions.

In his study of Marina Takalo's life history, Juha Pentikainen identifies a "religious frame of reference" which is "actualized" for the believing person during periods of crisis or transition (121). For many of the women I interviewed imprisonment is not the first crisis they have faced, and at other turbulent times in their lives several have experienced visions. Within the prison community, though, there is a real difference between the woman who has witnessed one or two unusual happenings in her life and the one who can recount a lifetime of visionary encounters. Pentikainen characterizes these latter individuals as "more sensitive and susceptible of having supranormal experiences" and identifies them as "homo religiosus" persons, those who have had frequent contact with the supernatural and who welcome such crossing of boundaries between the ordinary and the extraordinary (122). The women discussed in chapter 6, "Gifted Women," fit Pentikainen's model. Though it is impossible to construct the outline of any single coherent belief system from these diverse narratives, it is, nevertheless, possible to make one generalization: behind these stories lies the ardent belief in fate.

3. Signs

Claims of supranormal experiences are common findings for the student of folk belief. (See, for example, the work of Dégh, Vazsonyi, Honko, Hufford, Bullard, Rojcewicz, and Danielson.) But accounts of these experiences have a precarious existence. Some gain acceptance by the folk group and travel from member to member as legend (Brunvand); others remain in the private world of memorates, unblessed with orthodoxy. That is not to say that they vanish; they do not. Rather, they lie dormant, distant memories to be produced and recited usually in the intimacy of a conversation between two people.

The longest and most extensive study of these narratives began in 1882 with the founding of the Society for Psychical Research in London. In an effort to rationalize accounts like those collected in this study, Edward Gurney, Frederick Myers, and Frank Podmore categorized two thousand first-hand testimonies relating experiences regarded by informants as "inexplicable by ordinary laws" (lxii). Whereas spiritualists had claimed the cause of these extraordinary experiences to be spirits returning from the dead, Gurney, Myers, and Podmore looked to the percipients, themselves, for the cause.[1] Certain psychic abilities, according to these scientists, allow some individuals to sense what others cannot.

Myers, the father of parapsychology, attempted, with Gurney and Podmore, not only to rescue this material from the "sensationalists," nineteenth-century women novelists (Gudas[55]), but also to rescue it from the tellers themselves. The fact that most of their informants were women (a situation which continued in parapsychological research into the twentieth century) played no role in their analysis. They sought to decontextualize these accounts, to "neutralize" them by removing them from the life story, the family, and the community which gave them life, to sever them from all belief systems and to neuter them as well. They endeavoured to deracinate these visions and treat them as anonymous data that could, if amassed in great enough numbers, be framed by the rules of science. They strove to bring "objectivity" to the investigation of strange occurrences, ghost stories, apparitions, and, thus, to chart a science of the unseen. Their purpose in gathering and categorizing so many accounts of the marvelous was to erase any sign of the teller from the tale: "This book has been compiled . . . with a view to correcting or neutralizing individual fancies or exaggerations, of leaving as little as possible to the unchecked idiosyncrasy of any single thinker." (xxxvi)

It was important for this work that the stories these scientists examined were based on some "real" experience and that they represented facts on which sound hypotheses could be based.[2] But the preoccupation with the event, itself, rather than its cultural context carries with it the burden of verification, of somehow distinguishing "real" experiences from imaginary ones. In his review of the Gurney, Myers, and Podmore book, *Phantasms of the Living,* William James considers the possibility of hoaxes: "It therefore comes back essentially to the investigator's instinct, or "nose" as one might call it, for good and bad evidence" (26). Ultimately, then, what this science rests on is the researcher's "nose" which enables him to judge the truth of each story, only admitting as evidence those with the smell of authenticity. Anyone who knows anything about storytelling (not to mention the realist novel) knows that truth can be chimerical, that the most authentic-sounding narrators are often the biggest liars.[3]

By the twentieth century, investigators began to assess the limitations of anecdotal evidence as a function of the imprecision of human memory and turned to the examination of these phenomena in the laboratory (Evans). J.B. and Louisa Rhine founded the famous Parapsychology Laboratory at Duke University in the 1930s. (See Mauskoph and McVaugh.) Through card guessing, mind reading, and automatic writing experiments, researchers studied subjects with extraordinary powers so that they might gather reproducible evidence that would allow scientists to explain the unexplainable. But the failure of parapsychologists to do what they set out to do — to explain these phenomena according to scientific principles — renders them modern alchemists inventing new metaphors rather than new truths, spinning their own yarns of sixth senses and telepathetic moments, of mind-over-matter and clairvoyance, of astro-travel and psychokinesis. Accounts of these experiences rightly belong in the realm of folklore and anthropology where they share with earlier traditions (and contemporary ones as well) an uneasiness with rational answers, craving more than the real and the mundane, forever slipping from empiricism's grasp.

Second Sightings

Many of the accounts I gathered detail clairvoyant or clairsentient experiences in which a woman claims to have "seen" or more vaguely "sensed" something happening in another place. Typically, the recipients of these intelligences passively witness scenes of family members in danger. Although powerless to intercede, these women can, at least, use their knowledge to comfort and sometimes to prevent further disaster.

Such is the case with Jenny Risk, who in a dream witnesses her cousin's trucking accident:

I was home and I dreamed this. My cousin was going with the circus. He was a young kid that got outa school to go with the circus. He run off. He woulda been sixteen, and he didn't want to go to school, so he left with the circus. I dreamed one night while he was gone that there was a highway with an overpass. I dreamed that a circus wagon, a big red and white truck, was going on there, and all at once, it was gone. It wrecked and fell off. And then here David, my cousin, was climbing out going up to get onto the highway, and every time I'd put out my arm to get him and hold onto him, he'd slide back. And we'd do this all over again. I never did catch David. I never did get ahold of him, but I remember he wasn't hurt. He was climbing and reaching for me; he wasn't hurt.

He was due in the night that I dreamed this. So the next morning, soon as I got my husband off to work, I gets my automobile and drives it over to my cousin's house — it was her son. She said, "Why, you're early." I said, "Yeah, did David get in?" I never let on about the dream, see. She said, "No, David didn't get in, and I'm worried. Didn't sleep all night." I said, "Well, I'll tell you something. I knew that he didn't get in before I come over here. I dreamed he had a wreck, but he wasn't hurt. He was in a white and red circus vehicle, and it went off an overpass, but David was all right. He didn't get hurt because he was crawling up to me, and I was trying to get his hand to pull him up with me. I never did get ahold of his hand, but he wasn't hurt. That's the reason they're delayed." I said, "Well, I think I'll just hang around. I imagine he'll be

in after awhile." And I stayed, and David come in. I said, "Don't say a
thing to David when he comes; let him tell you why he's late."

And when he did get there he said the very same words that I saw.
He told us that they drug the truck into Millray, a little town right there
by Rushville by a junkyard to be fixed.

She said, "Come on, Jenny," and we all got in that car and drove over
to Millroy to this place where they pulled the truck in. When we first
started into town and I saw this big yard, I said, "There it is." It was a
big red and white vehicle. I'd seen it, see, in my dream, and I'd never
seen it before in my life. [Risk]

This is an unusually complete account: beginning with the identification of her cousin as the "young kid" who ran off to join the circus,
followed by a detailed description of the dream, and concluding with
a record of the next day's confirmation of that dream. From one pre-
spective, this might be read as a feminine version of the prodigal son,
who, in rejecting the security of the maternal world, charts a course
through the more dangerous, transient circus life. He has broken the
feminine grip that once held him home, a grip that the narrator tries
to restore in an effort to pull him up from the ravine into which his
circus life has cast him. The mother's inability to prevent his departure
and the narrator's failure to secure his safe return illustrate the powerless roles assigned to women in the dream. Although neither is able
to affect the world of masculine action (the narrator must see her husband off to work before rushing over to confirm her dream), the narrator takes from the actor control of his own story. The tale is hers to
tell, the evidence hers to identify. She, as witness, then, becomes more
central to the recapitulation of the story than its primary character.
The boy's telling is merely the redundant affirmation of the truth of
her dream: "he said the very same words that I saw."

The affirmation of one's reliability as a narrator, the evidence that
one underwent such an unusual happening, concludes this narrative
and many others. Often the voice of that authentication is masculine.
Risk retells the boy's story as her own but then must finally cede to
him the role of verifier. In another narrative, a letter from her husband
corroborates her testimony. In this way, the feminine is authenticated
by the masculine and the mysterious grounded in the everyday.

My husband was in World War II in the Eighth Air Force, and I was canning cherries. I ran the place by myself, picked the cherry tree, and I had them in a big aluminum canning dishpan. I thought, "Well, I'll go in there where it's real nice and cool." So I went in the dining room, and I just thought, "Well, it's so nice in here I'll just sit here, look out the window, and do my cherries."

I started outa the kitchen and had to step up to the dining room. I started to step up, had this dishpan in my hand, and a plane flew right in front of my face afire, a B-17! It disappeared right up in the left-hand corner of my dining room, right in the corner! It just disappeared. It just went into the wall in the corner. This was in Carthage, Indiana. I'd been going to the post office there every day and getting my mail. My husband was in the war, and we wrote every day to each other. But I didn't get any mail after this happened, and I thought, "Well, something's radically wrong." Finally, I got eighteen letters all at once. They'd been held up because of combat, see. He was in weather reconnaissance. And then he told it in his letter; he said that the plane had been fired on, and his ball turret gunner'd been killed. The ball turret gunner was a Lithuanian, and he'd been cut through in the middle, cut right in two! The plane had caught on fire, and they had to fly a crippled plane back to the base. [Risk]

This is clearly a vision and not a dream. Two levels of reality operate simultaneously: the normal and the supranormal. The narrator establishes a static scene of domestic order, one totally under feminine control ("I ran the place by myself"), where the cyclic activities of harvesting and preserving take place. Upon this tranquil scene is superimposed the B-17, agent of destruction that is itself destroyed. This narrative juxtaposes nature and culture: the former female, private, and hidden, the latter male, public, and devastatingly open.

For visionaries there is no contradiction in the coexistence of ordinary and extraordinary states of consciousness, of the simultaneous perception of both the local and the distant. Nor is a vision considered less significant if its full interpretation remains temporarily hidden. The eighteen letters held up by the fighting abroad confirms Risk's vision and provide the missing pieces to the puzzle of its reading.

Other accounts of clairvoyant moments are briefer than Risk's and typically devoid of character and plot:

I have gotten feelings about my family. Several times, I've been at work and something had told me, "Go home; there's something wrong." Just little things like that. And maybe I ignored it, but when I did get home, I found that there was something wrong on several occasions. I guess it's a type of clairvoyance in a way. [Murphy]

One woman's coincidence is another woman's psychic moment. What such accounts illustrate are the conflicting responsibilities of family and work. Separation anxiety manifests itself in the unambiguous command, "Go home; there's something wrong." When she acts on these signs by abandoning work and returning home Murphy confirms her fears. When she ignores them she learns later of their validity, possibly too late to resolve a family crisis. Murphy had learned to trust these warnings not because she believes them to be messages from some divine or benevolent force guarding her family but because they confirm her ability, her clairvoyance (technically her clairaudience), to be at work and yet "keep an eye on things" at home. In a magical world one can read distant events in local signs.

But to what extent is it possible to reconstruct this magical world in prison? Prison is a ruled place. The only movement visible is the rigidly patterned passage of women to jobs in the sewing room, laundry, upholstery shop, and kitchen; to typing and cosmetology classes; and to meals. Their quiet lines trace the same design day after day. Women daily come to the prison through jail and leave through parole, but within this walled and double-fenced community, all physical motion merely exaggerates the hard fact of stasis.

Designed to permit total surveillance, the modern prison monitors an inmate's location within the prison grounds at all times and strictly regulates her communication with everyone inside and outside the prison. Staff ration and supervise her visits with family and friends, read all incoming and outgoing letters, and limit phone calls, which take place in an open hall near a guard station. It is usually days before a woman learns of events at home. Much of the pain of imprisonment is the awareness that time continues to pass at a faster pace on the outside: styles change, friends move, relatives die, children grow. Only a person in prison truly knows the terrible pathos latent in the common phrase, "life goes on." Yet, though prohibited from participating in that life, experiencing that change, the prisoner is at least insulated from direct perception of it. Because she must imagine any life she cares to live, she can associate on her own terms with the world from which her crime has divorced her. The imagination, resisting confinement, remembers and invents a world which it alone patterns and supervises.

Messages from Home

The modern prison, a temple to rationalism, is an extreme example of the institutional machine: every minute is scheduled, every space surveyed. Despite the fifteen-foot-high double fence topped with razor wire sharp enough to cut paper, despite the taller guard towers and television monitors, despite the rarity of escape attempts on the part of women, all activity ceases for an hour six times a day for the counting of prisoners, prisoners who themselves are numbered, live in numbered rooms down numbered hallways. Everything in a woman's possession is counted: her articles of clothing, her pencils, her books and magazines, the minutes she may talk with a visitor, and the time she spends at dinner, in the rec room, and in the shower.

Built according to a secular humanist line of radical individualism, this prefectly ordered world assumes that one is responsible for one's actions and that certain actions produce certain consequenes. But no matter how clear the logic of the institution, a prisoner may refuse to live according to its rationalist principles of cause and effect, action and consequences. She may embrace instead an anachronistic belief in the correspondence between events in the external world and personal sensations. Removed from the world, she reads its events as personal signs. Public and private flip-flop: the most public world of the state institution becomes the most exoticly private.

Although separated from her family, the prisoner sometimes receives messages from home in unofficial ways: through visions and dreams. These communications keep her in touch with those she loves, often warning her of imminent harm. They allow her to protect and comfort those she has left behind, thus fulfilling family responsibilities from prison.

The sense of urgency felt by the woman who receives such "messages" is rarely shared by the officer in charge, who may prohibit her call home because that officer has no legitimate reason to believe that there is an emergency at home or because she may think that the prisoner is willfully deceiving her. The ability to see what others cannot see, to know what is happening at a great distance produces scoffers as well as believers. Although officers are generally skeptical of such mysterious messages, these warnings are unambiguous in the minds of those who receive them. So strong are the sensations of trouble, that those who experience them often panic if not allowed to telephone home.

One woman, according to three other inmates, received a pain in her leg when there is any danger at home.

> There was a girl here that could tell when somethin' happened at home. Her name was Gwen. I remember one day when we were in the cottage. She got complainin' about her leg was hurtin'. She say, "It's my mother."
>
> I say, "Your mother?"
>
> "Yeah, every time somethin' happen to my mother, my leg hurts."
>
> As soon as she called home, they had just took her mother to the hospital 'cause her mother's crippled and she had fell down the steps.
>
> Every time something would happen at her home, it would be like something would just all of a sudden hit her and she would jump up.
> [Johnson]

Interestingly, the site of the "sign," this woman's leg, allows her sympathetically to sense her crippled mother's distress and to respond quickly with expressions of concern. Such action in response to clairvoyance, often in the face of skeptical officers unwilling to trust an inmate's "intuition," is a motif that runs through all of these accounts. The powerful message of trouble at home makes its way magically, without interception, past warden, assistant warden, chaplin, classifications counselor, shift supervisor, and hall officer: a simple and direct line of communication between mother and daughter. Reverse communication is not, however, so efficient. While the clairvoyant receives her message unmediated, she must often negotiate the intricate network of overseers in order to respond to the warning received.

Accounts like these express the fear that there may be trouble at home. This fear prompts a call home or other communication which, in turn, confirms the original anxiety. The feeling has its object, and narrative is born in a scenario of random emotions and events which seem, upon the reflection of the narrator, to be linked and to be subject to some mysterious principle.

> One night before I laid in bed and I was physically tired as well as emotionally drained, I just kept thinkin' about my daughter and thinkin' about her, and I knew that she either had to be sick or she had to have done something to herself, because that's the only time that I really really dwell on it. And I called home the next day at lunch time, and she had wrecked herself goin' off the porch.
> She fell off the porch. She was playin' "Evil Kneevil" (she's a real tomboy now). Angie was playin' "Evil Kneevil" off the porch. I know there was no use in tellin' her, "Don't do that, you're gonna hurt yourself, you're gonna get scars." So I said, "Go tell your uncle to get you one of the car ramps." He gave it to her, and now it's safer. She's gonna jump, so give her somethin' that she won't kill herself with. [Frank]

Most women come to prison with minor children at home, and the greatest pain they experience is separation from those children. The greatest guilt they feel is the guilt of the absent mother. In the visionary moment, that absence evaporates, fantastically linking prisoner and home. The mother is both apart and there at the same time. Sensing danger at home, Frank calls and from prison negotiates a solution to her daughter's problem, thus preventing further disaster.

There is, of course, another interpretation of these events. It would not be unusual for any absent mother, prisoner or nonprisoner, to call home and learn that her young child had fallen and cut herself. But Frank, like many women in prison, subscribes instead to a belief in the connection between her thoughts and events at home. Such a belief bestows power and confirms the sense of themselves as good mothers and good daughters even in captivity.

Worries about the welfare of children are constantly shared in prison conversation. A woman who was sexually abused by her father from the age of eight until well into her teenage years fears that her daughter, now in the custody of her parents, may be similarly abused. Another must negotiate with guardians who refuse to bring her children to the prison to visit her. Another must explain to her three-year-old son that she really is his mother despite the fact that his uncle insists that the boy call her "aunt."

Visions of danger to a child are particularly common among prisoners. In her description of danger to her son, Luscious tells of other adults who are taking her son from her:

The other night I was sitting on the bed and I was thinking about my friend (she had left) and I saw this, like a moving van. It had "North American" and "Von Paris" on it. And in the back of the van was my son. These people, this man and woman, were trying to kidnap him, and I saw the numbers, the black numbers on the back of the truck. The van opened up to the trailer part, and I saw all these barrels and boxes. I was running after this truck, and then they stopped it, this black couple. They put my son out, and I ran and grabbed him. He was crying in the back of the van. But when he got out he wasn't crying; he just wasn't the same. He was motionless.

Later I was talking to Lumberjack, and Lumberjack says, "You know what's going on, so you know why that was shown to you, that your son may be in danger." I said, "Yeah, I know why but sometimes, Lumberjack, I get so tired." But then I think about all that's happened to me, and I think hatred is what keeps me going. That's sad. Usually some people have an inspiration: a person, flowers, or something. Hatred is what motivates me.

So Lumberjack says, "I hope that what you saw really doesn't happen." And I says, "But if it does, it's just a deeper web, that's all." I says, "It doesn't matter; they didn't hurt him." And she says, "Yeah, but just the fact of him being missing." But I says, "He won't be missing. I will know where he is at every moment of the day." [Luscious]

What should be a joyful occasion, the release of an inmate, is often a sorrowful one for her prison friends. They may hear from her for awhile, but they will most likely never see her again. The release of her prison friend provides the context for Luscious's vision about the abduction of her son.

Luscious does not at first tell whether the scene "shown" to her takes place contemporaneously (technically, a clairvoyant moment) or foreshadows an event to come (a premonition). Only in the subsequent conversation with Lumberjack does it become clear that what Luscious sees is a premonition. Commonly, women like Luscious who receive visions with some frequency experience both clairvoyant visions and premonitions. Commonly, too, they make little distinction between these two kinds of visions, one often reinforcing another. More importantly, Lumberjack's conversation with Luscious illustrates the typical way in which women communicate visions in prison: as confessions generally to a single, sympathetic listener. The friend in whom Luscious confides is Lumberjack, a masculine partner in a lesbian relationship (a "stud" in prison parlance). Not a lesbian herself, Luscious is, nevertheless, proud of her relationships with several of her "preference friends," as she calls them. She enjoys kidding them about their practiced male walks, their butch haircuts, and their makeshift codpieces, while at the same time she values their loyalty and their trust.

Second, Luscious's account illustrates the conflicting emotions of confinement: the passivity ("sometimes, Lumberjack, I get so tired") and the anger at others in control—those who control her children, her home, her daily life. She can reassert control only imaginatively.

The examples cited so far illustrate mothers' anxiety about the safety of minor children usually left in the care of a relative, but women in prison also sometimes fear for the fate of older children. Karen Johnson, for example, recounts a dream about her son which she comes to believe is a sign that he is in danger:

I was restin' one night. I had a dream, and I dreamed that somebody came after me and that my son came outa nowhere and put his arms around me, "You're gonna be all right," he said. Whoever it was was trying to kill me, my son had saved my life.

I know that sometimes you gotta reverse dreams. Now, my son's in prison too. He's doin' five years. After I had that dream I kept sayin', "Who is it that's tryin' to harm me and Tommy's tryin' to protect me from?" As it turned around—well, this is how I look at it—I get word that it happened to him, that somebody was tryin' to harm him up there. He was the one that had got stabbed. That's why I tell you I was dealin' with somethin' heavy that week. I was the only one he could reach out to. He couldn't get a call out to my mother, because he couldn't trust nobody on the phone, so he snuck, a letter out to me.

You know, my mother's another one that gets those visions like that. My mother say, "Oh, all day long I kept knowin' that some harm was comin' to my child (first she thought it was my brother), but come out to be, it's my other heart [her grandson]."

Two people in her family got killed in Cleveland, and she saw it before it happened both times. And in '74, somebody tried to kill my brother, and she saw it before it happened, but she dreamt he died. She would go into a sleeplike dream and have a vision real plain. Everything that happened to my brother she saw, except the part that he lived. When he got to the hospital the doctors kept tellin' her, "This boy's supposed to be dead; it's only the grace of God and his strong will that kept him living." My brother told me that he felt himself dyin' and his eyes closin'. He had major surgery 'cause he got stabbed up real bad. My brother fought real hard to keep his eyes open. He wouldn't go to sleep 'cause he said if his eyes hada closed, he woulda died. So, the same way she saw this when it happened was like how I dreamt it with my son. Soon as I got the letter, I went straight to the officer and I said, "I gotta call somebody right now."

She said, "It's count time, can't call during count time." I said, "I don't care." My exact words were, "Fuck the ticket! My child could be somewhere dead or gettin' killed." [Johnson]

The high incidence of catastrophe of various sorts in the lives of women who end up in state prisons and in the lives of family members renders such foreboding visions less extraordinary. Viewed in the context of such lives, imprisonment (a family calamity as well as a personal tragedy) would seem to have the immediate effect, at least, of removing one from harm's way. Such is not the case for Johnson's son, whose existence is as precarious in prison as it was on the streets. Separated from him, both mother and grandmother manifest their anxiety in similar ways. Visions are sometimes shared family experiences.

Just as visions may be shared, so also may the interpretations and misinterpretations of visions. It is interesting that the grandmother and the mother are incorrect in their first readings of the warning they receive and must revise their interpretations, substituting the correct family member in their visions. In this case at least, dreams are understood in a structuralist fashion: roles and functions within dreams may be filled by a number of performers. To interpret dreams and to know how to act, one must cast the correct player in each role. One must decide who is in danger and who must come to the rescue. Dreams are timeless plots that provide as much reassurance as empirical validation.

Even though a woman can arrive at a right interpretation of dreams through such substitution and role-reversal, she cannot alter the inevitable tragedy that dreams forecast. Dreaming is fatalistic: the dreamers of this family remain helpless in the face of the dangers that befall other family members. The only change that occurs is made by the prisoner, who breaks *not* the rule of destiny but the rule of the prison: "Fuck the ticket!"

In one sense then, visions are as much a curse as a blessing; they impart a dreadful superior knowledge before which the seer too falls victim. The grandmother has visions preceding the deaths of two family members in Cleveland but is powerless to prevent these deaths. Even though her 1974 vision in which someone is trying to kill her son prophesies a greater tragedy than the actual outcome, the dreamer plays no part in rescuing her son from death. His strong will to live and the "grace of God" alter the outcome and demand a revision of the dream narration. Though dreams do not impart the power to reverse fate, they do provide the mothers and grandmothers who experience them a way of "watching over" their children who are away and in danger. Though powerless to prevent the violence that will come to their child, Karen Johnson and her mother can, at least, comfort that child.

Premonitions

Many women receive signs of their coming to prison in a dream, a vision, or by means of a mysterious feeling. Wilma Bond's premonition of coming to prison is a typical account.

> I knew that I was coming to prison. I could see it; I even visualized bars — even though I wasn't behind bars per se — but I even visualized the bars, and this was even before it happened.
>
> I could see myself in a prison. This dream was like a dream that come to me several times, and I knew somewhere down the line — I didn't know where or when — that it would come. And sure enough, I'm here. [Bond]

Forseeing one's imprisonment even before a crime is committed removes the actual imprisonment from the logic of crime and punishment and allows a woman to absolve herself of final responsibility for her crime. Her actions are not the cause of her imprisonment; fate is. Instead of a narrative which begins with motivation for the crime, the details of the crime itself, its detection, followed by punishment, Wilma Bond tells a story that begins with a premonition and ends with imprisonment: any account of her crime is conspicuously absent.

Fate may not only be blamed for a woman's first prison term; it may also explain subsequent sentences. In the narrative that follows Sonja Briggs tells of a voice that forecasts her return to the Maryland Correctional Institution for Women.

> When I was here before in '75, a certain voice spoke to me. It was like a ESP. It was really wild. I was just talkin' about this the other day with some of my roommates.
>
> I was in Horigan Cottage at the time C [cottage] was not yet finished; it was being rebuilt. It was late at night. I was on the front, and I was looking towards C cottage back in '75 and something said to me, "Sonja, you're going to be here again. You're going to come again and you're also going to be in a talent show and you're going to do well." Well, that happened. I won the talent show playing my guitar. And Sue Malone, who sang. Bang! It come true about "Sonja, you will be in C cottage." Well, I did. I come back in '82, and I went promptly to C cottage. [Briggs]

Ironically, the narrative of a second prison term is told as a success story. The vision allows the prisoner to transform a curse into a blessing, or at least to balance the misfortune of returning to prison with the good fortune of winning the talent show. Visions of this sort clearly serve the purpose of those in authority by encouraging passive acceptance. An "adjusted" woman according to prison authority is one who accepts her confinement and makes the most of her time.

Premonitions may even allow her to prepare for incarceration. When former inmates and a police car appear to Luscious with special prominence, she knows that she must get her house in order for imprisonment will inevitably follow:

> When I would normally see people on the street who had been down here before I would say, "Hey, how you doing?" and keep going. But every time I get ready to fall, every time I'm about to get picked up by the police, I know because these people stick out like a sore thumb. When I meet them and they say, "What's up?" I says, "I'm going again." I always know. The policemen of the area may not be looking for me at that time, but it's coming.
>
> Like this last time, before the police were looking for me, they hadn't

had the warrants out then 'cause they didn't know who they were looking for. I was downtown, and I saw this police car pull up behind
another car, and the police car just appeared to be all stretched out. I
says, "Oh well, there I go." So I started getting the house in order.
I know when I'm going; I can feel it. It's an instinctive ability I guess; I
don't know what it is. [Luscious]

Even before the state knows it is looking for her, Luscious receives
a warning that she will be sought, apprehended, and convicted. The
process is inevitable and operates totally outside of her control. Any
suggestion that imprisonment is the result of her actions ("every time
I get ready to fall") is quickly qualified. Lest the listener interpret her
fall in moral terms as a slip back into crime, Luscious makes clear that
she is talking about a fall back into the hands of the police ("every
time I'm about to get picked up by the police"). This denial of responsibility for crime is a common (and psychologists might even say so-
ciopathic) reaction of many women in prison. They often speak in articles rather than possessive pronouns of "the crime" or "it" and of
their husband's "death" rather than of his murder.

But once in prison, what one dreads most is being put "on lock,"
in a tighter, more secure prison-within-prison. The fear of more restrictive confinement generates a frequent dream for many who are imprisoned. The fact that their nightmares come true is not amazing;
what is amazing is that some actually manage to avoid time on lock.
Among even the model prisoners I interviewed (prisoners who had
long sentences but who had adjusted well in the eyes of the authorities) I found few who had not spent some time in solitary confinement. Ronda Miller's dreams articulate the fear shared by many women,
the fear of being more narrowly confined in Solitary:

When I was downstairs in Horigan [quarantine] before I moved upstairs [maximum security] I had to rec [socialize for one hour] with the
people that stayed upstairs, and I used to look down the halls and say, "I
could never make it up here." The doors were slotted. I would wake up
in nightmares findin' myself in one of those rooms. I would wake up saying, "No, please don't let that happen." But eventually it did happen.
When I got up there I was angry again for havin' to move up there and
to have those slots slammed in my face time after time. We weren't
allowed to communicate with each other. [Miller]

Dreams forecast the inevitable deepening of punishment — isolation in solitary. By understanding punishment not as the consequence of misdeeds but as the inevitable outcome of fate, women abstract themselves from the prison and from their jailers.

Most accounts of premonitions I collected warned of misfortune to come, but a few were actually good omens. In her interpretation of various physical sensations, Anna May Lee reads particular messages:

> I can·always tell when I'm getting ready to go somewhere strange — my feet itch! See, lately my feet have been itching off and on. Every time my feet itch, I'm going to walk on strange ground. Like before I went to court, my feet were itching. The week before I was supposed to go for sentencing, my feet were burning on the bottom. They was itching so bad I said, "I'm gonna walk on strange ground." I knew I was not going home. I knew I was coming here. It wouldna been strange ground at home and my feet wouldna itched like that.
>
> Burke: Is it both feet?
>
> Lee: They alternate between the two. One day might be this foot; the next day it's the other foot. If they itch simultaneously, it's gonna be real soon. Right now they're alternating.
>
> A hand itch is always money. The right hand'll itch if the money is coming directly to me. If it's coming in the mail, then my left hand'll itch. It works every time.
>
> And my nose means that someone's comin' that I haven't seen.
>
> Burke: Do you have any relatives who have a similar ability?
>
> Lee: My mother does. Her hand itches and her nose itches. Her eye jumps, too, if someone's gonna make her angry. Mine does too. Whatever I do to try to stop it, it will continue to do it. I might not get angry today; it might be tomorrow, but that eye always prepares me for it. And when the issue's over, my eye stops jumping.
>
> My mother and them, they attribute some of these things to the old-time saying about having a veil over their face because they can see things. My mother has extra sense, too. She's really good about being able to tell what's going to happen. I don't know whether she dreams it or she sees a picture of it. My grandmother did it, too. My mother's mother was part Indian. [Lee]

Lee's narrative demonstrates the persistence of folk beliefs in prison: the belief that those born with a caul enjoy psychic powers and the belief in the supersensitivity of the female body. For Anna May Lee, the body contains sites upon which signs of the future may be written.

Unlike palm reading, such bodily signs need no expert to interpret their significance. Like her mother and grandmother before her, Lee is her own interpreter.

Signs of riches to come require little interpretation. Visions of lottery numbers and winning horses clearly chart the path to fortune. Though the prisoner is in no position to act on these omens, she can recall a time when she was free to follow such gambling lore and can assist others on their quest for fortune. The accounts of Sonja Briggs and Luscious that follow show how a dream and a vision, when heeded, bring riches and how the "seer" enriches the lives of those around her.

I won't ever forget this one dream I had. My sister-in-law called it the work of the devil, but I don't think so, because it brought me money. My mother used to own a race horse, and we used to go frequently to the race track—Pimlico and where have you. January of '79 I believed it was, January 12th, I had a dream that I played 681 (which is on the back of my license plate on my car) in the 9th race. Well, I played it and it hit for something like two thousand and some odd dollars. And I told my mother to play the numbers and she did. Me and Michael and my mother went, and Michael played it and I played it, and it hit just like that [*snaps fingers*] and it won eighty to one! I'll never forget it. [Briggs]

One particular officer, I told her about a number that came up in the lottery. It happened, the number came to me when I was getting my tray. I was in my cell, and when I reached for the tray a funny sensation came over me. And I says, "Oh God, here it comes again." And you know, it was like a movie screen, just like I was seeing a theater movie. I saw it, the whole thing, and I told her about it and she says, "What's the number?" I says, "210," and she says, "That's the number I always play." I says, "You're just saying that 'cause I told you 210." She says, "No, and then she played it for five dollars, and she hit! It was about two weeks ago, and the pharmacy tech, he played it too.

Sometimes when this kind of thing happens I'll be staring at one particular spot, and Lumberjack and them will say, "Oh, God, here she goes checking through the country!" But they understand it; they accept it. This one girl, Gloria, she's a very bright, very intelligent young lady (well, she doesn't like to be referred to as a lady—young woman) she told me there was an institute in Washington, the George Washington Institute or something, that did studies on some people that had these characteristics, but I says, "I don't want to go and dig up something; I might find something out." She says, "No, they research and they bring

it out to its fullest potential." I says, "It's all right the way it is, Gloria."
[Luscious]

Outside of prison, the ability to predict the winner of a race makes
one money; inside it wins one an identity as someone with powers
even the officers heed.

But sometimes it is best not to inquire too far into the mysterious.
The superstition that one may jinx a sign of good luck by speaking
too much about it is a belief shared by those women who attest to
the power of premonitions. Premonitions of good to come are very
rare, and if a woman experiences one, she is usually hesitant to tell
about it, perferring instead to speak in general terms about her wish
or her hunch that something desired will come true.

Melissa Stone has applied for a special therapy/education program
available at a neighboring male institution and knows that only a
handful of women will be allowed to participate in this three-year
project. She fears that speaking about the event before it occurs will
jeopardize the outcome.

> I keep havin' one. Right now, me sittin' here, I got a good feelin', but
> I'm not gonna say it 'cause I'm scared it won't happen. I'll tell you. I
> really wanna go to Patuxent bad. It's a real good program; they got real
> good education. It's a tough program, but it's gonna make me move; it's
> gonna get me out. [Stone]

Whether promise or warning, these signs define a realm beyond prison control. In a system designed to erase individual difference, women
living in prison discuss past premonitions and welcome new ones as
uniquely personal communications unmonitored by authority.

4. Return of the Dead

Revenants

Accounts of returning spirits abound in both classical and popular literature. These revenants appear for a variety of reasons: to assist or reassure the living, to trouble or injure them, to complete unfinished business, or to have sexual relations with the living. A restless spirit may also cross back into the land of the living as a result of an untimely death (an accident, murder or suicide). If survivors have failed to observe proper burial rites or if they have disregarded the final wishes of the diseased, a disquieted spirit may visit the living. But whatever their reason for appearing, revenants dramatize the permeability of boundaries between the living and the dead.

Several of the women I interviewed told of receiving comforting apparitions or disturbing nightmares. Their ghostly visitors might appear with all, or just part, of their spectral form; they might not be visible at all but merely speak; or they might make their presence known with a sensation. When invited to "explain" such visions, several women described them as isolated mysterious events that could not be interpreted; others viewed them as the unambiguous efforts of spirits to communicate with the living. Narratives of these experiences, like those of other visionary happenings, tend to be short accounts with little detail and scant explanation. The following is a typical narrative of a sense of the presence of the dead before burial:

> It was a true experience on my part. I was not sleeping. I was fully awake, sober. My mother's boss was very good to us. He had passed away. He had a heart attack at six in the morning and died within minutes. We all witnessed this. The paramedics came, but there was nothing they could do.
>
> Later on that evening we were discussing funeral arrangements at the table. Now, the house was brand new in Waverly. We were sitting

around the table. There was no wind that night, but the door blew open. Of course I jumped. But Dusty (that was his name) he had a habit of blowing in our ears as a joke, and I had felt that right at that moment—I felt him blow in my ear, "whoooo," and my hair stood up. I reached for my sister. Oh, I was frightened.

When I seen him at the funeral home I had to turn away: I thought I could see him rising up, but I think that was my imagination. But what I felt at that kitchen table was definitely real.

My mother also—she does not believe in the occult or anything like that. She's a Pisces. She had told me that she had seen her mother come to her. When she told me, it gave me goose bumps because I never heard her talk like that. And I could feel with her. [Briggs]

This narrative illustrates the common belief that, soon after death, spirits of the dead visit the people and places they frequented in life. In some accounts the newly dead linger only until burial; in others they inhabit the vicinity for some time.[1] This narrative illustrates, too, that although revenants may have kind intentions, percipients often fear them. Blowing into ears, a playful, affectionate act on the part of the living, becomes grim and chilling when practiced by the intruding dead. In response, the narrator, here seated with female family members, retracts from the deadly presence as if pulling tighter the circle of the living seated around the kitchen table: an inner circle of living drawn together by the dead.

Upon reflection, Briggs is careful to distinguish the sensation of the return of the dead man's spirit from the vision of him rising up in his coffin at the funeral home. The former, she maintains, is a "real" event, the latter, a product of her imagination.

Typically, one finds in these accounts statements that both uphold and challenge their veracity. "It was a true experience on my part" at once insists on the truth of the experience and qualifies it with the relative disclaimer, "on my part," leaving open the possibility that someone else might view it as false. As further proof, Briggs places her story in a family tradition of revenants, thus domesticating the otherwise exotic and strange. Her dead grandmother returned to her skeptical mother, someone supposedly less susceptible to the mysterious and the occult than herself. But even this characterization of her mother as rational is itself based on the antirationalist system of astrology: "She's a Pisces." In a sense, Briggs attempts the rhetorically impossible—

proving the unprovable, presenting in objective terms the totally subjective. In an effort to authenticate her report she supplements it with additional evidence that such unexplainable events really do take place.

Although the return of the dead is often a family affair, it may be nonetheless terrifying. Anna May Lee never saw the body of her dead father, but spent the troubling weeks after his death frightened by visions of him:

> When my father died, it took me a long time to get over it because I was carrying guilt around. I was saying, "Well, maybe I shoulda paid more attention to my father." He had been dead almost a week before they found him. "Did he cry out for somebody? Why didn't he call me and let me know he was sick? Maybe if I had been keeping in contact with him more often, maybe I woulda known." All those thoughts were running through my mind.
>
> He had a car, and for a long time after he died it seemed like every time I looked out my window, I could see him setting in his car. And I kept the lights on for weeks afterward because I was nervous. Even now, every now and then, I see him in my dreams. I dream that I see him in that black bag they put him in.
>
> He had started decomposing so badly because when he fell, he fell next to the radiator and the radiator was going full blast at the time. And I envisioned how he must have looked, because when we went to the morgue to identify him, my mother did it because she knew that I was a weak person when it came to death. She thought that she could stand it more so than me. So, she did it. She told me—'cause she almost fainted— she told me later on that I woulda never gotten over it. I woulda went off the deep end, because she knows how weak I am. I'm stronger now, much stronger than I was, and I've gotten that way because of that and because my mother's so sickly now. She's by herself. She's an only child too.
>
> I think about her as if to say, "What's gonna happen if something happens to her while I'm in here?" So I'm learning how to be able to face things. And that's something I've never been able to do before. [Lee]

Lee feared her violent father; why then should she welcome the vision of him after death? After all, he comes in a car as if to take her with him. Appearing outside her home, the specter inspires both guilt and dread in the daughter after his death. This is a narrative about the disintegrated nuclear family: the spectral father who terrifies both in life and death, the surviving mother who had once been strong enough to identify the badly decomposed body of her husband is herself now weakened, and the imprisoned daughter whose guilt and affection mingle in this family narrative. Having made the painful transition from child to adult and prisoner, Lee acknowledges a new strength, one that allows her to contemplate the death of her mother and to displace the intrusions of her dead father from waking vision to dream.

Whether frightening intruders or welcome visitors, manifestations of the dead seem to have a will of their own. They perform, usually as the sole actors on the visionary stage, before a passive audience of one, with the viewer rarely violating the dramatic distance separating herself from the specter before her. They alone seem to control their comings and goings, inciting fear, consolation, or annoyance. They bear messages for the living but never seek any communication in return. Representatives from another realm, they are rarely under human control. One never touches a revenant but may be touched by one.

Only a rare informant maintains that she has any influence over their manifestation. Such a woman is Violet Star. Through thought concentration she can "bring back" the dead, and conversely, through distraction, she can avoid their materialization. Even though the spirit of her dead grandfather forecasts freedom for this death-row inmate, she is wary of spiritual incarnations. Some are bothersome feisty creatures; others appear in grotesque form.

> The spirit of my dead grandfather has come here. He came to tell me not to worry, everything was gonna be all right, that I'd be free. I feel him a lot. I don't know all the time if it's him or not 'cause sometimes I don't check to see; I just cover up my head and go to sleep 'cause the spirits annoy me. If I start to think about him a lot he'll appear, but I try not to do that 'cause I don't wanna bring nobody back. [Star]

Revenants are "spirits" according to Star who are both self-willed and responsive to the will of some (such as herself) tutored in the arts of witchcraft. The practices of witchcraft over many years have increased Star's sensitivity to spirits. More intrusive than welcome, they disturb the prisoner's repose with their insistent demand for her attention by disturbing the contents of her room in poltergeist fashion, polluting the room with their foul odors, and sending blasts of cold air her way. Constantly aware of their irksome presence, Star only occasionally expends the tremendous psychic energy necessary to enlist these impish demons. Mere thought can invoke them, but only great energy can direct them.

A more welcome spirit is Wilma Bond's grandmother who returns to reassure her surviving granddaughter:

> I knew when my grandmother was gonna die; God revealed it to me. It was on a Saturday. He came to me and showed me two faces, and there was no body attached; it was just their faces. It was my mother's mother's face and my father's mother's face, and I was told that one of them was gonna die within the next couple days. He didn't say which one; He didn't specify which one, but those are the two faces I saw. So that Monday my grandmother, my mother's mother, she went in the hospital. She was havin' pains in her stomach and she went in the hospital. By that Tuesday evening she was dead. She was sufferin' from ulcers, and she had like a knot in her side. There was a hole and her intestines had protruded through this hole, and it looked like a balloon. It burst inside of her and poisoned her whole system. That's what took her away from here.
>
> She had had this problem for years, and you just don't think it's gonna all of a sudden get worse. But God had showed me that one of them was gonna pass away, but I didn't know which one. And I could not tell my mother or father that somebody's gonna die within the next couple days 'cause that would've frightened them, so I kept my mouth shut. I felt that God didn't want me to reveal this to anyone. He revealed it to me.
>
> So, when my grandmother passed away, I went down to North Carolina for her funeral and everything. The first night that I got there to my mother's house I was in bed with my husband layin' beside me, and my grandmother, who was dead, came in the room. She touched me on my big toe, just like I touch your hand now. She touched my toe and just called me by my middle name, "Anne." All I saw was her face, but I felt her touch my toe, my toe that stayed numb that whole day.
>
> I got outta the bed and went and told my momma, "Guess what, Grandma just came in the room!" She said, "Oh, you're kiddin'." And I said, "No, honestly I am not kiddin' you. She was here. She touched my toe and it's numb right now." She just like passed on out the window and went on. I wasn't frightened or anything; I was just relaxed and didn't worry about her 'cause I knew that she was all right and was leavin' this life.
>
> Since then, she has come back to me. I was always told through my other Indian grandmother that if anyone dead come back to you, mark their words whatever they say to you. She has come back another time, and she had on this beautiful white lace dress. She came back to my

mother's house. We were sittin' on the couch, and she told me she came
back to have dinner with my mother.

She always like lima beans and ham hocks. This was her favorite dish
my mother used to fix for her. She'd always tell my mother, "I'm comin'
over, and I want you to fix me these lima beans and these ham hocks."
So my mother would prepare this dish for her. So after she died she
came back to let me know that she was okay and she came back to have
this meal with my mother with these lima beans and ham hocks. She
was in this big lace dress just like she came down out of the sky, and she
sit there and ate her lima beans and ham hocks. She told us that she
had to go back in heaven before five o'clock 'cause that's when the gates
close. [Bond]

Wilma Bond's account of the return of her dead grandmother differs
from those that precede it because of its complexity. Really three stories,
this narrative proceeds from premonition to nocturnal appearance and
to the final meal with the dead—from partial vision, to revenant touch,
to fully realized revenant.

Superimposed on the domestic story of separation by death and subsequent reunification is the tale of divine disclosure. God communicates
to Bond through both words and images, but His intelligences are far
from exact. God's doubling of elders mystifies rather than enlightens,
producing a seemingly intentional ambiguity. But such partial revelations illustrate for Bond the proper relationship between God and hu-
manity: the former sees widely into the future, the latter only narrowly.

But what is Bond's relationship to her paternal, Indian grandmother?
Surviving Bond's maternal grandmother but dead at the time of this
interview, the Indian grandmother surfaces as a kind of phantom of
belief, confounding the narrative rather than clarifying it. She advises
her granddaughter to mark the words of a revenant, but the revenant
in this narrative speaks few words to mark. She calls her granddaughter
"Anne," presumably asks for lima beans and ham hocks, and tells her
daughter and granddaughter that she must be back in heaven before
the gates close.

The two grandmothers represent two figures of spiritual woman: the
spiritual "woman in white" and the ancestral Indian gifted woman.
The former is domesticated. Like the souls on All Souls' Day she returns
for dinner. The latter, representing matriarchal, pre-Christian wisdom,
is framed by the Christian narrative of death and resurrection.

Bond's narrative illustrates that visions are indeed family affairs (particularly female), but that different family members may have different reactions to them. Even though her husband is in bed beside her, Bond goes to her mother to report the first appearance of her dead grandmother. Her mother's reaction is disbelief; hers is welcoming acceptance.

Bond welcomes all revenants. Returning with the blessing of God, revenants do not frighten her. Instead, they often reassure:

> My father came back to me. My father, he was a good-lookin' man, handsome I thought. When I buried him we buried him in a blue suit. In this vision I remember me goin' to the grave site where my father was supposed to be. There was a guide that met me, and there was all this red dirt like a hill that I had to go down before I could come to the grave site where my father was. The guide was tellin' me to go to box 300. This is what was told in my vision, to go to box 300. So I go and I'm pullin' this box open, and here my father is in this box. He's layin' there with a little black turban on the top of his head. He had on his blue suit, and he looked so beautiful. I said, "Dad, are you all right?" And he said to me, "Baby (he always called me his baby) don't worry about me; I'm OK." And I knew right then and there that God had taken his soul and that he was gonna be all right. [Bond]

Distinguished by Bond's keen sense of detail, these vision accounts place her in the role of participant. Her prominence in the stories rivals that of the revenants. The premonition of her grandmother's death is a divine revelation which she alone receives, the secret she keeps until the appearance of her dead grandmother at the foot of her bed. Bond functions in her family as mediator between the living and the dead, assuring the living of the dead's salvation by way of sacred knowledge disclosed to her in visions. In communications from prison, Bond also reassures members of both her immediate and extended families that she is serving God in prison, not serving her time. The results of a divine plan rather than the consequence of human misdeeds, her incarceration transforms temporal trials into holy acts.

Oppressive Forces

The most common mysterious occurrence, related by young and old, black and white, straight and gay, is the experience of an oppressive, paralyzing force. What all accounts of this type share is the emphatic claim by the narrator that she is conscious at the time of the experience, even though she is lying down. A force, either accompanied by a vision or consisting simply of a pressure, prevents her movement and escape. In some accounts she wins her release by prayer or by concentration; in others, the force vanishes of its own will. Sometimes she associates this occurence with the return of the dead.

In his "experience-centered" work, *The Terror That Comes in the Night,* David Hufford seeks to establish an empirical basis for accounts of this sort (characterized by immobility, pressure on the chest, perception of surroundings, and sometimes the sound of footsteps). Because of the striking similarity of accounts by his Newfoundland informants, who refer to these attacks as the "Old Hag," and narratives related by Americans who did not have a name for their peculiar incidents, Hufford concludes that the "basic elements" of such experiences are "independent of culture" (15). Hufford's concept of culture is deeply reductive. He begins with a positivistic notion of an "experience" as a sense datum, and though he cautiously postpones a causal explanation of that datum, the explanation he forecasts is restricted to the options of physiology (the experience is the result of sleep paralysis with "hypnagogic hallucinations") or the supernatural:

> Many readers of this book will in part respond to what I have reported in terms of its usefulness in reducing apparently supernatural events to physical explanations; other readers will be concerned with whether my findings can be used in arguing for a reality beyond the physical. Looking back over what I have presented, I feel that there are some grounds for each argument. [256]

The alternative explanatory models of material and spiritual causes that Hufford advances to account for the experience of the "Old Hag" are, like rationalism and irrationalism, ultimately mirror reflections of each other. By restricting himself to these abstract options Hufford ignores the anthropological fact that these "experiences" are discursively produced and reproduced. That which ceaselessly mediates between these imaginary extremes of brute materialism on the one hand and ineffable spiritualism on the other is the loom of meaning called culture.

Even though the prisoners I interviewed report no consistent term for their similar experiences, neither those experiences nor the informants' accounts of them can be meaningfully engaged in isolation from the storytellers' characteristic way of inhabiting and constructing their social world. What experience, what narrative can? Some women describe these oppressive forces in terms of traditional beliefs in presences, harassing spirits, attacking demons, and disturbing revenants. Others seek explanations from fellow inmates. Murderers tend to explain these experiences in terms of their crimes. All set their attacks in the context of crisis, turmoil and tragedy. Although a few women recall incidents that happened before incarceration, the majority locate these encounters in the first year of imprisonment, sometimes in the early weeks of confinement, a time of isolation, fear, and depression.

Hufford's analysis of this phenomenon ignores the place of such narratives in the individual lives of their tellers. Even when he encounters striking evidence of the importance of context, Hufford dismisses it perfunctorily. In one of his interviews a female informant associates the easing of these attacks with the taking of anti-depressants. Hufford reluctantly concedes the link between depression and his "Old Hag": "it has been suggested to me that depression may have an effect on either the frequency or the nature of these attacks" (47). But once he entertains the interesting possibility, he hastily abandons it:

> Any drug that acts on the central nervous system might have an impact on a sleep-related experience. But victims of the attacks are naturally anxious to discover a cause for them and thus tend to associate them with any unusual variable in their lives. No depression-related effect has been indicated in the information I have collected so far, and any drug effect would be difficult to establish. [49]

Hufford asks us, on the one hand, to accept as legitimate the woman's account of her experience but, on the other, to reject her observation about its relation to depression. Far more willing to acknowledge as valid data the narrative portions of informant testimony than statements of belief, Hufford assumes the posture of medical examiner, admitting as evidence a patient's chronicle of complaints but dismissing her speculation as to its cause. For the folklorist, such distinctions are arbitrary. After all, one man's Old Hag might be another woman's depressive episode.

These experiences occur, according to Hufford, and then culture steps in to interpret them. But the question of the reality of these experiences which Hufford takes to be an important issue is not an issue at all. What is important is the meaning these accounts hold for the individuals who relate them and the groups in which they are told. Are they true? is a question for the metaphysician, not the folklorist. The folklorist must give an account of the cultural production of these narratives. And any account of their cultural production must recognize the role of gender. Hufford assumes that choosing a term is neutral, pretheoretical and precultural, and therefore fails to see that his gender-laden term, "Old Hag," is not simply descriptive but interpretive from the outset. The subordination of culture in favor of experience is analogical with the discrediting of women's accounts in favor of a preconceived notion of what an experience is. That is, in Hufford the subordination of culture is part and parcel of the silencing of women.

Gender, personal psychology, and environment play a greater role in these oppressive visions than Hufford is ready to admit. Murderers, for example, are twice as likely to report such happenings, often reporting them as the assaults of their previous victims. Confrontations between murderer and victim abound in folk and popular tradition, with the dead often returning to execute their revenge (Rogers, Rockwell). In prison narratives, a husband or lover whose abuse the prisoner endured and then revolted against returns after death as vengeful phantom.[2] The following three accounts by a woman who killed her husband illustrate not only the range and type of prison encounter but also the variety of experiences related by a single informant:

A

It's like I was paralyzed. I was in my cell, but I thought I was back in my own bedroom, back home. And the bed kept going from corner to corner, wall to wall. It was like it wanted to take me into the closet. It was a big black force that was pulling me. I couldn't move; I couldn't scream. The closet was like a big mouth, and a force was in there pulling me, me and the bed. [Walsh]

B

The other night, a week ago or two weeks ago, after I said goodnight to my next-door neighbor [in prison] I was so relaxed. I didn't have nothing on my mind, and I felt like I could really get a decent night's sleep. All of a sudden, I just laid there, and I rolled over and my eyes just flipped up, and I looked. Where my bed is, it's against the wall, but I had maybe a couple inches space. And I noticed a hand. It was like a force was there. I was paralyzed. I knew what was going on, but I couldn't move. It was like I had to scream, and it wouldn't come out. And the hand just kept on turning. I didn't recognize the hand until I seen Bill's ring. He wasn't buried with his ring because his inlaws have it, but that was the only way I could tell it was his hand. I started gasping for air. It was like I couldn't breathe.

And Pamie, my next-door neighbor, kept on calling me 'cause she kept on hearing me hitting against the wall. I was trying to push it away from me.

I'm afraid of Bill. I'm afraid that he's going to come back and harm me. So the next morning I was talking to Violet [Star], and I mentioned that dream to her, and she said that she went through the same thing when her daughter died. It was like they come back. It was like a force holding me down, but I was aware of everything. And Violet, she said, "When you feel relaxed, lay in bed and call out his name. Quietly call him to appear and see what he wants." But I'm afraid to; I'm afraid that he's gonna harm me. I know it's not possible that he could do it, but I'm petrified.

I keep on thinking about it. Somebody said that they can come into any form. It could be half of their body or image, but it's like they're trying to tell you that they do forgive you for what you've done so that you can feel peace. I know I shouldn't do this. They say that you will really never be free, not unless you accept what you've done. [Walsh]

C

Sometimes I'll be walking and I'll smell a certain odor of cologne and I'll think Bill's there. I'll get real jittery. I believe that he's out to kill me because he died in a violent death, and I think that he's out to do the same thing to me that happened to him. But everybody says, "Don't feel that way; he can't harm you."

One night—I don't know if I should even talk about this. Oh God, I even turned around and told Violet and she said, "That was a spirit."

I was laying in bed (usually I don't sleep on my stomach), and me and Pammie [in the next cell] was talking. I got real tired, and I just put my arms up over my head while I was laying on my stomach. While I was laying there I just felt this pressure on my whole entire body, not my front but my back. And it was like I couldn't move. I knew my eyes were awake 'cause I could look in my room, but I couldn't lean up enough to see if anybody was on me.

But I told Violet that I actually felt that I got screwed! I looked at her like, "Am I going crazy?" But she says that there are demons that will come in and do that to you. [Walsh]

When I heard the first of these three accounts I was struck by how dreamlike it appeared, with surroundings shifting from prison to home, but when I raised this with Walsh, she insisted on her wakefulness throughout. Ernest Jones, Freud's biographer and author of *On the Nightmare,* describes a set of experiences that in every way appear like the classic nightmare and "run their whole course during the waking state" (26).

As evidence of such a violent attack, one of my informants claimed to have been left with bruises.[3]

In '63 I tried to put it on my father because my father didn't like me. I was scared to sleep in the dark. Every night I would sleep on my stomach, and I'd be layin' there with the shade open and the light would shine in from the lamp outside. I was scared to go to sleep in the room. I would doze off, you know, a cat nap, and a pressure would grab me and just hold me down. I would try to get up, and the only way it would go away — I had to pray. I had to pray.

A couple of times I was pulled sideways by this force. It would make me hit my mouth on the bed and bang with my mouth. It was trying to hurt me. And I mean I'd be wide awake! I know what it is to have nightmares, and this was different. The power was tryin' to cut my breath out so I couldn't breathe, and I had to pray. I had to pray to get up outa that; that's the only way I could get up. And I'd be soaking wet, and I KNOW I wasn't asleep. I know the difference between havin' a nightmare and when somethin' is puttin' pressure on my body holdin' me down. [Jones]

Both Betty Jones and Walsh attribute the repressive, life-threatening force that haunts them to dominant males in their lives, men who have brutalized them in the past. A reform school resident, Jones describes herself as the victim of a suffocating violent force, more real than the phantoms of dreams, more dangerous than human power.

If in these narratives there is any resistance on the part of the passive female, that opposition takes the form of prayer and the solicitation of a more powerful male figure, God.

The male who threatens Walsh, she says, is her husband, the man who subjected both her and her son to regular physical abuse and the man she killed. Like Betty Jones, she cannot escape her tormentor. Even in visions he continues to play the role of brutal oppressor and she, the part of helpless victim. Her crime wins her no liberation; the violent force within the home has merely altered its form and seeks her out inside the walls of her prison.

Walsh sought the counsel of another inmate, Violet Star, to help her make sense of these confusing and frightening experiences. Until recently, Maryland's only woman on death row, Violet Star is an avid believer in witchcraft and spiritual advisor to a small group of dedicated followers, interpreting their dreams and waking visions as workings of a spirit world, a world with which she is in daily contact. In an interview with me eight months prior to my interview with Evelyn Walsh, Violet Star related a similar experience:

> I was just laying in bed and I looked up and this hand was like right up there. The closer it came, the bigger it got. And I couldn't really see what this hand was attached to, but it looked like a black robe or something. And it had a hood, but it was just the hand that was coming towards me. And the closer it got to my face, the harder it was for me to breathe. It was right there, and I couldn't breathe at all. If it touched me I guess I would of died. And there was someone in bed with me, and I could not move or speak or nothing. I was terrified 'cause I didn't understand what it was. But my daughter had died three days before this and she was like two months old when she died. At that time I wasn't into what I'm into now [witchcraft], and I didn't understand.
>
> That was when I was about eighteen, and I never forgot it. We were living in a trailer, and we moved out the next day. But you know, before I moved out, it was weird. Even though I didn't understand what I do now about the spirits and all, after everything was out of the trailer I went back by myself and went into the bedroom and tried to communicate with whatever it was.
>
> But the strangest thing about his experience is that it happened at night when all the lights were on. It was really weird. Nobody's really explained it to me yet. 'Course if it happened now, I could relate to it.
>
> Since I became knowledgeable about spirits I've seen my daughter. I

know that she's all right, she's content. She only lived two months and
sixteen days; she died of crib death. I didn't know what that meant
either, so I asked the doctor and he told me about crib death. I
remember I had gotten up and I was feeding her, giving her a bottle,
but she couldn't hold her bottle, so I propped it up. It was just like ten
minutes of twelve, and I walked in the kitchen, put on some coffee or
something, came back, and she was dead — just like that. I tried to bring
her back by mouth to mouth, and my husband went and called the ambulance. When they got there they just took her; they didn't tell me she
was dead. That's weird, isn't it? Just like that!

She was still warm and everything. But her death didn't destroy me
emotionally because of my upbringing, but I missed her. I didn't want
any more children, and I won't have no more either. I felt like that was
the one, and we were going to be tight 'cause I had had a lot of miscar-
riages. I guess I was too active to carry or something.

But I feel like whatever it is that my daughter has to do to work her
way back, she'll be back. I know that we're gonna meet again, if not in
this lifetime, in another one. So death to us is just a passing into
another life. I have no regrets about death other than the fact I might
miss somebody. [Star]

Violet Star understands this vision in terms of her belief in witchcraft and her Native American heritage. According to Star, both traditions affirm the existence of spirits who may effect either good or ill
upon the living. Skilled in the manipulation of spirits, Star advises
the new admittee, Evelyn Walsh, to address her oppressor directly and
thus to rid it of some of its menacing power. Spirits, according to Star,
often plague the living, seeking something in particular and can sometimes be placated by a simple prayer, the performance of a certain
ritual, or a straightforward conversation. Once confronted, they will
often depart. But to communicate with spirits in order to learn the
cause of their unrest requires the summoning of one's courage. A gesture common in stories of revenants (Brunvand, 163), this prescription
by Violet Star can release one from the dead's domination. Practicing
as priestess and therapist, Star helps her young, vulnerable followers
begin the process of adjustment to prison.

Star's and Walsh's accounts share the image of the oppressing hand.
The single human, always male,[4] hand and the shrouded head or bust,
its features obscured, are the two predominant images in the accounts
I collected from women prisoners. Again my findings are at odds with

those of Hufford, who claims that eyes figure most prominently in the data he surveys. In the thirty-seven accounts of oppressive forces I collected, not a single one mentioned eyes, and only one contained the sound of footsteps (an important element in Hufford's research).

By repudiating culture, the discursive production of knoweldge, in favor of a culture-free or transcendent "experience," Hufford also repudiates the possibility of a gender-inflected discourse of this phenomenon. But culture, when ghosted, often returns. Hufford's (and his Newfoundlanders') gender-laden term for this phenomenon, "Old Hag," unites the evil spirit in female form with the witch and night-*mare*, into the image of the suffocating female, the female on top. Hufford fails to acknowledge the sexual implications of both informants' accounts and of the term he takes as his own.

I have found the term "Old Hag" inadequate to characterize the experiences of my informants. Only one woman in this study describes her oppressor as female; in other instances if the oppressor has a gender, it is always male. Male demons as well as dead fathers, husbands, and lovers oppress these women and sometimes, like incubi, attempt penetration. Victims' reaction to these sexual episodes differ greatly. Walsh's oppressor seems more domestic, less frightening in her third narrative. When relating this episode Walsh smiled at the recollection of its pleasure; when describing the others she was visibly shaken and nervous.

Like Star, Luscious interprets such a prison experience for a younger woman on her floor. She relates their conversation:

> She [the young woman] says, "I wasn't asleep, and I couldn't move. My body, it felt like something was gonna penetrate me." I says, "You had a incubus experience." She says, "What's that?" I'm thinkin' everybody knows, you know.
> "It's a demon that takes on a male form that preys on sleepin' women," I said. "It feels like you're just rooted to the bed and you know what's going on but you can't break the spell of it?"
> She said, "Yup!"
> "That's a incubus."
> Burke: Where did you first hear about this?
> Luscious: The demon in the night?⁵
> Burke: Yes.
> Luscious: When I was eight years old and I had that experience.

Burke: When you were eight?

Luscious: Yeah, and the day after that, my cycle started. My sister and I, my little baby sister and I, we used to sleep in a bed together. That particular night she was down the foot of the bed; I was at the top, and the incubus came. Well, I didn't know what it was then. I was wide awake, but I couldn't move. It felt like a numbing sensation. I was trying to break the grip of it but I couldn't. I could feel my legs being open, but I had no will to stop it. I think it was after me actually because I was untouched. [Luscious]

Luscious describes how she threshes about, nearly hurting her sister sharing the bed, and manages to counter the force of her oppressor, but in this case, as in the case of her friend, even after the spirit has backed off he still hovers in the room.

The sexual content of these terrifying scenes presents itself so unambiguously that it is hard to imagine one would dismiss it. But Hufford criticizes Jones's insistence on the sexual nature of dream:

The presence of overt sexual content as a frequent feature of the nightmare proper is also highly debatable. I have encountered a few explicit sexual details in Old Hag accounts, but these are rare and not typically major components of a given experience. Some overtly sexual accounts have appeared in the course of my investigation, but these differed from the Old Hag in that they have lacked the paralysis feature and, in several cases, fear. These probably constitute either a distinct subtype of the experience or a different phenomenon altogether. [131]

With the ambiguous distinction of "subtype . . . or a different phenomenon altogether," Hufford sets aside the sexual. By excluding the incubus from his type, Hufford conveniently exempts this phenomenon from sexual implications. He argues for an empirical reading unconstrained by the Freudian yoke which burdens Jones's interpretation.

What Hufford fails to take into account are the ways in which his own methods infect the pure empirical enterprise. In order to refute the incubus interpretation, Hufford claims, for example, that when he has encountered sexual accounts they have lacked the elements of fear and paralysis key to his definition of "Old Hag" (131) What he fails to consider is the possible self-censorship of his informants when it comes to sexual detail. It is likely that informants (particularly women) who had experienced such sexually explicit "Old Hag" assaults might be more reluctant than other informants to come forward to be interviewed by a strange man.

To ignore the sexual implications of these narratives, to see them as simply experienced rather than produced is culturally misogynistic. Women construct experiences in light of the culture in which they find themselves. Like the prison, itself, these suffocating, malevolent forces keep women in their place as victims. The only means they have of curtailing their power is through belief in a more potent force — through God or through Satan, Violet Star's god of witchcraft.

Prison Ghosts

Besides the ghosts that women bring to prison with them, the prison houses its own. Noises that cannot be accounted for, lights that turn on and off for no apparent reason, and doors that miraculously lock and unlock are the work of prison ghosts. But who are these ghosts? At the Indiana Women's Prison they are generally believed to be former inmates and officers who have died while at the prison, according to Officer Verna Brown:

> I used to go around at six in the morning to get the girls, and one morning I came in and it was real foggy. I'd come all the way up the grounds and pick the girls up. So that morning it was real foggy, and I opened the door and one of the girls said, "Mrs. Brown, look under that tree over there. Don't that look like a woman?" I said, "It is a woman." There was eight of us there, and we hung in the door. I couldn't get the door opened. I wasn't scared, but they started running, so naturally I went with 'em. When the supervisor opened the door, she had to pluck us out of the door one by one. We were just hung there, and they were hollering, trying to get in. I would see this woman, a Yugoslavian girl who died out here, and every morning at six she'd leave the side of the building and go toward the laundry. I'd see her.

The fear of ghosts keeps prisoners in their places, according to this officer, clinging to the door of their prison building like frightened children "hollering, trying to get in." Acting almost as agents of social control, the ghosts help this officer do her job. Even when the administration seems to be working against her (when they order the removal of needed suplies from the kitchen she oversees) spirits appear to negotiate their return:

> And about eleven every day there was a big woman, had her hair cut short, and she had a jumper and a white shirt on. She would appear up in the dining room, so I asked an inmate who she was. She told me who she was, but I said, "No, she's in the spirit world." I found out later she was dead years before. She was an officer. Any time anything was wrong or trouble or somebody'd press me, she'd always show up, and I'd always know what to do.
>
> So one day, they came in and cleaned out the pantry—took everything out and left me nothing to work with. I don't know what happened, but, anyway, a lot of stuff was coming up missing, so they cleaned my kitchen out, too. But I didn't get upset about it. The girls said, "Mrs. Brown, aren't you gonna try to get it back?" I said, "Don't worry; it's coming back." And it did. The next day, they had orders to get every bit of that stuff back. When they come back and put the stuff down, my eyes, you know, looked toward the pantry. One of the girls looked at me and she said, "Mrs. Brown, who was standing by you?" I said, "Nobody." She said, "Somebody went across the floor just then. I was looking at you. When she left your side you watched her go to the pantry." It was this woman she saw. [Brown]

Although generally willful and unpredictable, prison spirits aid Officer Brown by warning her of potential inmate disturbances, disclosing cures for inmates and staff, and protecting her from harm. With their help she maintains security and nurtures those in her charge. (For further evidence of Brown's spiritualism, see chapter 6.)

Ghosts at the Maryland Correctional Institution for Women are thought to be the spirits of those buried in a small cemetery upon which the prison stands, but accounts of this cemetery differ. Most inmates and a few officers believe that graves exist within the prison compound. Some staff members, making light of inmate superstitions, hold that the graves are not on the prison grounds at all but might be found (though they have seen no graves themselves) up the wooded country road that leads to the prison. Still other members of the staff view the idea of a cemetery anywhere in the vicinity of the prison as complete fabrication. Despite such contradictory claims about the existence and location of a cemetery, old inmates tell newcomers of having seen or heard the ghosts from this cemetery as they wander about the grounds, disturbing what peace exists in prison.

You know we're over top of a graveyard. I've never experienced it my-self, but back in the winter the girls claim they were seeing things. Their TV's would come on. They knew they had turned 'em off, but they would wake up and the TV'd be real loud. It would wake 'em up. Even the officers said, "I know I locked that door," and would come in, and the door would be open. Girls would almost get tickets [write-ups for in-fractions of prison rules] for that, because the officers thought the girls had rigged up a way to open the door.

I've heard talk of it; I really have. Even a few of the officers are scared to be upstairs by theirself at night in that hallway 'cause they be hearin' noises, people walking and strange noises. They say upstairs in Horigan where "the lock-ins" were, they said that place is spooky. Even the nurses that work over there at night say that. So it's something going on — I'm serious. [Chambers]

They say the buildings are built on a cemetery. I've heard this from the officers and from the inmates, inmates who have been here before. And I've heard them talk about Horigan. They say strange things have happened in Horigan.

This one woman said that once it go so hot in her cell that she just kept praying and praying that the door would come open. And she said, next thing she know, the door popped open. And I've heard them talk about the lights flickering off and on and nobody's messed with the switches because everybody's on lock in Horigan. [Star]

According to these two inmates, prison ghosts work in typical haunt-ing fashion: generating strange noises at night, manipulating the build-ing's electrical devices, and unlocking doors meant to be locked. Un-like Brown's ghosts, these work to subvert prison order rather than to sustain it.

Horigan, mentioned in both these selections, is the building that was replaced in 1986 by a newer, cleaner, more mechanized building. But for years Horigan housed the new admittees as well as women in solitary confinement, placed there for disciplinary reasons. All would agree that before its closing Horigan was the most unpleasant place on the grounds. The constant traffic of food trays into rooms three times a day allowed a roach population to flourish. The cries of new admittees, the shrieks of the disturbed, and the curses of those rebel-lious inmates who have nothing to lose (they had lost it all by violating prison rules) contributed to the daily horrors of Horigan. Though a most inhospitable place for the living, Horigan was the most likely place for prowling ghosts. It is not surprising that the place most women feared to be sent was the place where the most fearsome creatures resided.

Not only did the proximity to grave sites give rise to accounts of ghosts, but the death of an inmate two years before my interviews at the Maryland Correctional Institution for Women produced several accounts of the appearance of her ghost. Due to be released shortly, this woman lived in the pre-release trailer on the prison grounds, where she died of a drug overdose. There was, and still is, much discussion of the incidents surrounding her death, but it was her wandering spirit that troubled a number of women (including at least one officer). Restless some nights, she walked the grounds and looked through windows at the living.

With the help of psychics in England, California, and Philadelphia, inmate Violet Star claims to have liberated this woman's wandering spirit from the confines of "the earth level" so that it might enter the spirit world:

> A good friend of mine, Debbie, died here two years ago. Her trailer that she died in was right across from my window. And after her death, I could feel her. I had made a couple of phone calls to other people knowledgeable in working with spirits because I felt her, but I wasn't positive. I made a phone call to England and one to California to some psychic friends of mine and asked for their help. And Debbie did come. She wasn't in form or anything. The only thing that I could understand was, "Help me." She couldn't get beyond this level here, so the two people that I called contacted some more, and we all worked together. There was one in Philadelphia that was called. At a certain time we all worked together. And after that, I never felt her no more, so I guess she went on.
>
> When something like this happens it's kind of like you go into a trance and you're guiding that spirit through the levels to get her off the earth level. It's like your mind is a box, and you take that box and open it so you can send that spirit home. You see the start and the end of a tunnel, and you send the spirit to the end. I've seen this done before with other spirits, and it worked for them, too, if a spirit wanted to go. Some spirits linger, and they never ask to be sent on. I wouldn't try to send one unless they were willing to go. But with Debbie I didn't feel that I was capable of all that by myself, so I got some help. [Star]

Many of these prison ghost accounts express the belief that those who die on prison grounds before the completion of their sentence wander within its confines, eternally serving time. But Star, marshalling psychic forces in America and England, executes the ultimate spiritual prison escape and succeeds in accomplishing what death did not: release from prison.

Prison is a place haunted by the spirits of its dead and the memories of its living. To communicate with both the ghosts of the present and the ghosts of the past a handful of gifted women serve as psychics or mediums, counseling individual inmates about the personal spirits that trouble them and acting as intermediaries with the spirit world.

5. Gods and Demons

Prison visions may appear as warnings of the future, comfort for a painful present, or the resurgence of haunting images of the past; they may console or alarm. Although these sometimes idiosyncratic accounts of spiritual events do not yield themselves to rigid categorization, two types of vision narratives fall comfortably within Christian orthodoxy: accounts of a tempting or frightening devil and those of a loving and merciful Christ. Poised between the promise of divine deliverance and the distraction of earthly temptations, the Christian autobiographer narrates a tale of the struggle between the mind, fixed on eternal rewards, and the body, prone to temporal pleasures. Fighting for possession of the soul, the devil attempts to gain control of the individual, of her home, or of her room. Alone, she is powerless against this evil, but by enlisting God's help she can free herself, her home, or her room from the devil's power.

Visions depict good and evil not as criteria by which to judge human action but rather as personifications before the passive recipient of visions. But not all recipients of visions passively watch a scene unfold before them; some enter the drama. They travel to heaven, to the sites of exotic primitive rituals, to times past, or they actively engage the spirits that appear to them. Though not a first-hand account, the following identifies the typical lore that flourishes in prison: the prisoner's struggle with demons:

> There's been different sightings of apparitions here. I'll tell you about this one girl. She was real Christian when she came in here, but she got into a spiritual battle with demons. They supposedly beat her up in her room. I never met anybody as unchristian afterwards as she was—sailors couldn't match her!
>
> Another girl sighted Satan sittin' on the fence post.
>
> Another time several girls were locked in their rooms. Something was with them, but they couldn't holler, couldn't scream. My one girlfriend, she said that this guy was in her room, and he was strangling her with

clothes hangers. She couldn't get free. She couldn't get anybody to pay attention to her, she kept banging on the door.

There are a lot of creatures walking around this place. Most of them take the form of males. [Fitton]

This brief account illustrates the general myth among prisoners that inmates enter prison as good people and are corrupted by the institution, a belief ironically opposed to the societal assumption that prisoners are bad people imprisoned certainly to be punished and possibly to be reformed. But for inmates, the prison harbors its own evil in both human and spiritual forms. Interestingly, fellow prisoners, even those convicted of the most violent crimes, never appear in visions as the agents of evil. Rather, evil takes the form of gatekeepers or fence-sitters, figures who can open locked doors.[1] Read in one way, these visions express an inmate fear of those in charge. Prisoners report instances of the use of violence by guards (generally male guards); they allege rapes, tell of bruises, and recount the screams of women in other cells. Through vision narratives prisoners might, in fact, be attributing supernatural agency to real violence, and thus, furthering the institution's goal of maintaining security. An officer, after all, can be fired or reprimanded for striking an inmate; a spirit cannot.

When asked about visions of demons or gods, women often relate experiences that happened in their homes. Gladys Chambers tells of a troubling time after the death of her daughter:

When my daughter got killed, I just kept blaming myself 'cause I kept saying, "If I had been a better mother, took care of my kids myself, this never woulda happened." Right before she died, I could tell she was going through changes 'cause we had talked and she had begged me to stop doing drugs and get it together. This was like on a Saturday night, and Sunday night she got killed. I had brought all her graduation things (cap and gown) home. She had moved her clothes back home; she was coming back home.

After I left the viewing of her body I came home, and I just couldn't go in the house alone. I couldn't face it; everywhere I looked it was memories of her. I had to take her pictures down. I would look at her clothes hanging in the cupboard, and I would just jump up outta my sleep and just start screaming. I said, "Well, I shouldn't be afraid of my own daughter because I know she loved me and I loved her, but maybe she's blaming me because she's dead. I didn't know what that was. I just kept seeing something like the devil was in the cupboard. Every time I would go to the cupboard and see her cap and gown hanging there, this face would be in there, it was something in that gown with these blood-red eyes and these little points on its head. The way I had it hanging, the cap was on top of the gown and the tassel was hanging down. I looked up and I saw these eyes and these points, and I said, "That's gotta be the devil." I just jumped up. I was scared to death.

I went and told my mother. About this time my mother had started getting into the church; she was reading her Bible and all. She says, "I'll tell you what; we're going back to that house and we're gonna pray together." She said, "Maybe it'd be best if you just took her stuff and let me keep 'em or just get rid of it." But I just could not let go. I had to just cling to 'em. The cap and gown was the last thing that I remember seeing her in. So me and my mother just prayed together, just prayed together. She stayed all night long that night, and we just prayed together to God. That next morning I got up, that gown was still there.

When I went out to the store my mother had taken her clothes and packed 'em up, said she was taking 'em home. I said, "No," and she said, "Every time you look at it, it scares you." I said, "Just try it again tonight; I got a feeling it's not gonna happen. I'm gonna be all right." Sure enough, when I went to sleep that night I slept peaceful. When I did think about her, did have memories, they were good memories. But I still carried that guilt around a long time.

They say that the devil can be just as powerful as God can be in some ways, but God can always overpower the devil. And I believe that 'cause he is busy twenty-four hours a day. I'm not kidding! [Chambers]

The daughter never comes home to her mother. Instead, the mother, haunted by guilt, encounters the horrifying image of the devil, superimposed on her daughter's clothing. This terrifying vision can only be overcome with prayer, and so two generations of women, grandmother and mother, seek the assistance of God to overpower the devil. Prayer keeps away the demonic vision and restores to the narrator pleasant memories of her dead daughter. Prayer banishes the devil as it lessens the mother's guilt. Had Chambers given up drugs as her daughter pleaded, her daughter would be alive. Unable to care for her daughter because of her addiction and previous incarceration, Chambers entrusted the care of her daughter to a friend, a Baltimore drug "kingpin," and a vengeful drug dealer killed the child, mistaking her for the daughter of this man. The sign of Chambers's failure as a parent is the graduation costume with no body to fill it. Facing this horror, Chambers retreats into daughterhood, becoming the humble child of her reassuring mother and of God. Prayer erases the nightmarish vision of the devil's "blood-red eyes."

The power of prayer to counter witchcraft, the work of the devil, is the message of Nancy Madison's account of her eccentric neighbor:

> I believe in heaven. I believe in hell. I believe there's a devil, and I believe there's a God. I'm a God-fearing person, and I try to do things as right as I possibly can. I also know there's a devil, and I do believe that he can make people do things. I believe he's there. And I believe in witchcraft and stuff like that. It's very real. I don't think that a lot of people know what they're getting theirself into when they mess with it. I've had some dealings with people who were into witchcraft pretty heavy. My oldest brother was one of 'em. I seen a lot of things that he went through and things that happened in the house that couldn't be explained. But he's a born-again Christian; it's been fifteen years.
>
> This girl that's here now, Marie Berger, you mighta read an article in the paper on her. She's a juvenile, came in when she was fourteen for killing this boy. She's eighteen now. It was really weird. She would write me from lock and tell me about this guy who wrote her from the penitentiary and how he said he could see her in his dreams, how he had to come to her, how they can trick, use their minds to communicate all this. And I would tell her, I said, "You know, just because he doesn't come out and say he worships the devil, doesn't mean that it's not associated with witchcraft, 'cause even astrology is." I would tell her, "Don't mess with him." And he told her that if she ever left him, he would do terrible things to her and that he could do these things through witchcraft. I kinda talked her outta witchcraft. I believe there is power in it and people who are really into it can make things happen. They really can. I believe that.
>
> I had this experience—it's hard to believe things when you read them, or see them in movies that are supposed to be true, but to really experience something—it makes you believe. What I experienced with this guy who lived next door on St. Paul and 28th—he was into witchcraft—really, really into it. Just to walk into his house, it just felt so weird. It was a friend of mine's friend, and we went over there and smoked a couple joints. This guy, I couldn't believe how he lived. He was like an animal! His apartment was filthy. Dirty! I don't think your imagination could ever think up this kinda dirt. The sheets—you knew they used to be white at one time—they were black. He had a waterbed

in there and all these pictures of disfigured people, people with horns, and statues of the devil.

He wore jeans that he probably had on since he was twelve. He was in his twenties. Oh, he was just filthy. He had real long hair, mustache, beard. His eyebrows even grew up at the ends. Sometimes he gave me the creeps. He would look like he was in another world. He was a jeweler, and I couldn't believe he lived like this. There were bowls that food used to be in, and you used it as a ashtray and the cigarette butts were on the floor. I didn't want to sit on anything. I'd sit down and just couldn't stand it. Roaches would start crawling on me, and I'd pluck 'em off. I was trying to act like it didn't bother me, you know: I'm used to roaches. But the ones I'm used to, you turn the light on and they run. These, you turn the light on and they come out. It's like, "Hi, my name is Ralph."

And his refrigerator—I just gotta give you a description of it. It broke, it hadn't been working for like six months, and he must have had food in it when it went out. And there was still that food in it from that day. And when you opened it up, roaches were an inch thick on the stuff. The sink was backed up, and it just had this thick scum on the water where the roaches would walk across it. It was so filthy. He had this parrot, and there were parrot droppings everywhere. Oh, I couldn't stand it.

Anyway, he was moving, and I lived next door. He said, "Well, look, I got some books that I would like you to keep until I can come and get 'em; would you mind?"

"OK, OK."

They were all on demonology, astrology, witchcraft and you name it. He had this old box with antique little bottles and corks with all these herbs in 'em. And he asked me to keep his iguana and his cat. His cat scared me. The cat was possessed. I really believe it.

Well, I called my brother up after I'd had these books for a month. My brother's real intelligent; he's got a master's degree, plus he's a born-again Christian. He's really into it. Plus, he used to be into this. He knows about it and how dangerous it is. So I called him up and he came up and looked at the stuff. He said, "Get this stuff outta here. Do you know what you're doin'? Do you know what you're inviting into here?" And he started praying. He said, "I'm gonna pray, but you really need to get rid of this because I can get whatever's in here to leave, but it'll come back as long as this stuff is here."

And I said, "OK, OK."

I hadn't heard from this guy since the day he moved them books into my house. But that day my brother come up and prayed on that stuff, half an hour later, this guy come banging on my door. I opened the door. He said, "Are you gonna be here tonight? I'm coming to get my stuff." It's like he knew my brother had been there. It just gave me the creeps. He came back that night and got all the stuff—everything. I couldn't believe it. When he came he was hysterical. The look in his eyes—it's like he knew my brother had been there. [Madison]

Grotesque pictures of disfigurement, filthy sheets, a foul refrigerator, and vermin become, in a retrospective account, evidence of spiritual befoulment. Even the books and herbs left in Madison's safe-keeping threaten to infect her home. A born-again brother, himself once infected with unholy beliefs and practices, effects the exorcism. His prayers recall the neighbor who practices the devil's art, who removes the contaminating books, bottles, etc., from Madison's apartment. The neighbor's return, according to Madison, is clearly not a coincidence; the look in his eyes reveals that he is responding to a superior power. Invoked by prayer, this superior power cleanses the home of corruption, and fundamentalist Christianity triumphs over occult forces.

Within this tale of pollution and purification Madison embeds an account of advice given to a younger inmate. The relationship of advice account to exorcism story is one of belief statement to exemplum. Isolated from fellow prisoners, Marie Berger corresponds with Madison and with a male inmate in the nearby Maryland House of Correction.[2] Madison's narrative affirms one form of correspondence (the illegal—according to prison officials—exchange of letters between Berger and Madison) and cautions against the other. Letters from a male inmate confessing psychic beliefs and threatening telepathic harm infect in the same way as occult books and herbal bottles and must be shunned.

Stories of ridding the home or the prison cell of corruption by prayer and ritual cleaning are common. The following illustrates the correlation between spiritual and physical purity in prison:

This one woman, she had like a witchcraft about her with God. She did certain things and she'd get certain results. For instance, she told me to fast for two days, be completely in prayer, read your Bible and keep reciting different psalms. Then she said, "When you get up in the morning, you take a shower, mop your floor, take a package of salt and dump it in the water. Then you mop your floor while you say the Twenty-third

Psalm. At the end you ask God to lift all the evil spirits from your room." [Miller]

Some prisoners also routinely anoint their rooms with holy oil to free them of evil spirits: "If we feel there's something spiritual in our room binding or something that shouldn't be there, we'll anoint the room with holy oil" (Fitton). Such ritual cleansings rid the eight-by-six-foot prison cell of repressive or "binding" forces and establish for the prisoner a small territory under her control. But that control is, of course, illusory, for at any moment guards may ransack a room searching for contraband; at any moment a new inmate may be added to her cell. The establishment of private and holy spaces within confinement is a rich and understudied phenomenon. Even in double- and triple-bunked cells women are quick to demarcate even the smallest space as private, carefully displaying family photographs and magazine illustrations or erecting religious shrines.

The ritual cleansing of one's room to prepare for a holy encounter is as common in the prison as the "trashing" of one's room in rage at one officer in particular or at the sinister institution in general. In the former act, the woman transforms her cell into a temple, a holy place free of the evil that surrounds it. In the latter, her room suffers the effect of her rage; everything loose becomes a projectile in this violent rebellion against the institution. After such an outburst the woman is generally punished with more "lock time" (time in solitary confinement). To make of one's room a shambles and to transform it into a sacred place are two ways in which women rebel against their narrow confines. The first is punished by the authorities, the second tolerated.

But in prison women not only testify to the power of prayer to dispel evil forces, they also give accounts of prayer that produces a reassuring response from God. In one such narrative Gladys Chamber's prayers for a resolution to her daughter's problems are answered by God:

> Shortly after I got here and I got to praying about my daughter at
> home, because they say my daughter is one of those troublesome
> children, used to having her way. And nobody seemed to know how to
> deal with her but me. When I left I left her in the hands of my oldest
> brother and his wife, and they were gonna raise her, send her to school
> until I get out.
> I would call her, and every time I would call her I'd say, "Veronica,

how's everything? Are you all right?" and she said, "Oh yeah, I'm fine."
And I just knew something was wrong. I could tell because I knew her.
And I said, "What's wrong; you don't like it there?" She said, "No, I'm
very unhappy here, but I'll be happy for you." "I used to tell her, "Just
be happy for me, 'cause if you're sad, you're gonna make me sad and it's
gonna be harder for me to do this time here, so try to be happy for me."

Even though she tried to be happy, I knew she was not happy. She
said, "I just wanna go back home with my sister because she's the only
one that love me." At that time her sister was living with her boyfriend
and their little girl, and she was working, trying to get on her feet, and I
just didn't want to put all that on her. She had just kept her sister eight
months when I was here before.

After I had talked to her (she was so unhappy) that night I just kept
reading my Bible and saying, "Lord, there's gotta be a way; there's gotta
be a way." And I laid there, hall lights out, and this particular night (I'll
never forget it) it was a full moon out. It was so bright. I had finally
dozed off to sleep a little bit, and I had to get up to go to the bathroom. When I got up something just drew my attention to outside my
window, and I saw this big pretty moon. It was really bright and real
pretty! It felt like the moon just came so I could reach out and touch it.
Then something just went on through me, and a voice said, "Don't
worry Gladys, it's gonna be all right. It's gonna be all right." And I knew
then that it had to be God speaking to me. I had heard of other experiences like that, but never had I experienced anything like that. At that
time, I just got on my knees and started praying. The tears came, and I
was praying and praying and praying.

The next day I called home, and my daughter said she had my little
girl with her and it was gonna be all right. It was a nice experience; it
really was. It was just beautiful. [Chambers]

God does not appear to Chambers physically; rather, He speaks
words of reassurance to her so that she knows He has heard her prayer
and will solve the problem. Over and over narratives of supernatural
experiences in prison testify to the occurrence of magical solutions to
family problems. Unable to fulfill her role as mother in person, Chambers can, through prayer, solicit God's assistance. Although prayer
does not restore the mother to the home, it does bring together her
two daughters. In the crisis of trial and sentencing, mothers make
provisions for minor children, but when those arrangements fail, a
woman must negotiate an alternative from prison, often with neither

support from the outside nor help from within the prison. Through prayer she finds solutions to seemingly insoluble problems.

Prayer can also make the divine word transparent, transforming the opaque text into the solace one seeks:

> I read my Bible a lot. I find a lot of comfort in it 'cause sometimes things are troubling me, and if I can't sleep, I'll get up, open my Bible and read it. It's interesting though. When something's bothering me I'll know that I need to reach a certain scripture, but I don't know specifically where to find what I need. And when I don't know where to look for it, I lay the Bible down and pray on it before I look in it. Then all I have to do is just take the Bible and open it up, and what I need is right in front of me. I don't know why, but it does every time. If I'm reading it before I say a prayer and I don't understand something, I close it and then I say a little short prayer about the opening of my eyes so I can see. Then I open it back up to that passage again, and I get it every time.
>
> I don't know why—maybe I'm not receptive to it when I first open it, but something says you're not goin' about it the right way. So I try another way. [Lee]

Visions of Heaven and Hell

Another kind of vision that has dominated much of Christian literature and iconography is the vision of heaven, and its counterpart, the vision of hell. Lana Murphy tells of waking, after a short nap, to the startling vision of hell:

> I was married at the time this incident happened, and my cousin, him and his wife were really having a hard time. And they'd bought 'em a new home and they had these two small children. One was still a baby. Joanne had to go back to work to help get 'em out of debt. Because the children were small, she didn't want to have just anybody in there taking care of them, so she just begged me to come and take care of the children until she found somebody she could really trust, which led into quite a long while.
>
> Anyhow, I went over. It was early, and the children were asleep. It was daylight, but it was still kinda dusky out. I was laying down on the couch and dozed off to sleep. I woke up and was laying on my back. I was awake, but I couldn't move. I tried, but I couldn't. I could just look down at me. And I saw what I always considered to be a vision of hell.

Before me, when I first opened my eyes, there was a ball right in front of me, but yet it was off at a distance. It was nothing but fire, flames going every which way. And inside of it there were people. These people were screaming. (Although I couldn't really hear anything. I didn't really hear nothing, but I could just see it, and I knew they were screaming.) They were just like in a whirlwind. Their bodies were going every which way. I thought, "I'm dead."

Then that just left, and I looked around, but I couldn't move. I had my hands crossed over on top of my stomach, and I could see my hands. I could move my eyes, but that was all. So I looked around the room and thought, "Well, if I'm dead, I wonder why I'm here." And I thought, "Well, maybe I'm not dead." I tried and tried what seemed like an eternity to make myself move, and I couldn't do it. I kept watching my toes which I could see and my hands. Finally, my right little finger—I was finally able to make it just barely move. I was really in a shock there for an hour or so thinking, "God, is this a dream? What did that mean? What happened?" [Murphy]

This vision of hell takes place "off at a distance" before the speaker and serves primarily to represent hell to her much in the way oral and written descriptions of hell might be told to a child. The screaming people in the vision are not people she knows, and she takes no active part in the vision. Rather, she assumes a dual perspective of the observer and the observed: "I was awake, but I couldn't move. I tried, but I couldn't. I could just look down at me." Such a dual perspective is typical of narratives recounting out-of-body experiences.

As in most vision accounts, the speaker describes herself as passive. Her only part in the drama occurs after the vision is over and the opening setting (her cousin's living room) is restored. Looking at her corpselike body, Murphy struggles to gain control over her muscles and to make sense of the vision: "Is this a dream? What did it mean?" With visions comes the need to interpret.

The reason for Geraldine Jackson's vision of heaven is painfully clear to her. The dazzling vision of heaven defines the holy, solitary way that God invites her to follow, as opposed to the earthly life of lust and homosexual intimacy that resides in prison.

When I was little I used to go to church every Sunday. I used to go with my aunts, and I used to like goin' to church. The best part was the eatin' afterwards.

After I grew older and I realized who God was and what I was to Him, I always wanted to be close to Him. I started goin' to church after I got here. I went to church under the Baptists. Then I went into the Catholic and the Presbyterian. And I been baptized by Baptists and Presbyterians. When I got older, they had a Catholic sister here and a Baptist minister and a Methodist, and I went to all three. I was just searchin' 'cause I really didn't understand. I knew that God was a good God; He was a forgivin' God; He was merciful. I really wanted to know about Him, so I went to church. The experience that I had with Him; it was magnifying. I felt so good. I was goin' to church every Sunday, and I was doin' Bible study. I used to read the Bible to pass the time, and I felt good. I used to be in a group of ladies, young girls like myself and a couple older people. We used to come in at lunch break everyday, and we would pray.

I always wanted to know how to pray. When I laid down at night I always talked to God through my mind; I'd never say the words out. I always wanted to pray so everybody could hear me, so people would know I meant what I said.

After I started goin' every Sunday and was doin' my studies, I prayed for Him to give me a sign to let me know that He was real 'cause I didn't understand why He would let somethin' like this happen to me.

He came to me one night. I was layin' in bed, and I could feel my soul leave me, but I was awoke. I saw the whole thing. I felt it. He took my soul into the heavens with Him. Everything was just—it wasn't dark but it wasn't light—and it was just—I don't know how to explain it—it was just magnifying, magical. I was there with Him, not my physical being, but I was there. And He told me that I could be with Him or I could be down here. And I came back, and I felt so good. Nobody bothered me. I didn't have any worries. My mother came every weekend. Everything was good.

That's when I met this girl named Laura, and I just decided I was gonna be in Jessup with everybody else. If you're young like I was when I came in, I can't see homosexuality not comin' into a part of your life. If you're older, it's different; you're already settled in your own ways, and you may not do it. But anybody who's young will be curious. I was curious even though I was reared that it was wrong. The Bible says you're not supposed to do that. Even though it was wrong, I still wanted to do it. I wanted the closeness of somebody; it didn't make any difference.

I thought that it was ugly at first. Then I saw that the gay women were people just like me. And then I felt like I was gonna get punished for this, and I have been. I really feel in my heart that once I made that decision that I was marked. Just little things started happin' that were unexplainable. I think that my heart is good, that I believe in God, and that He allowed me to make a choice to be of the world or to be of Him. And when I chose to be of the world and live in lust, then everything just went haywire for years.

But I remember that feelin' when He came to me that night. And whenever I become real, real troubled about anything I always go back to that moment, to that sight of heaven, where I know that it was really good. There's not a word in the dictionary that could describe what I felt that day, that night.

After I chose not to be with God but to be part of the homosexual life of Jessup, I started havin' more complications in my life. Not that my visits stopped comin' right then and there, but gradually my mother stopped comin' so often. I started havin' health problems. I became more confused. I wasn't smilin' as much. I was hurtin' inside, and I didn't understand what was goin' on.

I explain it now that I had to make a choice and that I made the wrong choice. I believe that in myself. Even though all the pain that I've suffered not understandin' why I'm here or why He allowed that to happen to me, I still know that I'm supposed to be with Him and live right by Him. I just know it. Life before my experience with God was better than to have made the wrong decision and have to live with it. [Jackson]

Geraldine Jackson turns away from the promise of liberation that would transform her sentence into a calling and, instead, selects "the closeness of somebody" and a life that damns her, or so she believes, to a prison existence with fewer and fewer visitors from home, deteriorating health, and depression. Although her vision is not unique, her response to that vision is. Hers is the only vision of the divine I collected in which the narrator not only fails to heed the clear message of the vision but consciously chooses to disobey it. But to reject the holy and embrace the worldly is, from one perspective, the most radically human response available to her. Most visionary experiences defy the authority of the prison by defining a power superior to the state. Geraldine Jackson's fall from the path to celestial happiness promised in her vision repudiates the power of such enchantment. She turns from the only happiness possible in prison—the mesmerizing happiness of personal visions—and accepts the reality of prison and the life of lust which it defines. Rejecting visions is for Jackson a sin that brings with it the punishment of guilt and sorrow. The punishment she endures in prison is not, then, the result of a crime against society; it is the price she must pay for apostasy.

Wilma Bond's vision of heaven, on the other hand, confirms her faith. Through it, God speaks personally to comfort and instruct her. Unlike Lana Murphy who is passive in the face of her vision, Bond plays an active role. Assumed into heaven with the rest of her family, she moves about initiating conversations with her dead brother and father:

> God has been good to me in showin' me these things to relax my mind because He knew I was bothered about my father's death. I'm still here in Maryland, but yet I see myself in North Carolina with my mother. My mother was going to the doctor's, and we were sittin' in the waiting room waitin' for her to see the doctor. She had not yet seen the doctor, and my daughter was with me and she says, "Mom, I gotta go to the bathroom." So my daughter gets up, walks outta the room to go to the bathroom, leaves me sittin' with my sister and my oldest brother. We were all in the room with my mother. All of a sudden — it was just like this: my mother looked up, and she saw somethin' like the moon, red as a ball of fire in the sky. She said, "Look at that! Isn't that strange?" We all looked up. It was just like the whole sky opened up and just burst and took us up into it.
>
> I know that I left my daughter behind, but my sister and my brother and my mother, we were all taken up into heaven. When we got there — and I'm gonna tell you exactly what I saw — I saw all these people there in heaven. Here was my brother that died. He was there, so I've been relaxed about him. I know God forgave him, and he's there.
>
> So here's my brother. He was walkin' down this little path over a stream of water. He had two books under his arm like a scholar and these little old-fashioned knicker pants that came to his kneecaps with plaid socks. This is what my brother had on, and I looked at him and I said, "Johnny, what are you doin' with books?" See, my brother went to the twelfth grade and dropped out of school two months before he was supposed to graduate because this girl said he got her pregnant. He wanted to do the right thing and marry the girl, but yet she lied to him; she wasn't pregnant. But he still dropped out and never went back to graduate. I always held that against my brother, not finishin' school.
>
> So in heaven, I see that God's makin' my brother finish school. He had these two books in his arm, and he had these knicker pants on with

the plaid socks. I was shocked 'cause he had never dressed like that in this lifetime. So here I see him like this, and I laugh and I say, "Hey, what are you doin' dressed like this?" And he says, "I'm goin' to school; I'm doin' real good. I'm enjoyin' it."

Then I looked under a tree. I see my father with all these other people. I see him sittin' like on a picnic table with all these people around, and he is sortin' out neckties. One color that my father never really liked was brown, brown neckties, he never cared for brown. He was the gray, the blue, and that kind of person. But he had this brown necktie with some flowers on it. He kept on puttin' on this brown necktie, and I looked at him and said, "Dad, what are you doin' with that brown necktie? You never wore brown." He said, "I'm gettin' this necktie together for dinner tonight. We have to dress up when we go eat," and he was sittin' on this picnic table with a pair of bib overalls on and no shirt. He said he was settin' out his ties 'cause he had to get dressed for dinner.

And my mother was so thrilled that she could rejoice with my daddy again. They disappeared off into another room. But here we were left standing in heaven lookin' all around at these people. I mean, they were all colors: black, white, every color. They were havin' a good time, and I knew my daddy was preparin' for this big feast in the evening. God satisfied my mind to know that I don't have to worry anymore.

When I tell people about these things they be lookin' at me like, "Hey, she's gone," but I know this is true that has happened in my life. This is true stuff, and I'm not lyin' about it because I know these things have been revealed to me. I'm just glad that God has put me in the position where I can even talk about it, because people might see stuff and never are able to talk about it. [Bond]

Heaven for Wilma Bond is not the place for blissful strolls through Elysian Fields; it is the place where things are put right, where her brother finally completes his high school education and her father dresses properly for dinner. Although she sees others in heaven, people of "all colors," her attention is directed toward the members of her family. But one family member, her daughter, leaves the waiting room to go to the bathroom and is, therefore, not assumed into heaven with the others. Although this fact troubles Bond, she has no explanation for it.

Not only does Bond trust that the vision is divinely inspired (God's wish to soothe her troubled mind about the deaths of her father and brother), but she understands the ability to talk about these visions as another gift from God. Many, she believes, are given visions, but their stories of divine communications remain secret, imprisoned within them. God blesses Bond twice: with His revelations to her and with the subsequent ability to tell of them.

Divine Cures

Wilma Bond speaks freely and at length about the moments of divine intervention in her life and the lives of her family. One such incident occurs when she is miraculously healed following a bad auto accident:

> Every summer I would take my two kids down to North Carolina and let 'em stay with my mother and father, and they would enjoy their summers there. In the summer of 1979 I had just bought four brand new Firestone tires and had put them on my car. I had a '75 Oldsmobile Regency, one of the biggest ones that they made, and on the way back from taking my kids to North Carolina, my left front tire blew out. It was down in Brunswick County, Virginia. My car turned over five times and went down an embankment. My husband was with me. At the time I suffered a broken ankle and three fractured bones in my back, and my husband had a hole knocked in his head and a broken arm. He has a steel plate in his arm right today. They said that I would never walk again. They said that they would have to put a pin in my leg, that I'd be a wheelchair patient for the rest of my life. Well, I just couldn't see myself stayin' in a wheelchair the rest of my life.
>
> I guess I'm more or less, I'm very close to God because I pray a lot. That night, after I had the accident and I was layin' in bed in the hospital room—I was just layin' there just like I'm lookin' at you right now—and this man, this form of Jesus Christ came to me right at the foot of my bed. He just looked at me, looked at my leg, and then moved away and did not say anything. I knew Him as the form that we know Jesus Christ. This was Him that paid this visit to me.
>
> The next day my doctor came in and asked me to go down to X-rays because my leg was just pulled one way and it was supposed to be the other way on the bone. That's what the x-rays the day before showed. My doctor told me to go down to X-rays that morning at ten o'clock to have more x-rays. But what the new x-rays showed was the bone back together! The part that was separated was lyin' right back on the bone.

So the doctor, he said it looked just like a miracle; he didn't know how this had happened. He couldn't believe the x-rays; he thought that they had made a mistake, so he sent me back down at two o'clock in the afternoon to take more x-rays. And it came out lookin' the same. He said, "This is impossible; this can't be." He said, "Mrs. Bond, I don't understand what happened here; it's just like a miracle has happened with your leg. I was preparin' to operate and put a pin in your leg, but it's not gonna be necessary now 'cause your bone has jumped back on track. I don't know what happened." I just smiled at my doctor and said, "I know what happened. I had a visitor last night, but I'm not gonna tell you about it because you probably wouldn't believe me."

So within a couple weeks I was walkin' around, and my back healed. And I said that had to be a miracle that God healed me. [Bond]

The miraculous fusing of a broken bone startles the professional; the fact that x-rays, seemingly incontrovertible evidence, affirm such an overnight change renders Bond's recovery even more amazing. Unfortunately, her husband does not receive the same blessing, the same cure, and must leave himself in the hands of human healers. He endures surgery, suffers protracted recovery, and carries with him forever the evidence of human healing, the steel plate in his arm. Bond's narrative contrasts two types of healing: the ability of science to put a man back together and the power of God to make the narrator new, with the latter obviously more efficient than the former.

In another narrative of divine healing Bond acts on behalf of a family member to secure her cure. With her mother gravely ill, she proposes to bargain with God:

There's just so many things that's happened in my life. About ten years ago my mother was very ill, and the doctors had given her up to die. And where I come from, the hospitals operate a little differently than they do here. They had wrote my mother's name (she was in intensive care), they had wrote her name on a blackboard, "the deathboard" they call it. When my mother got up and she went to the bathroom, she looked out onto this board 'cause everybody in North Carolina know what this board is for. They say these patients are on their way out, they're not expectin' 'em to live. So she got up and she noticed her name on this blackboard, and that upset her, really set her back.

Out of the five kids that my mother had I am the only one that left home. All the rest of 'em are within a five- or ten-mile radius around my mother and father. So my sister called me at twelve at night and says if I wanted to see my mother alive I'd better come home. I was like five hundred miles away and workin' in the government at the time, and I said, "I gotta make some arrangements about my job and do a few things before I can jump up and leave." The only thing I could do was just pray that my mother would hold on. After I hung up the telephone I just started prayin'.

My father had called my sisters and brothers to the hospital at like ten o'clock that night, and they were sittin' there. My mother didn't even know that they were there 'cause she was just out of it. It was about twelve-thirty at night when I started prayin'. I prayed this type of prayer, and I never told—you will be the fourth person I've told this to—I asked God not to take my mother from us. I said, "She has five kids, and if it means that You have to take a couple years off of each one of her kids' life to spare her, I say do it."

At this time my father was sittin' beside my mother in the intensive care room, and he said that at about ten minutes after one o'clock that night my mother just rolled over and looked at him. And I was back in Maryland prayin' this prayer, and it was just like a shadow came over me to tell me that everything's gonna be all right.

My mother rolled over and looked at my father, and she said, "What are you doin' here?" She didn't even know that he had been sittin' beside her bed ever since ten o'clock that night. And he said, "Well, I came to be with you." She says, "Well, I'm okay. Don't worry about me. I wanna get outta this bed; I'm tired of layin' in bed." So she gets up outta bed and sits in a chair and tells my father to go home, that she was gonna be all right. So when I heard what happened I knew that God had answered my prayers.

Now, going back to 1970, my baby brother, the youngest (deceased at this time) was cheatin' on his wife. It was during the Christmas holidays, and my mother would always invite the family over for Christmas dinner. This one night she was in the kitchen cookin' pies. When she cooked, she cooked like seven or eight pies at one time. She just don't make one or two; she make a whole slew of 'em! So she was bakin' pies.

Earlier, my sister's daughter had saw my brother purchase a coat with a fur collar, and she just knew that he was gettin' it for his wife, so she told her aunt, she said, "I know what you're gettin' for Christmas 'cause I saw Johnny buy you a coat." My brother's wife was so excited about the fact that she was gonna get this coat with this fur collar, but when the presents were opened, she didn't get the coat.

My brother was angry that my sister's daughter told his wife that she was gonna get a coat 'cause he didn't purchase a coat for her, he got it

for his lover instead. He was so angry he slapped my sister's daughter
and told her when she sees somethin' to keep her mouth shut, she is not
to speak of it. My mother told him, "You didn't have no right hittin'
that child since she's not yours. If she should be punished, her mother
should punish her, not you." My brother was drinkin' too. When they're
doin' somethin' wrong, they drink alcohol to hide their problems or
their secrets — this is what he did. And he told my mother, "Well,
Momma, I'll hit you." I feel he was lettin' his alcohol talk at that point.
And she says, "Oh no you won't!" and continued to roll her pie crusts.

So he jumps up and hits my mother. At that time, my mother was
runnin' about a hundred and ninety pounds. She fell when he hit her,
and the force of the lick knocked her down on the floor and crushed
her knee bone. She had to be rushed to the hospital, and the doctors
wanted her to file a charge against my brother because he was responsible for her injury. And my mother, she cried about it and prayed about
it and told the doctors, "No, he's my son; I wouldn't want him to go to
jail because of knockin' me down." But right today, my mother has a
limp from this, and every so often (they call it fluid on the knee) she has
to go and have them pump this fluid out of her knee.

I was livin' here in Maryland when I heard my mother was hurt, and I
got in my car in the middle of a snowstorm and took my family and we
went down to North Carolina 'cause, like I say, I love my mother dearly.
When I got there and I found out what happened, I was very upset. My
brother refused to see me. I went home two years in a row, and every
time he would find out that I was comin' home, he would not come
around. He could not face me. It took him three months to come back
to my mother and apologize that what he had done was wrong. He
knew he was wrong. But each time that he knew I was comin' home, he
would disappear and not come around even though he only lived like
five miles away, and I would not go visit him when I went home.

I told you that I prayed this prayer asking God to take a couple years
off each of her kids' life so that she could live. But God didn't do that;
what He did was take my brother's life instead. My brother died of
pneumonia. My mother has had pneumonia three different times and
gotten over it, but here he has pneumonia once, and his lungs collapse
and he dies. On a Tuesday he was in the grocery store shoppin' 'cause he
was workin' a three-to-twelve shift. He went in the grocery store around
eleven o'clock in the day to shop, and he passed out in the grocery store.
The manager of the store called an ambulance and sent him to the
hospital. He went to the hospital on Tuesday, and by Thursday, he was
dead. They said it was inflammation of the lung. They called it the old-

fashioned "walkin' pneumonia" and said he'd probably had it at least a couple of weeks or a months and didn't even know it. His wife said that he'd been complainin' of pain in his back and muscles and joints but that he just ignored it.

When my sister called me and said would I come home that my brother had died, I thought someone had killed him or that he was in a car accident. Nothin' of this magnitude crossed my mind 'cause at his age (he was younger than I was; he was the baby), you just don't look at your baby brother dyin'. But when I heard what had happened, a voice came in my heart. It was just like God flashed a warnin' to me to say he had taken my brother's life to give years to my mother.

Here is my mother now seventy-three years old and in pretty good health. I thank God for everything. I told my father what I knew about my brother's death immediately when it happened, and I told him not to tell my mother 'cause I don't think my mother would've been able to handle it. Three months later, my father died. My brother died in April, and my father died in June. [Bond]

This long narrative incorporates an account of a mysterious experience within a fuller family history. Although removed from her family, Bond changes the course of family history by proposing a bargain with God: a couple years off hers and her siblings' lives in exchange for the prolonged life of their mother. But God alters the conditions of the contract so that it becomes an even exchange: her brother's life for her mother's. Bond explains such an adjustment in the context of the larger family saga in which the mother's miraculous cure is just a single event. The brother, who sins against wife, mother, and niece, is required, according to divine justice, to pay the full price of the speaker's bargain with God. An interesting mixture of blessing and curse, this tale demonstrates that one is not always in control of the terms of a wager with God.

What is particularly interesting about this narrative is the method of telling. The speaker suspends the mother's domestic, holiday pie-making through an account of her brother's misdeeds, only to have him perform the greater sin of striking the privileged mother while she makes Christmas pies. Although the speaker is absent both times that her mother is in danger, she manages, through prayer, to direct events. Hers is, finally, the prayer that cures and kills.

What is missing from this account of family crime is any discussion of the relationship of the misdeeds of the brother to the narrator's own crime. The omission of Bond's crime is necessary, for without it, she can reconstruct family history so that her brother alone plays the role of the bad child and she the part of the protector. His attempts to fracture the family are countered by her efforts to sustain it. Her stories defy reality. The only child to leave home, the only child to serve a prison sentence, she presents herself as a better member of the family able, imaginatively at least, to oversee things from afar, even from her prison cell.

The conclusion of this narrative, a family history in which men die and women live on (with the briefly mentioned death of the father), is premature. Its real conclusion might be found, in fact, in the narrator's own crime, the attempted murder of her son. But Bond, like most of the women I interviewed, refused to conceive of herself as the agent of crime. This silence about crime may explain why women do not tell life histories celebrating their lives of crimes as men do. To deal with the world they must take refuge in unreality. For men prison is largely a highly social working environment; for women it is often a meditative one in which the boundaries between inside and outside break down. By denying the reason for their imprisonment, women attempt to transform prison into a dream.

Angel Helpers

Another type of vision story is the angel helper story. Unlike the other visions of the divine presented here, the angel helper story generally describes a realistic tale of rescue with realistic human actors. Only upon reflection does the narrator realize that the rescuer was actually a divine envoy. One angel helper story appears in the final chapter and is presented in the context of Betty Jones's life story. Another and longer narrative of this type accounts for a short period in the life of Kathy Moore.

Kathy Moore recounts a surprisingly detailed story of mental collapse and subsequent rescue by a kind and mysterious man whom she can only imagine was an angel. Raised by a submissive mother and a verbally abusive, alcoholic father, Moore suffered insults which became most intense as she reached puberty. Like many incarcerated women, she describes a father who found it difficult to deal with his daughter's physical development. Most likely finding her both attractive and repulsive, he attempted to exercise tyrannical control over her comings and goings. He calculated the number of minutes it should take for her to get home from school and later from work, and if she took more than the allotted time, she was greeted by an outraged father who called her "slut" and "whore." While still a virgin, Moore was already convicted of promiscuity by her obsessive father.

After the breakup of her first marriage, Moore returned home with her daughter to the wretched family life she had sought to escape. Her father's insults intensified; he criticized any contacts she made outside the home and accused her of being a negligent parent at home.

> I finally met a fine young Jewish man, and I probably would have married him. We would go to lunches because that was a time when I wouldn't be late getting home. I was home at the exact time, unless I was working overtime. He begged me and pleaded me to go to a meeting with one of his district supervisors. He said we'd make arrangements for the baby, take her to another sitter, anything. He wanted to adopt the baby; he adored her. His parents adored her, and they liked me too. He made me feel like a young Jewish woman as opposed to a Catholic woman. I was totally accepted. It was beautiful. This was the first time I was accepted by a different race.
>
> At this time I'm living at home and being labeled by my father. I'm finding it more and more difficult to go home. If I'm five minutes late, it's like a traumatic scene: neighbors coming out on the porch, "What's going on?" I'm obviously sober, so I'm not drinking or doing drugs. He'd say I was a slut, I was a whore, there could be no way I was working. I don't care if I was five minutes or a half an hour late; I couldn't even be late due to the traffic. "You get off work at five. It's only twenty minutes away; why aren't you here?" He would be drunk, and maybe the baby would be crying. "Your mother's had her all day." My mother was delighted to have her. I think they hated the fact that I was coming home.
>
> Then I told him I had met Nathan. Now I'm really a slut, "How could you even look at another man? Your child's not even two years old. What kind of whore are you? You've got to be sleeping with him; you're probably not even working. You're probably laying up in a hotel all day," and all this other kind of devastating name-calling, obnoxious language, constant carrying on.

The night of the function we were to be home by nine. I had told Mother, and she had begged me not to go. I said, "I have to go. I'm going to marry this man. He wants me to meet these people." I had the engagement ring, the whole nine yards! We were ready.

Well, when the function was over, which was slightly around eight, I couldn't go home. I just could not go home. I think I had my first nervous breakdown then. I knew in my head the baby was all right. It wasn't like she was with a sitter that I only saw while I dropped the baby off and picked her up; she was with my parents. Everything we owned was in that house.

I had Nathan carry me to the Greyhound bus station, and I asked him to come back for me in about half an hour. I remember going to the bus teller and asking him for the next bus out. He said, "What do you mean, the next bus out?" I said, "Which one's going?" And I remember him saying to New York. I have no recall of getting on the bus, but I do remember waking up on the bus going over the George Washington Bridge and a lady saying, "You kept hollering you were so cold, you were so cold." I can see this lady's face, a black lady, real grey hair, putting a sweater over me. And I also remember waking up again later with the same lady saying, "Honey, I'm going to take my sweater now. I'm going to take my sweater now; we're in New York." And I remember not really verbalizing anything. I remember walking a great deal and not really being sure where I was and just walking and looking and walking.

I found out later that Nathan had come back to the Greyhound station for me after half an hour. He had a brother that was living up the street from the bus station in Mt. Vernon, and he had ran over to see him for a minute and then come back to get me. Of course, I wasn't there.

This is real weird too. I remember seeing a person, a young guy, a white guy with black hair, real light skinned, real milky white, saying to me, "What is wrong?" and I saying, "Nothing." He says, "You need some place to stay?" And I said, "I'm all right."

"Just come with me; we're going to get the subway." I remember getting on the subway, but I don't remember where we were going. I remember getting off the subway, and I remember going into a basement area. I remember him saying, "I won't be back the rest of the night. You're in Brooklyn. There's a bunk over there. I'll turn the light on, and you can stay as long as you need to get yourself together." I remember him going and coming, but I don't remember him staying. One time I remember waking up, sort of, and he was ironing clothes.

He said, "Oh, you're awake finally. I'm going to go to work now, but there's food. You do whatever you need. Take whatever you need out of the refrigerator. If you decide you have to leave, leave me a note." I remember waking up several times, apparently on different days and him saying, "Oh, you going to wake up now?" And then I remember waking up and saying to him, "I have to go home."

I know to this day that I have not had relations with this person. By this point in my life I knew about sex. I knew I hadn't had sex with him. I have no recall of being on any chemicals. I had stopped taking Valium when the baby was born. But the night that I left Baltimore I remember having two drinks at this function with my friend, Nathan. They were scotches with soda and a twist of lemon (I got away from the soda scene later, but at this time I had not started drinking).

Anyway, this gentleman put me on a bus to come back. But the way he put me on is interesting. I remember him taking me to the bus station in New York, giving me some money, saying, "I'll wait at the end of the line; you go get your ticket." I turned around to thank him again, and he was gone. To this day (nobody believes this story either), I believe that I actually had an angel in my life.

When I got back to Baltimore an instinct was telling me, "Don't go home." So I went to see my girlfriend. Her name was Susan, Susan Donohue. I knew that she was working at the Lord Baltimore Hotel, had a discotheque lounge in the basement at this time in the middle sixties, and she was a bar maid there. I said, "Oh, God, please let her be working tonight."

So I walked from the Greyhound station down to the Lord Baltimore Hotel thinking everything is fine. I don't know why all these people are looking at me and everything; I figure I'm okay. I walk in the Lord Baltimore Hotel and into the lounge, and she says, "Oh my God! Oh, Lord above! Jesus, you look like shit!" I thought I was only gone three days, three days and two nights at the most. I find out I was gone for fifteen days!

Well, I also lost twenty-five pounds. I still had on the same dress, and it's like hanging on me. (Honey, I tell you, baggy wasn't in then!) But I think I look fine. So I say to Susan, "I haven't been home for awhile, and I need some place to go to sort my thoughts." It's like late at night, real late. She says, "Oh, no, please don't go home; your parents have had the police looking for you. Oh, God, you look terrible; where have you been?"

"I was in New York, I think. And then there was this guy."

"Oh, don't tell me now; here's my key to the apartment." And she gave me the address: a little studio apartment on Eager Street.

"Go on up there. Do not open the door for anyone. I get off work at two, but I won't be home 'till about four. Go to sleep; there's food in the refrigerator. If you want something to drink, there's something to drink."

"Oh, I don't want anything. I just want to go to sleep; I'm so tired."

So I go there. I remember waking up now and then. I remember her saying, "God, I got to have a conversation with you; would you please wake up? I got to go to work." So then she would leave for work. Close to a week passed, and then she started filling me in about my parents.[Moore]

Moore's angel is the mysterious, nurturing male who leads her to shelter and, for a brief time, provides the protective home she had never known. Like the "fine young Jewish man," he appears and then disappears in the narrative. In such a story the narrator becomes the child of providence, passively accepting both the protection and the harm that providence metes out. Responsibility for her fate no longer rests with her but is beyond her control, in the hands of One who provides, at least for an interval, a divine caretaker.

The angel helper narrative is an episode that Moore places in her elaborately detailed life history between the account of an uncaring first husband and a brutal second one whose beatings nearly kill her. Moore's life story, retrospectively reconstructed from the point of view of prison, presents moment after moment of passivity leading ultimately to the eclipsing of her crime, a murder which seems to have no agent, a horror she dreamed rather than lived.[3]

6. Gifted Women

Although many women in prison experience visions, only a few inmates are widely acknowledged to be spiritually "gifted." These women frequently assume the roles of maternal counselors and spiritual advisors for their followers. This chapter will look particularly at four such "gifted" women: Luscious, a forty-two-year-old black woman from Baltimore, a repeat offender, serving a fifteen-year sentence for "bad checks"; Violet Star, a forty-year-old Native American who was, at the time of my interviews, Maryland's only woman on death row; Wilma Bond, a forty-eight-year-old black woman from the Washington, D.C., area, a first-time offender sentenced to life for attempted murder, assault with a deadly weapon, and theft—a woman who regards herself as a devout Christian, who often leads Sunday services and small prayer services; and Verna Brown, a black woman now retired from her job as correctional officer at the Indiana Women's Prison. Whether feared, revered, loved, or merely tolerated by those around them, these "gifted" women are not dismissed as mere eccentrics. They command attention from both inmates and officers.

Three of these women are in their forties, old by prison standards. Where the majority of the population are in their twenties, they have the status of elders. These women have experienced a lifetime of visions. Although they sometimes choose not to speak about a particular vision or to reveal only part of the specific intelligence disclosed to them, they make no secret of their "gift." It distinguishes them from other inmates and staff and puts them in touch with powers that transform the time they serve into revelation and ministry.

Their ability to function as mediators between the human and the divine endows the gifted with conspicuous stature within the prison community. Dream interpreters, priestesses, spiritual advisors—these women convince their followers of the presence of powers greater than the state operating within the prison and of their unique skill at invoking, manipulating, and interpreting these powers. They regard themselves as having been special children chosen by the divine to possess a superior knowledge. From a childhood during which they were considered "special," through a period of training and achieving spiritual perfection, to the present, these women understand their gift as the vital force directing their life story.[1]

They anchor their special gift in a family tradition.[2] Like their mothers or grandmothers before them, they receive warnings or strange visions which they learn to interpret and to heed. The special province of a few, this psychic knowledge comes to them through maternal blood lines, rendering them sensitive to supernatural or paranormal forces at work in the world. Though their capacities may become more acute at different times in their lives, and though they may, as in Violet Star's case, acquire their skills by studing the techniques of witchcraft, none questions that her gift is innate. Each acknowledges childhood visions as evidence of a natural rather than an acquired phenomenon. However, both Verna Brown and Violet Star narrate the events of their adult lives more vividly than incidents from their childhood. In interviews, Verna Brown eagerly detailed her professional history as a prison guard but evasively deflected questions about family life, and Violet Star, always more eager to discuss the doctrines of witchcraft than actual experiences, responded vaguely to the question of childhood visions. "I don't remember," she said, "my memory's kind of bad because of my drug use a few years ago. My childhood's sort of blurry." Although Star assured me that she did, indeed, experience visions as a child, she was unable to recall the details of such experiences.

Luscious

Luscious, on the other hand, volunteered a full account of her intial vision:

> The first time I had one of these experiences I was maybe eleven or twelve. It was like a time I'd been there before, like a déja vu. I was looking up at the balcony in a place like Bourbon Street in New Orleans, and I saw this woman. She was brushing her silver hair. I looked up, and I said, "Miss Silver." She didn't like me. I think because of some kind of status or something in the alleyway in Sterling Street in Baltimore, but the vision took me to New Orleans. I didn't understand it then.

> I asked my mother, "Who's Miss Silver?" And she got a funny look on
> her face and said, "I don't know—why do you ask that?" I says, "I don't
> know. I just want to know. Who is Miss Silver?" She says, "You are a
> strange child—I knew that from birth."
>
> My mother knew. I didn't know then what she was talking about.
> And my daughter, she knows that it's uncanny because she gets away
> from me. That's why we don't get along, I guess, because she's so afraid
> of me. She's so normal.
>
> Visions never frightened me. I knew what I saw, what I felt. What I
> *lived* is what frightened me. A lot of times, the things that I saw
> I would never speak about. I like dissolve them. I have to. [Luscious]

In this narrative both figure and ground shift before the viewer. The
setting of Sterling Street, one of Baltimore's oldest streets, shifts to
Bourbon Street where the mysterious lady, "Miss Silver," appears on
a balcony. What is at work here is the dreamlike power of the uncon-
scious to weld sterling and silver into the dazzling image of the re-
mote, enigmatic sterling silver woman. The speaker's reaction, her
bewilderment and her subsequent search for interpretation, is lacking
from most accounts of visions. The mother's interpretation, that her
daughter is a "strange child," authenticates the narrative and instructs
the child in the risks of talking about such strange sighting, but fails
to answer the child's question, "Who's Miss Silver?"

As an adult, Luscious later confronted her mother with the possibility that Miss Silver might be someone from her mother's past whom
she had wronged. Although her mother did not confess this to Luscious, her evasive reaction admitted as much to the daughter. Even
three years after this series of interviews Luscious reaffirmed her belief
that her mother knew but would not confess the real identity of Miss
Silver. The disparity between the strange child's truth and the adult's
resistance is a familiar one in these narratives. Spirits can sound so
"soothing and seducing" that they may appear benevolent, especially
to children, when their intent is really sinister. They return often to
settle a score. Wronged in life by an ancestor, they execute their revenge on subsequent generations. Thus, the sins of the mother are
visited on the daughter in the form of hauntingly ambiguous visions.

By claiming to report visions like those experienced by her grandmother, Luscious estranges herself from two generations: her mother
and her daughter. Prison presents her the opportunity to construct a

new family on her own pattern and bonded by her charismatic authority. This family values her gift. She functions as knowing, comforting, and loved mother, sending psychic messages to new inmates and reassuring those who are put "on lock," in the solitary confinement wing where Luscious has spent most of her recent sentence:

> They're very possessive of me. The whole wing is very possessive of me. It's like a neon sign outside my door. There's a little girl that came here recently. I feel for her; she's not going to last long. When she came in the first night and she was crying, she told me, "I just knew you were the one."
>
> I said, "The one *what*?" I knew what she was talking about, but I didn't say.
>
> "Luscious, I knew you were the one to touch me on the back of the neck just before I came here and tell me that everything was going to be all right, that you were going to make me feel better."
>
> I said, "How did you know it? This is the first time I laid eyes on you."
>
> "No, it's not," she says.
>
> I knew she was coming. The night before she came I saw a vision of her. I told Shelley, "A girl is on her way."
>
> Now, when I talk to this little girl I say, "You know what? You're like a little monkey, a chimpanzee, that mimics everything I do. But you can't do that because it will get you in trouble, Little Girl." I have to watch myself, how I act around them because they easily pick it up. [Luscious]

Luscious's light flashes like a neon sign, like Miss Silver's hair, in contrast to the drab monotony that surrounds her. Not the mysterious inner light of some special knowledge but the bright advertisement of her charisma, Luscious's gift binds younger women into the simulated family and political worlds she constructs in prison, worlds in which she functions as warden, mother, and counselor.[3] The responsible parent for a group of troubled, temperamental young women suffering the intense boredom and frustration of solitary confinement, Luscious (from her locked cell), comforts them, gives advice, tells stories, teaches scripture, and even leads the whole wing in dramatic productions, each woman speaking from her cell.

These impromptu plays, sometimes referred to by prisoners as "radio plays," can be quite elaborate. Alone in their locked cells, women sometimes create makeshift costumes. One dresses as a "hoola girl" and another as a "dude," and they describe their costumes and stage directions (where they're standing, any props, etc.) before speaking their parts. A play may live only for a single performance, or it may be performed repeatedly over several months.

One of the most popular plays "on lock" is "Radio Man." A prison tradition rather than an invention of Luscious's, "Radio Man" is quite simple in format. It begins at one end of the hall with the first speaker describing a handsome man who has come to visit her in her cell. She tells in elaborate detail what this welcome visitor looks like, what he says, and what they do together. After a short time the prisoner in the next cell interrupts and demands that the man be shared with her. This woman, in turn, reports her own version of their private encounter. Prisoners pass the imaginary man (like a talking stick) down the hall. When he happens to visit at the cell door of a "stud," she demands that he bring his sister with him. All variety of sexual descriptions are welcome, and fellow prisoners reward the most entertaining speakers with cheers and catcalls. If one speaker becomes boring, the next in line insists on the floor.

Luscious and dynamic women like her often organize the women into such performances. Luscious views such group activities not simply as ways of passing the time but as necessary safety valves for release of the pressure that builds up from twenty-three hours a day in solitary. In addition to directing such plays, Luscious often demonstrates her skill as storyteller by narrating detailed and chilling ghost stories. Amazingly creative and instantly adaptable as social chair, she sometimes directs events aimed to instruct as well as to delight. Her raucous production of "Ezekiel and the Valley of Dry Bones" was a favorite of fellow prisoners but resulted in "write-ups" for Luscious and another inmate because the ecstatic delivery of this biblical story offended the officer on duty.

But what the officer found offensive, Luscious understood as a poignant comment on the plight of prisoners and the offer of a message of hope. In Ezekiel 37, the prophet is carried away "by the Spirit of the Lord" to the valley of old, dry bones and by repeating the words of God restores life to the dead:

So I spoke these words from God, just as he told me to; and suddenly there was a rattling noise from all across the valley, and the bones of each body came together and attached to each other as they used to be. Then, as I watched, the muscles and flesh formed over the bones, and skin covered them, but the bodies had no breath. Then he told me to call to the wind and say: "The Lord God says: Come from the four winds, O Spirit, and breathe upon these slain bodies, that they may live again." So I spoke to the winds as he commanded me and the bodies began breathing; they lived, and stood up—a very great army.

Like Ezekiel, Luscious delivers the messages contained in her visions to those around her—sometimes as warning, sometimes as promise. And like Ezekiel, she restores hope and a sense of community to those convicted and condemned. But although she claims the authority of a prophet, Luscious declines the subservience to a higher power. "It doesn't have anything to do with God," she tells another inmate. Her visions bind people to her, not to God. Nonapocalyptic, they predict the local and the domestic.

Often the recipient of several visions a week, Luscious witnesses not only the activities of her own family but also events taking place in the families of other prisoners. More often depicting misfortune than fortune, these visions sometimes communicate messages of which even Luscious is not fully aware. One such account communicates the betrayal of a young woman by her lover:

There is one little girl I can't get rid of; we call her "Rajeem." When we were in Horigan I was sitting on the bed and we just got quiet. Rajeem was sitting in the chair, and I was sitting on the bottom bunk. I was leaning over, and I don't know why, I just told her what I had seen. It just come out, and she burst out crying. She says, "Luscious, I was just sitting here asking God to give me some message of something, to tell me what to do. I says, "Well, it doesn't have anything to do with God. I don't know why I told you that. I apologize." She says "No, you know what? What you just described to me is true."

I can't get rid of this girl now. Every time she sees me, "Luscious, did you see anything about me?" I had described to her a scene with her boyfriend, her baby's father, the man that she lives with. The scene was a store, and this woman was coming out of the store, and I described the woman to Rajeem. I saw her get in a car. I described the store; I never been to this place before. Later, when she was telling me that she knew this little roadside store and she was telling me about it, she says, "The girl you described I know. Now I know who my boyfriend's running with." I says, "Oh my goodness, I didn't mean—" I says, "Look, what do I know? Maybe I'm wrong."

So a week later, he wrote her and told her he had this girl pregnant, the very girl I described, and I says, "Oh man, this is uncanny! This is really weird!" [Luscious]

Like many of these narratives, this example concludes with the bit of external evidence that adds legitimacy to the vision and grounds the extraordinary event in the ordinary world of letters from home.

As further proof of her powers to see into the lives of fellow inmates Luscious recounts a vision of the contents of her friend's closet at home. According to Lucious, this conversation took place when these women were in adjacent cells on the solitary confinement wing of the prison:

I had one that was really weird. I called Deana "Little Girl." One day I says, "Little Girl, do you have a pair of yellow pants and a white and yellow blouse?" And she says, "Yeah, at my grandmother's house." She says, "What are you doing over there, Luscious?" I says, "Little Girl, tell me the truth, please I got to know. When you got locked up, did you leave a pair of yellow pumps underneath your pants hanging down? And a blouse over top of it?" She says, "Oh my God!"

It'd be weird, a lot of times I see a lot of stuff and I don't say nothing. I don't want anybody to think I'm weird. [Luscious]

Those who believe accounts of Luscious's visions regard her as special; those who don't consider her either amusing or weird. Like many who claim visions, she carefully weighs the situation before disclosing to others the content of her visions, fearing their disbelief and their ridicule.

When I first asked Luscious about her visions she spoke to me vaguely, relating few details. Once I had won her trust, her narratives grew longer and more elaborate, but she still remained hesitant to relate visions that she had experienced between our visits. The more recent the experience, the more enigmatic she was in her account, seeming to judge whether or not to tell all the details. With the privilege of visions comes the responsibility of weighing their messages, sharing them only with those who will respect them and, in Luscious's case, be entertained by them.

Luscious's visions inform all aspects of her special relationship with fellow inmates. They allow her to know often before the officers that a woman is coming on lock, insuring for her a control over the operations of the segregation wing that appears, at least, to rival that of the authorities. But of course her power doesn't rival the authorities; it provides an imitation of them—a power that, though familiar, is finally as mysterious for fellow inmates as Miss Silver:

> Someone made a statement the other night. She says, "You have full control of the officers here; we don't understand."
> I'm saying, "No, I don't,' but I'm thinking, "It's true a little bit." It's not a control thing. They're just attracted to my light I guess. [Luscious]

Light as a metaphor for spirituality is as universal as the trope of wisdom unheeded. Although descriptions of her visions were not welcome during her childhood, they fascinate those who make up her prison family and give her prominence within that community. Luscious not only tells other prisoners of events taking place in their homes but also prophesies things to come, and entertains them with accounts of her out-of-body experiences. Her narratives provide a form of cultural resource and simulated political structure: storytelling to some, psychic revelation to others.

Upon her return from some of these out-of-body experiences, Luscious draws images of her experiences which she shows to other inmates and favored staff members. Her songs, poems, and pencil drawings all find their inspiration in her visions. Although they can be productive for the recipient, they can also exhaust and frighten:

> This place can make you nuts. You have to dominate psychic projections, take a rein on. Everybody has a psyche, but some people, they don't want to bring it up; it's scary. [Luscious]

Receiving visions is not something done lightly. Encountering images of oneself (of one's past, present, and future) requires a great deal of energy.[4]

The task of interpreting visions is far less demanding than experiencing them. Sometimes visions will embody transparent messages;

other times messages will reveal themselves over time. But far easier than the interpretation of visions is the interpretation of other's dreams. Prisoners come often to Luscious and to other "gifted" inmates soliciting their interpretation of dreams:

> I have girls who tell me their dreams all the time. They say, "Luscious, I had this dream," and I tell them what it means. It's a knowing thing. I think it's two people inside me, or something—my identity and something else. I don't know how to explain it. Sometimes when they come to me I just know before they get it out. Sometimes it's like I'm not just a mere mortal or mere human. Girls come to me and they're perplexed. They bring their dreams to me and I know what they are. [Luscious]

The dream interpreter has her own authority in prison. With the time of counselors almost entirely taken up by administering tests and paper work, dream interpreters serve as unofficial counselors who offer women an alternative reading of events of the past and of things to come. These generally older women quickly become the motherly figures in the institution, soothing the depressed and quieting the often hostile younger women.

In the long narrative that follows, a woman in her twenties tells of overcoming her skepticism about an older psychic woman who interprets her dreams and forecasts her eventual deliverance from prison:

> Back in 1980, it was a lady here, she claimed she was psychic. She was sixty-some years old. They raided her house and, because it was her house and drugs was found in her house, she just got caught up in it. But she wasn't here no more than about ninety days. And she used to always read cards and the palm of people's hands and stuff like that.
>
> I used to see everybody goin' up to her, and she would tell them about theirself, right? I was scared 'cause I don't believe in stuff like that. I don't have any reasons as to why I don't believe in it. I just don't feel comfortable with it because I feel that they could just tell you anything they think you may wanna hear. But this woman was really tellin' them girls and scarin' 'em, right? And I would never let her do me, right?
>
> So one day, she said, "Come here, I wanna do you 'cause you are so quiet."
>
> I said, "No, I don't want to."
>
> And she turned up these cards and she said, "You've been hurtin',

you've been hurtin' real bad." Even though I was walkin' around with a smile (it had been about five months and I'd kinda got out of my shell) she said, "You been hurtin' real bad." She said, "Money. This card is money. Somebody took a lot of that from you." Which was my lawyer, right? By this time, my heart is goin' like this [*taps her chest*].

She said, "You're in here for somebody really, really close to you." And she said, "You had a dream, and that dream was something that dealt with your mouth." And I'm like, "How does this woman know this?" I did, I had a dream that I lost all my teeth, and I was walking around and I didn't have any teeth in my mouth. It scared me and I woke up. She told me about that dream. She said, "You dreamed something that dealt with your mouth, kissing or something, but it deals with your mouth."

I say, "I dreamed I lost my teeth."

She say, "You lost somebody very close to you by your own hand." Which was my boyfriend.

She scared me so. By this time, I'm like, "Please don't tell me no more."

She say, "Have you been havin' any more dreams lately?"

I say, "About two weeks ago, I dreamed of a man without a head. He didn't have no face, but he had Tom's body, and I would cry the whole day because I wanted to get back [*snaps fingers*] in that dream. When I realized it was Tom [the boyfriend she killed], I was woke then, right? I could see his physique and all that, but they never showed his face. I cried for two days after that dream wanting to get back in that dream so I could tell him how much I loved him."

Another dream was, I had this basin of water and I was sittin' in my room, and he was layin' across my bed I had this basin of water, and I was washin' him up, playin' with him, washin' him up and stuff. And he was layin' in the bed. He kept talkin' and the captain that worked here walked in my room, and she say, "What are you doing?"

I say, "I'm givin' Tom a bath."

He told the captain, he say, "Well, can't she give me a bath if she want to?"

I said, "Be quiet, she ain't even talkin' to you."

The dream went on off. So when I told this old lady this, she say, "Your dream signify that one of these days, somebody of some high authority will come and wash all your blues away." Every time I think about it, goose bumps come, because I really believe her. She said, "It's gonna come in sixes. I don't know whether it's gonna be six years, six days, six months, six hours," she said, "but it'll be in sixes." I'll be here six years this year.

> I come up for parole this year. I'm supposed to. This had been a real
> good year for me. She say she don't know whether it'll be six years, six
> days, six months, six hours, but I see that it's sixes. And sixes is sup-
> posed to be the sign of the devil, but this has been a real, real blessed
> year for me; it really has. [Jackson][5]

The fact that this older woman knows the subject of Jackson's dream
even before she mentions it confirms her authority as psychic interpreter. In the loss of teeth she reads the loss of a loved one and Jackson's crime. For Jackson the confession of dreams to an older, maternal
woman eases guilt and offers her hope that someone will someday
"wash all your blues away." What hope there is in prison one finds in
dreams.

Several years ago dream books, those newsstand paperbacks detailing elaborate systems of dream interpretation, provided the most
popular methods for decoding dreams at the Maryland Correctional
Institution for Women. But two years before I began my fieldwork such
publications, along with packs of tarot cards, were confiscated and
banned. My informants could recollect no reason for this censorship
but speculated that the dream books and tarot cards encouraged a
kind of private talk that made the officers nervous. In spite of official
censorship, fortunes and dreams continue to be lively topics of conversation among women in prison, a daily topic for some.

> A lot of people told me their dreams. Like my roommate, she has a
> lot of dreams, and she doesn't understand them. They usually come to
> us in distorted form, and if you can break it down, it makes sense. And
> a lot of dreams do come true. Like say you, for instance, you'll have a
> dream about a wedding. A wedding usually means death or a birth. It
> comes true like that, it really does.
> Burke: How do you break down dreams? How do you interpret them?
> Briggs: The simplest form I know how. I used to read about dreams
> and remember, rapid-eye movement stage, and everything. And with
> you knowing about the literature a little bit it helps you form it. I forgot
> the dream she told me, it was a whacky dream, and I explained it and it
> happened. Something about a phone call — I forget. But I broke it down
> into an easier form for her and she understood it. [Briggs]

Although I have conducted no formal study, discussion of dreams appears more frequent in prison than out, a factor undoubtedly of increased idle time, of the concentration of individuals living together

under the same roof, and possibly of the increase in dream activity itself. Sleeping is a way of doing one's time, and many prisoners choose to spend the time when they are neither at work nor at "rec" napping.

Although the authorities could rid the prison of dream books, they could not eliminate the persistent talk among inmates about their dreams. But with no dream books to aid in the interpretation of dreams, prisoners at the Maryland Correctional Institution for Women have relied more and more in recent years on the skills of gifted women like Luscious who profess a psychic knowledge of a realm more vast, more varied, yet more personal than the regimented, indifferent world of the prison.

Wilma Bond

Raised in rural North Carolina, Wilma Bond describes a childhood in which she overcomes the scoffing of skeptics and is able to give accounts of her premonitions to willing listeners.

I remember, I was young. I was very young when I first really could see things happening, when I knew something was going to happen before it happened. If I visualized something and I knew it was going to happen, sometimes I would go to that person and tell them that such and such a thing was gonna happen. And a lot of times they didn't pay me any attention.

They'd say, "Hey, she doesn't know what she's talking about. This is not going to happen."

But then, it would happen to them exactly the way I tell them, and then they'd come back and say, "You know that child said such and such a thing was going to happen, and it happened just the way she said it. How did she know it was gonna happen?" This happened to me a lot when I was young. I would tell people that I see something that was gonna happen, and at first they didn't believe me. But then after they saw that I could really tell them something that was gonna happen, then they started paying attention to me.

And a lot of my family would come to me and say, "Well Wilma, what's on your mind today? Is there anything we should be aware of? Anything that you know about that we should know about?" And this type thing. And if it was something that I felt they should know about, I would tell them. I would give people warnings about things 'cause I could see things happening in the future. I would tell them that it was gonna happen, and most of the time when I told someone that these things was gonna happen, it would happen exactly the way I told it. And I would give warnings to a lot of people. But sometimes if I fell that the person can't handle the warning, I won't tell 'em. I just tell 'em to be careful, something is gonna happen in their life, but I won't reveal to them what it is. It's like God has told me when or who to reveal whatever I have to reveal. Like I know I can't reveal to my mother about me knowing what time to really expect that she might die, because I don't think that she could handle it. If I felt that she could handle it, then I would tell her. [Bond]

Bond avoids specificity with expressions like "anything," "something," "sometimes," "such and such a thing," and "this type of thing." Rather than recount actual incidents that illustrate her gift of divination, she generalizes about making believers out of skeptics and about the subsequent attention bestowed upon her as a child. Although vague about the content of her pronouncements, Bond emphatically identifies their source: God. Personal and Christian, Bond's God speaks directly to her the message of things to come.

A child with knowledge that surpasses that of the adults around her, Bond apparently bears only bad tidings. She possesses the gift/affliction of the "death-seer" (Jaffe *Apparitions,* 18), one who peers into the future to see the death of a friend or relative. The "death-seer" stands, according to Jaffe, as a threshold figure between the present and the future, between life and death, between the human and the spiritual. Her position sets her apart as special.

Read psychologically, Bond's narrative sounds like a child's fantasy of revolt against adults who everywhere control her life. She has the power, after all, to wound them by disclosing the doom that is to befall them. By demonstrating her power, the child wins the attention of the adults around her, who come to solicit her forecasts. Although the child is obviously still dependent on adults and under their control, she nevertheless inhabits the privileged role of "seer." By assuming such a role, the child, like the prisoner, inverts (imaginatively at least) the normal hierarchy and exchanges her dependence for spiritual mastery.

In her analysis of spiritualist "Rita M.," June Macklin offers a psychological reading of another child, one who retreats into the fantastic world of magic and trance. Inhibited by strict parents from reaching "self-realization," Macklin's subject projects herself into a world of benevolent spirit guides where she can play the roles unavailable to her in daily life: "By employing a series of defense mechanisms throughout her life, she has been able to reduce and control magically the tensions created by a series of inter-personal conflicts. Although she is coping with the various problems of living and helping others to cope, she could be judged to be suffering impairment of psychological, social, and cultural functioning" (54–55). Macklin thus domesticates the spirit world of her subject, reading it as the fabulous creation of a child frustrated and overlooked by those around her. One could venture such a psychological interpretation of Wilma Bond: the child, seeking attention, invents a spiritual world which she alone mediates. Such a reading, though, presumes that an informant's remarks about childhood experiences are, in fact, more trustworthy than her accounts of supernatural events. If we, however, consider a life story in which the extraordinary shapes the ordinary, we can read an informant's account of childhood as a means of naturalizing, if not rationalizing, the irrational. Her vague account of childhood enables Bond to situate ecstatic moments in a tale of origins and ends. Born to receive God's word, the child learns that she will encounter skeptics, that over time they will become believers, and that she must be cautious in her predictions because all are not ready to receive her grim forecasts. She weighs what she relates, judging the listener's readiness to receive the sometimes harsh knowledge she has to communicate.

The withholding, then, becomes part of the telling. There is generally some part of the knowledge which the psychic keeps hidden, and this undisclosed portion adds to the mystery of the medium. This mystery, for Bond, is also part of God's plan. She and He share complete knowledge of an event to come; the recipient of her warning possesses only partial knowledge. This special ability to see what others cannot see, to hold privileged knowledge, sets the woman apart from others as a holy person.

Although men figure most prominently in the history of Judeo-Christian prophecy, prophetic women appear in impressive numbers among such early Christian sects as the Montanists, French Prophets, English Prophets, and Pietists, and later among Quakers, Shakers, and American evangelical sects (Garrett). These women experienced visions, preached the inspired word of God, and guided others toward enlightenment. Of the four women discussed in this chapter, Wilma Bond most clearly fits within this tradition of female prophecy. From unnoticed child to respected seer, from criminal to spiritual advisor, Bond is the Christian-made-new by revelation. Even the years she spends in prison becomes productive time in which to do God's work by guiding others:

I had one girl that was living next door to me. She's suicidal. She had gotten twenty-five years. I talked to her, and she was so depressed till by me talking with her, it brought her out of this depression. She drinked, and she set the house on fire. Her sister got burnt up in the fire, and this was what got her here. So she say she kept on hearing voices. I told her, I said, "Can you tell me what these voices are saying?" She said she don't really understand. She can't. When she wake up she don't understand what the voices said to her, but she keep hearing these voices in her head. And she said she don't know whether it's her sister's voice or whether it's God's voice or somebody's voice trying to tell her something. And she wakes up screaming, hearing these voices in her head.

So I told her, I said, "You gotta get in touch with these voices. Try to recognize what the voices are saying and whose voices they are." I said, "Just try to see if you can remember something that they are saying. Just try and if it's just a lot of mumbo-jumbo and you can't understand, then you gotta pray. Ask God to reveal to you what it is that you don't understand."

She didn't know how to pray, and she said, "Well, I don't know what to say." I said, "Well, I can't tell you how to pray; all I can tell you is to say what's in your heart. It might not sound right to you, but God will understand what you're saying. Whatever you want to talk about, whatever's bothering you, talk about it. If it's your sister that's bothering you, talk to God and say, 'Hey, I don't know how to pray.' Let God know that you don't know how to pray. He don't know this unless you confess it with your mouth that you don't know how."

And I said, "He will understand what you going through 'cause He know your heart better than you know it yourself. He will give you your blessings, and you can ask Him to forgive you for what you've done, because He know that you was gonna sin. You have sinned. You gotta confess to Him and ask for his forgiveness."

She said, "Well, I don't know how to say it."

I said, "Just say whatever, whatever comes to your mind. God know what's in you heart. You just have to confess it."

So she started praying, and we would sit in our [adjacent] rooms and I'd be sitting at the window and I'd call Lynn and say, "Lynn, I want you to look up in the sky and tell me if you can see it." Now, I would see a cross in the sky, and I would ask her, could she see it. But she couldn't.

And many a day, I have sit here and I saw the face of a man in the sky: the shadow of a man on his knees praying, the shape of a man and his face. And I would ask her did she see it. One time she told me she saw the cross when I was talking to her. I said, "Look, right at it this moment; you will see it!" She looked and she sid, "Yes, I see it too."

So I look in the sky sometimes on the evenings and I be praying. I have also asked God to reveal Himself to me. I be looking at the sky, and all of a sudden it would, like a cloud or a form of a man, would flash. And I can be driving alone in my car, and if something bother me, I can look to the sky and pray and ask God to show me a sign. And I see, it's just like a mountain side and a man kneeling beside it. I would see this several times. And I see crosses in the sky all the time. It's like a light, a glowing light.

I may live a long time before I really come to understand everything that God is wanting me to understand. This is the reason why I said I know that God is strong in my life because it's so many things that I see that nobody else can see. I know He's showing me these things for a reason, but I have yet to understand all the reasons that I'm seeing the things that I see.

Even though I've talked to people who have studied the ministry and explain these things to them, some of them I talked to say they've been ministering fifteen, twenty years and they have never seen a vision. And so I ask them how did they get started into ministry? "Is it a feeling, or did someone come to you, or just what did you feel? What made you become a minister?" And some of them say, well it was just something inside of them that made them say, "Hey, you know, I want to preach the word of God and tell others about His great works," and this type thing. They just got that gut feeling that this is what they wanted to do, but they have never really saw a vision or anything like this. But see, I am seeing these things, and it's not clear to me if He's calling me to the ministry.

I ignored things that I see. A lot of times I have ignored it, and I say maybe this was the way God wanted it to be. I feel that in here [*puts her hand on her heart*]. But maybe now I can have enough time on my hands to see and to do what He had in mind for me to do. I was too busy before I came here. I ignored a lot of things that was put before me. Now, it's coming back. It's coming back slowly. I can see it coming back. [Bond]

Wilma Bond sees prison as a place where her gift may flourish and her eyes open more fully to divine revelation. Incarceration allows her the time to pause and interpret rather than ignore the "signs" that God shows her.[6] Such a transformation of the prison from a place of physical confinement into one of spiritual liberation would have pleased the early Protestant prison reformers like the outspoken British Quaker Elizabeth Fry (Dobash, Dobash, and Gutteridge), but what would have frightened Fry is the simple, and fully Protestant, movement from personal enlightenment to preaching. Though Fry and others advocated prisons set up to insure the religious reformation of the prisoner, they were not prepared for the results of such spiritual transformation. To be filled with the divine light of God and to preach before others was one thing outside of prison; it was another within its walls. Such a practice could usurp the very authority of the institution, which is based on keeping prisoners in their places, places of silent, motionless humility. To preach as a reformed sinner might be welcome outside the walls of the prison but could not be tolerated within.

Although Bond's spiritual experiences seem to suggest to her that God is calling her to preach His word, the prison ministers she consults can give her no confirmation, for they are unable to witness, themselves, to any calling visions. Rather, their calling to the ministry was just a "gut feeling that this is what they wanted to do." From their perspective, the visions of Wilma Bond might be viewed as unorthodox, but there is nothing novel in this: the visions of evangelistic callings have often been viewed with skepticism by established churches, especially when those visions have been reported by women.

Like visionaries of the past, Wilma Bond often experiences visions after sleep deprivation and fasting. Refusing to sleep when the time for sleep is decreed by the institution and refusing the food offered by one's jailers are forms of passive rebellion rewarded by visions. The following account demonstrates the ways in which physical deprivation brings about spiritual rewards:

> When I first came here I felt let down because I said to myself, "If God loved me so well and so much, why did this thing happen?" But then, some peace came in my heart. When I first came I couldn't sleep. I laid awake sleepless nights, a lot of sleepless nights, yet I was not tired. I knew that God was trying to show me something, so I didn't force myself to go to sleep. I have never taken a sleeping pill in my life. Even

if I couldn't sleep, I said, "Well, it's because God don't want me to sleep. It's something he want me to see, and I gotta have my eyes open to see it. So if I can't sleep, I'll just lay down anyway and close my eyes and just lay there awake and pray."

When I got up the next day it's just like I slept, even though I know I laid there all night awake. But see, the rule is here that even if you are not sleepy they want you to lay down. They don't want you sitting up in a chair, and they turn the lights off, so actually you're like sitting in a dark, almost dark room. If they come by checking and they see you sitting up, they want to know what's going on and why are you up and not asleep. So I would lay down just to satisfy everyone around me that, hey, I'm OK, even though things are going on in my head that I can't explain to others. So I would just lay there and continue to pray and ask God to help me through it.

If something really bother me, then I'll fast for a couple days. I won't eat. I'll just drink liquids and I won't eat any solid foods. I'll just pray and fast. When I do that I'm not hungry; I'm full, just as full if I had sit down and had a three-course meal, even though I might not have anything but some tea or a little coffee or something like that. I might do that for maybe ten days in a row. And then all that time, I'm using this time to talk to God and to tell him to help me, show me whatever he want me to see and open my eyes up and my heart and my soul and let me know what he want of me. I try to do this at least a couple times a month. It's very helpful, to me it is. [Bond]

These practices of discipline and purification subvert prison control in subtle ways. The prisoner and not the institution decides when she will sleep and eat. Several inmates told me of the need to fast in order to feel an inner peace, to hear God's word or to insure that a wish might come true. In prisoner discussions of these rituals, the older, more practiced women like Bond often instruct their younger counterparts in the importance of such ritual, offering these women some sense of control over their fates.

In other small ways, Bond has appropriated control over her daily routine. Every morning without the aid of a prison wake-up bell or a personal alarm, she rises at four-thirty ("to God's call not the institution's"), prays, showers by herself and meticulously applies her makeup as if "dressin' up to go somewhere." She *is* going somewhere, she insists, out into the prison to do God's work. Bond prides herself on looking good. Every day she tends to her long, bright red fingernails, delicately ornamented with tiny stickers. Every day she finds some innovative way of transforming the same clothes she has worn many times before into "an outfit." Even though the prison prohibits plastic and silk flowers, Bond resourcefully fashions a flower out of a net scarf and pins it to her tailored blouse. Distinguished among six hundred women for whom the fashion of choice is jeans and a sweatshirt in winter or jeans and a t-shirt in summer, Bond appears every morning (hair carefully done, fancy blouse, plain skirt, heels, and stockings) like a woman going off to her middle-class job. She is distinguished, too, because of her disposition. In an institution in which staff and inmates alike exchange "prison stares" as the pass,[7] Bond projects a warmth that few share and some find annoying. "What you smilin' 'bout," they sometimes say to her.

Bond's physiognomy, her morning rituals, and her dress would signify nothing outside of prison, but within they constitute a position of defiant self-definition. Subversive in a very fundamental way, Bond maintains her separateness as someone not to be blended in or adapted.

Violet Star

Of all the women I interviewed at the Maryland Correctional Institution for Women, Violet Star enjoyed the largest reputation. Convicted of a brutal murder and sentenced to death, she was the subject of several articles in Maryland newspapers. Inside the prison, every inmate and every staff member willingly offered an opinion of this self-proclaimed Satanist. Her small group of followers, though reluctant to discuss beliefs and practices in any detail, credited Star with their spiritual enlightenment. Believers but not followers, others ascribed to her great power (particularly to do evil) and therefore tried to avoid her. Half-believers admitted her knowledge of psychic phenomena and considered her interesting and entertaining to talk with but believed she exercised no control over them. Still others saw Star as the creator of the most impressive con in the prison — one so successful that it even made guards keep their distance. Whether believer or nonbeliever, inmate or staff, all acknowledged Star's intelligence and charisma, the primary ingredients of a successful cult leader.

Star aspired to become a leader in the international Church of

Satan, a position not bestowed or given but achieved through discipline and study in the manipulation of spirits. What distinguishes Star from the other women in this chapter is the emphasis she places on craft, the acquired knowledge of psychic phenomenon. Although her spiritual practices may resemble those of other women, her beliefs certainly differ.

Like Wilma Bond, Violet Star prepares herself for spiritual experiences through loss of sleep and lack of food:

> I've had quite a few visions here. You can bring them on yourself. It comes through fasting, lack of sleep. If you're sleeping a lot, eating a lot, you're just caught up in a rat race; it's hard to catch one, but if you're sitting there and meditating, totally in tune with the universe, it can be brought to you. So a lot of times if I really need that inner strength, that's what I do. And then I can visualize or see things I've never seen before.
>
> But it's hard to receive visions in brick. You need to feel the sun or the moon. But the way the moon shines through my window, I can sit on my floor and get some of the strength from that. The sun never shines in my window, but the moon does. Once in a while I get out in the sun. The Indians have a technique which I used to practice when I was allowed out. If you're sick—and I been sick, like I am now—you go out and you lay up on your right side facing the sun, and you'll get well. Or we take grass, boil it and drink the water from it, but in here I can't get any grass. [Star]

Whereas Bond's visions are personal communiqués from an all-powerful God; Star's seem almost to exist independent of the perceiver, only visible when one is "in tune with the universe." Added to the ritual fasting and sleep deprivation is her notion of meditation (pirated from Eastern mysticism and reminiscent of the sixties), practiced to establish a more perfect balance within the individual. The ultimate aim of this meditation is to experience an absolute cosmic harmony, the individual in perfect tune with the cosmos. According to Star, visions are potentially available to everyone, but few people see them. Perceiving visions is an art that requires a disciplined body and mind. Out of the rat race, living a simple life, the prisoner would seem to be the perfect candidate for visions, but she sometimes lacks the all-important stimulus of sunlight, or its reflection in moonlight. Sunlight, according to Star, not only spiritually enlightens, it also physically heals. Like her explanation of visions, Star's theology merges elements of Native American belief, witchcraft and popular spiritualism.

Violet Star discloses the marginality of the holy woman in the proud account of her spiritual powers. She explains how witchcraft unites her belief in spirits, a belief nurtured by her Indian heritage, with her desire for a religion that gives women access to power. By careful study and discipline she learns to recognize and manipulate spiritual forces active in the world.

Drugs have blurred Star's memory of her early childhood in North Carolina where she was raised by a Cherokee mother and an Apache father. She claims to have experienced visions as a child, but is imprecise in her accounts. More communicative about her Cherokee grandfather, the most significant nurturer in her childhood, Star tells how he taught her the importance of living one's life in harmony with the spirits. Her first marriage at fourteen to a man ten years older than herself lasted three weeks. When her husband went to prison, she filed for divorce. She married and divorced two more husbands until she realized "that the heterosexual life was not for me." Even though she discovered her homosexuality after the breakup of her third marriage, she married a fourth time to allay the suspicions of others, "to keep people in the community from talking, that type of thing." Oppressed by the "domination" of all her husbands, Star found in lesbian relationships more equality, and, in some instances, an opportunity to become the dominant partner herself, perferring "real feminine-looking women" whom she could "protect and take care of."

Although vague about her past and evasive about her crime, Star freely discusses her beliefs, taking a delight in the fact that she has intimate knowledge of a subject that many fear.

> In '76 I turned more and more to the power of witchcraft. Witchcraft was something I'd kind of grew up around, but it was white witchcraft. My fourth husband was into it real heavy, and he really got me involved. He called himself a white witch, but yet he dabbled in conjuring, and to me there's conflict there. . . . Tony, my fourth husband, is the first one that ever showed that to me. He brought forth spirits in our house. Our house looked weird: skulls everywhere and everything because he was totally into witchcraft. Everything was done in ritual by both of us. He had a coffin he slept in when I met him. Once I met him I understood why. It was totally quiet and you could meditate. He had

this in his bedroom, and I thought, "That's unique; he's kind of cool."
And he was. But he was just—he was just a little bit leery to totally step-
ping over the line. . . .

But I went on farther than he did. I became really interested and
started studying and learning. Eventually I found out that there were
Satanic churches, Satanic bibles. I joined a church in California [Church
of Satan, founded by Anton LaVey in 1966]. When you first join you have
to go in under a sponsor. They sponsor you for a couple years, see that
you're legit, teach you things that you should need to know, and then
you're kind of under a sponsor for about three more years. So it takes you
about five to get where you want to go, unless you just walk in and join
and you're not interested in going nowhere. But my whole aspect behind
it: I wanted to be a priestess one day, and that included having all the
knowledge. I don't particularly want to just sit there and listen; I want to
teach. But, believe me, I don't have all the knowledge. [Star]

It is necessary at this point to distinguish white witchcraft (practiced by Star in her novitiate stage) from Satanism (practiced by the
mature, independent Star). The former, known also by the terms "wicca"
and "pagan," promotes what one believer terms "the moon principle . . . that from which springs the intuitive, the psychic, the mysterious."[8] Through the study of occult tradition and the practice of
occult ritual the witch (or "wise one" as the term literally means) gains
greater and greater access to heightened levels of awareness. Most ad-
herents of witchcraft today practice this form of benevolent witchcraft,
which combines a reverence for nature as the source of spiritual power
with a notion of self-development.

Believers in Satanism, on the other hand, elevate Satan to the level
of divine ruler. More sinned against than sinner, Lucifer, according to
Satanists, was unjustly cast out of heaven to rule earth below. The figure of radical independence, he symbolizes for all his followers the
rebel who usurps ordained order and establishes in its stead a revisionist order, one that insures the satisfaction of temporal desires. What
is condemned in Christian terms as the first crime becomes for the
Satanist an act of self-definition. The worship of Satan, first criminal,
wrongly accused and convicted (accordingly to believers) seems particularly fitting for a prison where many maintain their innocence even
while sometimes acknowledging their crimes. It is Satan's rebellious
powers that believers summon in black sabbath rituals.

In white witchcraft ceremonies members often cast a circle (a sort of psychic forcefield comprised of the channeled energy of individual coverners), invoke the elements, and banish evil spirits. In a typical Church of Satan black mass a nude woman acts as the altar and Satan appears in human form often to engage in sex with her, along with several members of the congregation. As opposed to popular belief, members of the Church of Satan sacrifice no animals or infants; they ingest no blood or human excrement. They celebrate, instead, orgiastic sex and the divinity of Satan:

> Sabbaths involve eating, drinking, prayers, dancing, sex if you want it, and politics. It's just like you're paying total homage to the one that you worship, Satan. Most of the worshipers call him "Master." When he appears at the sabbath he appears like a man, a good-looking man. All Satanists behold him to be beautiful because that's what he is to them. The only thing that would differ about him from a human being is his voice. His voice sounds like it's coming from all around. When he appears he sets there, and you're supposed to worship him. A lot of people have tried to say that it's the pope [the Black pope, Anton LaVey] or some other human being that appears, but it's not. I know that for a fact! But then I know for a fact that Satan can come forth to any one of his followers. [Star]

Rather than offer an alternative to repressive Christianity, Satanism directly inverts it. Satanism embraces, according to its detractors, the most vicious myths about witchcraft—that witches make pacts with and have sex with the devil. Promoted for centuries, these myths have sanctioned the brutal and often bloody treatment of proponents of witchcraft as well as of a miscellaneous assortment of women whose claims for spiritual experience church fathers deemed intolerable. It is no wonder then that most witches today resoundingly repudiate Satanism as the dangerous distortion of traditional witchcraft (see Valiente, Luhrman, Margo Adler). They reject a religion preoccupied with evil spirits, conjuring, and curses, sharing, in a sense, the popular abhorrence of what seems to most serious witches a perversion of the craft.

Acutely aware of the condemnation of Satanism by white witches and the fear with which it is regarded by the general public, Star avoids using the term "Satanic" with the uninformed (though inmates easily apply that adjective to her) because it suggests grotesque images of baby killing and other ritual violence. That is not to say that Star's practices are totally benign; she has, according to her testimony, harnessed the forces of evil spirits and put curses on people. But conjuring is not something one does lightly: "When you're messing around with demons you better know what you're doing to start with." Evil spirits, if not properly directed by the conjurer, can plague the witch as well as her intended victim. The practitioner of black magic knows that the real art is not in calling forth an evil spirit, a relatively simple operation, but in channeling that demon so that it will appear in an acceptable form—as a breeze or split candle flame rather than a grotesque being (its supposedly more natural state) whose frightening visage and putrid smell one never forgets.

When you've got everything together and you know what you're doing, a spirit will appear. He can appear in the form you want him to appear in. A lot of people think that's bull, but it's not. They really appear because those things exist, but you have to know what you're doing. I wouldn't want to be around an amateur who did it because number one, it might psychologically kill him.

You can ask spirits to appear in a certain form, a form that you can accept because they have to materialize from something. I mean, they're not material objects, and some of them you don't see. It depends on who's bringing them forth. It depends on what there is available for them to use. I've had them materialize in candles. I've had candles sitting there, and I've had the flame split in half. It was weird—we were having a seance that night. But I respect them. You're afraid to let them feel fear though, because if you're not 100 percent in control, you're in trouble.

They have appeared when I didn't call them. They're present and will pick up on your vibes, but I think they're probably comfortable in my room. When I was in the Delaware prison waiting to come here, people'd walk by my door and they wouldn't come in. I never knew why for a long time, and then they told me that when they came to the door it felt like a refrigerator. But I was quite comfortable in my room; it didn't seem cold to me. Some of the guards told me the same thing. You know how they have those little glass windows in the doors; well, the glass was busted in my door. If my door was closed, the guards would not come in; they would stick my mail through the door. They said it was like a refrigerator. I've had girls tell me that here. It'd be 90 degree in their room; it'd be cold as anything in mine. It was the spirits that caused that because they are cold.

> I've had people come in my room and tell me they've felt them, but I try to get these people to relax and enjoy it; they're not going to bother you. But I've felt them in other people's rooms. These people didn't know they were there because they can't distinguish the presence of spirits, but I can. [Star]

And Star describes the hierarchy of spirits one might summon:

> I wouldn't bring Satan forth unless I had to, because number one, you're scared with a demon. And besides, there's a lot of demons, so why bring the big man up? Demons hate people anyway. They hate to be controlled. When I was learning about demonology they have the demons all listed as to the status levels, and you get to know which ones are what. You pick one off the totem pole that's way down here if you want him to do a certain thing. Each one of them have a certain thing to do. [Star]

The most important word in Violet Star's discussion of witchcraft is "control," and it is the knowledge of spirits that gives her the illusion, at least, of control over her life and, to some extent, the lives around her. Acutely sensitive to spirits, Star can sense their presence when others cannot. Spirits insure an insulating distance between Star and the rest of the prison population. Entombed in her chilly cell, she inspires awe and fear in others.

Unlike the other women discussed in this chapter, Violet Star sees herself advancing in the hierarchy of an organized religion: the Church of Satan, founded by Anton LaVey, author of *The Satanic Bible* (1969) and *The Satanic Rituals* (1972). During our conversations Star spoke more than once of her desire to someday become a high priestess in the Church of Satan. Respected for her power and her skill, she would then instruct others in the faith. Star receives letters and publications from other members of her church and seeks their help in executing difficult spiritual communications. Although her psychic ability is a trait inherited from her maternal grandfather and mother, she enhances her gift by the practice of witchcraft. According to Star, the knowledge necessary to influence the spirits is available only to a dedicated and fearless believer, a believer courageous enough to "be one's own god" and to love what others fear and hate.

In prison Star realizes her desire to teach, preaching a theology of apostasy to all who will listen, mostly the young recruits and short-timers. Although her followers are few (fewer than twenty) they are certainly ardent. As testimony to her charisma, most inmates cite the example of the young woman who was sentenced to death like Star, but who, at the persuasion of Star, tried to convince her lawyer to desist in efforts to reduce her sentence.[9] Although Star entrances a few, most keep their distance from her, discussing the sixes tatooed to her ankle and referring to her with a mixture of scorn and fear as a "Satanist." Being distinguished as the practitioner of forbidden arts is not that different from being regarded by the community as the most vicious murderer housed in the prison walls. In both capacities, Star inspires in colleagues and guards both fascination and fear.

One woman, though sees in Star nothing to fear, just a masterful con who has managed to deceive even herself.

> I think she's into something because people don't understand it, and what people don't understand scares 'em. People don't mess with her because of it. I tease her all the time, and she laughs at me. I say, "You're nuts!" I like her, though, she's off! But she can be a real cruel person. You can't be friends with her 'cause she's cruel as shit! She's truly a cold person.
>
> I think Violet has psyched herself out. I don't think she can work magic. Now, I do believe in certain things like that, but I don't believe Violet is one of those people. I think she leans on witchcraft the way some people lean on religion and God to give her that personal inner strength to go from day to day. Where my grandmother would say, "God please" to release some inner strength in her, Violet use witchcraft. Plus the fact that Violet gets off on expressions, people's expressions. If you're smilin' and she can say something not hurting your feelings but just to trip you out enough to where you stop, she loves it. That's what this is about. She's extremely bright, so don't underestimate her. [Stone]

Intelligent, manipulative, and canny, Violet Star plays the role of jailhouse lawyer to many and spiritual advisor to a few devoted followers. Aware of the skepticism of those around her, she keeps hidden (the meaning of the word "occult") much of her clairvoyant wisdom and witchcraft.

> I can feel within myself if something's going to happen; I can feel it and ward it off. A lot of times I can maybe see it as a flash or something for other people. Mother has that ability too, somewhat. I've warned a

few people in my life, but I don't instruct them to do certain things unless they're into the occult because, number one, they'd think I'm crazy. I get magazines in here from some religious organization, and they've got the most beautiful prayers, white witchcraft prayers. I tell the women in here, "If you could just, when the moon is full, say this prayer, it would take away the depression you feel." But they're afraid of it. I said, "It can't hurt you. It's just a beautiful prayer." But they're scared to death because they don't understand. Believing is a very important aspect of witchcraft. When the moon's full there are special rituals that you do; I do them too. It's like a cleansing out of the body and the mind. It's great!

I feel energy a lot from the sisters, the sisters in witchcraft, out there when they have ceremonies. And then I write and tell them that when they had it I felt it the night they had it. Or when I get a letter from them telling me about a ceremony, I say, "Yeah, I knew that," and I'll write back and tell them.

Star looks beyond the prison community to the greater body of believers outside the prison, witches and Satanists whose support she sometimes enlists in executing difficult spiritual maneuvers, particularly the banishment of troubling spirits.[10]

Spirits are troublesome and unpredictable for the expert and life-threatening in the hands of the untutored. They can manifest themselves as visually horrifying creatures, often with putrifying smells, if the conjurer neglects to select a proper vehicle for their manifestation. A battle between spirits, according to Star, is the dramatization of emotional conflict between individuals, and such a battle can result in confusion in the home or in the prison. It is in mastering the many spirits which share her eight-by-sixteen-foot cell that Star claims most success. Though prisoners and staff speculate about her beliefs and practices, only a few have joined her. But her importance as a figure of spiritual power cannot be measured in the number of her converts. For the women around her she represents someone who can contact and, to some extent, command powers far greater than the power of the state.

Verna Brown

At the Indiana Women's Prison Verna Brown fills the seemingly conflicting roles of officer and spiritual advisor for the women in her charge. In her professional life story, recollected in several interviews the month prior to her retirement, Brown recounts what resembles a divine calling, a spiritual summons to come and work in the Indiana Women's Prison.

> I'm sixty-two, and I'm retiring. My body's tired. This is not the only job I've had. This twenty-two years is the longest I've worked at one job, though. Early in life I found out working with people was for me. First, I worked at a hospital off and on. I had those old people spoiled to death. Nobody could work behind me. One year I told 'em, I said, "You know that I won't be here another year?" They said, "Where are you going?" I said, "I'm going to work with another bunch of sick people." They said, "What do you mean?" So I told 'em the dream I had. I said, "I saw a prison. The sun was shining all around it. It was brick. I've never been there; I don't even know where it is. But that's where I'm goin'."
>
> We had a woman at the hospital, and she had sort of a cancer. It grew in a knot, and they had to take it out every three months. She had come back to the hospital, and she said, "Verna, you know I believe your dream is true." I said, "Yes, my time here is up. I have to work for other people." So, sure enough I came out here to work.

Brown tells how, with little preparation but great spunk, she began her first job as prison cook, refusing to be hampered by stringent rules. When, for example, she wanted some fresh fruit or vegetables but did not want to wait for the officer in charge of the prison garden to arrange for their delivery, she would put a ladder up to the wall and send a couple prisoners over to accomplish the task. This practice continued until one of the prisoners expressed her concern, lest she be caught by the "Mr. McGregor" officer whose task it was to patrol the grounds after working hours.

Brown advanced from cook to officer in 1956, only to spend her first weeks at her new job in monotonous confinement with the notorious Opal Collins, a prisoner who brutally murdered her husband, mother-in-law, and two sisters-in-law. The prison warden decided to keep this violent inmate (sentenced to the electric chair) in twenty-four-hour surveillance. Brown and another staff member were promoted from within to this task of dubious honor and another was hired from the outside. Each of the three took her shift during the early weeks of Collins's imprisonment. Brown and the other two women essentially lived the life of prisoners themselves, locked in a cell with no key, dependent on others to spell them for meals and bathroom breaks. And like prisoners, many times they were forgotten by other officers busy with tasks of their own.

But it was through this parallel experience, this forced intimacy, that Brown grew fond of and even tamed the most feared monster in the prison.

> I'd go in at six in the morning, and she'd lay up in the dark asleep. So when I got tired of it I said, "Look, you might as well uncover your head 'cause you're stuck with me, and I'm gonna stay in here so you might as well talk." So we started talking. One day I told her, I said, "You know, Indiana don't burn women. Something's gonna happen. Your sentence's gonna be commuted." See, God give me a gift of clairvoyance.
>
> But, heck, they were so long coming, I'm the one started losing weight with worry. So I go down and told the supervisor, I said, "Alice Mary," I said, "Time is running short; we haven't heard anything yet. If they have to come after her, will you tell 'em to bring an ambulance with oxygen 'cause I'm gonna have a heart attack?" I was, I was going down fast 'cause it was worrying me, I had gotten so attached to her. I said, "I hope to God they don't burn that woman—I'll die."

Several months later the governor commuted Collins's sentence from death to life in prison. But the prison administration was reluctant to treat Collins like the other "lifers." Even though she no longer required personal guards, Collins was, nevertheless, segregated from other inmates and heavily sedated. When she had to pass from one part of the prison to another, officers conducted stringent security checks at several points along the way.

Verna Brown mediated between prisoner and administration to withdraw the debilitating thorazine and to prepare the feared and fearful prisoner for passage from solitary confinement into the larger world of prison culture. This transformation of Collins from crazed monster to tractable prisoner illustrates for Brown evidence of God's work. So powerful is His work that when the doors on Collins's solitary confinement cell are first opened, Collins cowers in the corner, refusing to leave. The instrument of God and force for socialization, Brown soothes the savage beast. As further evidence, she tells how as arbitrator she settles disputes between resentful prisoners, preventing petty disputes from escalating into major feuds.

Called to the women's prison to care for and guide even the most abject prisoner, Brown uses her God-given gift in "holy" employment. Just as she predicts her own entrance into prison, she foresees the commutation of Opal Collins's death sentence and her eventual release from solitary confinement. Part and parcel of her faith, though, are moments of doubt. Because of the extraordinary amount of time it takes for Opal's sentence to be commuted, Brown begins to doubt her God-given clairvoyance. But her story, as does history itself, affirms the power of her foresight. It is this gift that during her tenure as an officer, is a force for good in the prison, a force inextricably tied to the mothering role she sees herself playing as an officer. The inmates of the Indiana Women's Prison, according to Verna Brown, need love and spiritual guidance, not warehousing.

The nineteenth-century prison reform movement both in America and England, which resulted in the creation of separate prisons for women, had as its basis the belief that women required different treatment from their male counterparts, that they must be treated as wayward children who need to be taught self-respect and respect for others. In these new, all-female prisons, wardens and guards were to guide those in their care back to the path of righteousness. Though the isolation of women from men generally created better physical conditions for the female prisoner and freed her from the threat of rape, these separate prisons by no means insured her spiritual and moral reformation. Though individuals in the system may care for those they govern, the one thing that institutions, by their nature, cannot supply is love.

Addressing this problem, the most outspoken critics of women's prisons in the beginning of the twentieth century, the British suffragists, publicized their own accounts of incarceration. A 1912 Fabian tract quotes one such account:

> The whole system is one to destroy anyone's self-respect and moral control. I observed the gradual hardening of certain of the prisoners who were quite obviously full of grief and shame on arrival. . . . The principal effect of the prison system as it now exists seems to me to be the

destruction of self-respect and initiative. I believe many of the wardresses who come into closer contact with the prisoners than any other officials take what opportunity they find of urging the women to a better way of life, but since the system works in the other direction, their influence cannot be very great. The wardesses are as much prisoners as we are.

Every endeavor is made to render the life dull, monotonous and dreary; all the surroundings are as hideous as human ingenuity can make them, the food unappetizing, and the whole tone brutalizing and hardening. [Blagg and Wilson]

Twentieth-century accounts of prison life reiterate the failure of prisons to achieve prisoner rehabilitation. Most recently, prison spokesmen have almost entirely abandoned the rhetoric of rehabilitation to speak exclusively of security. With the pressure of intense overcrowding and tight budgets, opportunities for counseling, education, and job-training have decreased in institutions across the country. More and more prison workers have resigned themselves to the limited goal of warehousing convicts. Viewed from this perspective, Verna Brown's attitude toward those she governs appears anachronistic. Although unable to transform a harsh, inhumane place into a home, officers like Verna Brown and her predecessors chose to view their role as that of guide rather than jailer.

Officers like Brown who played important roles in the older, matriarchal prison system are being replaced by young, more professional women receiving the same training as their male counterparts (generally a six-week program at the police academy). I am not suggesting that women's prisons of thirty years ago could not be cruel places in which to do one's time; rather, I am suggesting that there has been a change in the way officers perceive their role. They no longer see those under their control as wayward or disturbed children whom they must nurture and discipline. The new generation of prison guards define their task exclusively as the maintenance of order in the institution. To achieve this they are taught to remain aloof, to avoid familiarity with inmates, and to favor no one. To show concern for prisoners is to invite the erosion of discipline.

Verna Brown overcomes the contradiction between the impulse to nurture and the necessity to control through her contact with a spirit world that aids her in both roles. Her powers enable her to carry out the ministry to which she was called and to keep the prison secure.

It is her gift, she claims, that alerts her to dangers before anyone else. In the following account, slamming of doors is a sign to her that something is about to happen on the hall she is guarding. This forewarning enables her to perform her custodial role successfully, for the action she takes actually prevents the dreaded escape.

I'd work with 'em all. They'd come to me and talk. And if I "see" anything, I tell 'em what I see. People say when you "see" that you're crazy. I've had spirits show up before me in the bathroom. They'd be standing before the mirror primping, and I'd run out into the hall with my pants down. Or they'd come out of a room and disappear in front of the desk. I'm not lying!

And I hear doors slamming. I went on 2-3 [a wing of one of the "cottages"] about six in the mornin, and the doors, they been slamming. They was getting on my nerves. So I got the girls up; all twenty-eight come out of their rooms. I said, "Girls, I want to talk to you." They came on down, and I says, "Somebody on that end of the hall is gonna run. This morning after breakfast you go out in three's. You go out in four's. I want each girl to be responsible for the other. When you walk in the door at eleven o'clock I'm gonna check you in. I know, I suspect who that person is who's planning to run, and I want to tell her that she *is* gonna pass the board. You *are* going home."

So board day come. She went on to the board, and then she stopped at the desk, and said, "How did you know it was me?" I said, "Well, you didn't run, did you?" She said, "I'm glad I didn't." I told her, "They have a way of warning me." So people went to calling me crazy. I said, "Well, they wouldn't understand." So I didn't try to make 'em understand. The girls understood. And they still come to me.

I've had this gift all my life, but I got out in the street when I was a young woman, and God took it. But I knew it would come back in the later years after I started settling down. Now since 1970, He's been working on me stronger. There's always a warning. Oh, one time I called and told 'em there was something gonna happen in the building; and I said to the supervisor, "You think I'm crazy, don't you?" She said, "Yes I do." I said, "Well, I don't know how crazy you think I am, but watch this building for the next three days." Ten o'clock that day a girl left. If she hada been watching, the girl wouldn'ta left. I told her to watch.

A spirit had warned me. I come in the door downstairs, and I heard somebody groan. Well, I knew this Miss Hedley died. I stopped and started to tie that door behind me, but she was still groaning so I hurried upstairs. Wasn't nobody here. Then I realized who it was. It was this Miss Hedley who had died here in this prison. Her appearing was a warning to me that there was gonna be trouble. And the girls will tell you. I told 'em; I said, "Somebody's gonna leave the building, it's gonna be trouble—a girl'll run." When it happened, the girls said, "You said it was gonna happen." It happened at ten o'clock.

It gets more stronger by the first of the new moon than it is on the last part of the month. I said when I got older He would start using me more. But see, my job was trying to help, but the people here now don't appreciate that because of the fact that I didn't go to college. But I have sense enough to carry a job. Any job I had here on the grounds I didn't flub. Just my mouth wouldn't stay still. Evidently, I haven't done too bad. I've tried to help keep it on an even keel here, but they don't hear too well. I don't have enough education for 'em. But education is not what's important in this job; it's knowing how to use common sense. See, I said I went as far as the Lord wanted me to go. I can read and write. I can count money. I can do what I want to do. See, everybody don't have to have education. God has already got people that He educates Himself. I have Him in class when I go to sleep. [Brown]

This divine gift, according to Brown, has a certain fragility and must be protected from the corrupting influence of the world; it can flourish or wither. As a natural phenonmenon, it grows stronger with the new moon; as a supernatural phenomenon, it is ultimately dependent on the will of God. In the hands of a guard, this power can help preserve peace in the prison. The primary duty of an officer in a modern penal institution is surveillance: to account for every prisoner at every moment and to keenly observe for the signs of imminent trouble. Brown's claim is that her special relationship with the spirit world sharpens her ability to keep watch. Feeling eased out of her job by police academy graduates, Brown offers as her defense this special God-given ability which enables her to be a successful guard. Had the warden, or supervisor as she is called in Indiana, heeded her warning, there would have been no break.

When considering the close association between her visions and her job, it is not so surprising that the overwhelming majority of Brown's encounters with spirits involve doors opening and closing mysteriously. Thresholds between confinement and freedom figure prominently in her visions. As guardian of the threshold, or gatekeeper, a prison guard implements state punishment by insuring, at the very least, that doors and windows remain locked. But these doors and windows also confine

Verna Brown, and she must periodically negotiate her release from the willful spirits who control them. If heeded, these spirits aid her in the maintenance of order; if not, they work as forces of disturbance. These spirits dramatically illustrate Brown's ambivalence toward her contradictory roles of state disciplinarian and nurturing parent.

When I worked in quarantine a woman from the spirit world would come out of one of the empty rooms, take a shower, and she'd go back in. I never told the girls, and I met her at the sink one night. I said, "Oh, excuse me," and went on the other side and washed. And another time these people from the spirit world locked me in the bathroom upstairs. They wanted me to move in and live, and they hung [locked] me in the bathroom. I couldn't open that door, and I just sat down on the bathtub. I said, "You might as well let me out 'cause I'm still not gonna move up here." But when I changed my mind and decided I would move over to that hall, that door just popped, and I just pushed it open.

And another time the storeroom door locked for a whole month. When I got back from vacation they said, "Mrs. Brown, that door has been locked the whole time you were gone." So I said, "OK, let's see if we can get it open." We couldn't budge it, so I said to the spirits that held it closed, "Well, you can turn it loose now 'cause I'm back to work for another year." And pretty soon we heard, "Ploom!" and it give.

Those chain locks—one day every one of 'em was just swinging. I went across the hall, and I told the girls, "Come on I'm gonna show you something. You all say I'm crazy. Where's the wind coming from? (There was no wind.) Miss Hedley's in here letting us know there's something going on."

And another time, down on 3-5, that's when I went in the bathroon and come out and this woman was standing there primping, and I hadn't even pulled my clothes down. I run out in the hall. I think it was over a week before I'd go to that toilet. I asked about that woman that appeared and asked about her, and one of the old women who worked here wouldn't never tell me who the woman was, but every once in a while she'd ask me to tell her what happened again. [Brown]

Along with Miss Hedley, Brown has an Indian guide who frequently manifests himself; other spirits may also assume human forms but do not appear as people familiar to Brown. One discovers the identity of spirits over time with repeated appearances. Women who recognize spirits are often reluctant to identify them. When Brown asks an older prison employee the identity of a spirit she has seen, the old woman remains silent, appearing to know but unwilling to tell.

But Brown never questions the identity of her spirit guide, a consistent figure in her mythology. Like other spirits, he assists her clairvoyance, but unlike the other spirits, he assumes much more importance. For example, he discloses recipes for secret packets which she assembles, wraps in aluminum foil (sometimes no bigger than a postage stamp), and presents to the appropriate inmate or staff member as protection against some impending evil. The contents of her packets remain a secret between Brown and her Indian guide, a gift rather than the granting of a request. Brown reports no incubation, the ritual practice designed to invoke visions or dreams in which cures are communicated by the gods. (See Ratcliff on incubation.) Instead, these communications from the spirit world appear spontaneously. Although she would generally prefer that spirits not materialize because many are troublemakers who stir up the inmates and undermine the powers of the institution, her Indian guide seems innocent of such charges. Neither capricious nor perverse, Brown's spirit guide cautions and instructs. Unlike other seemingly anarchic forces, this spirit stabilizes Brown's world.

For Verna Brown, this emissary of the spirit world is a figure shrouded in mystery. Unwilling at first to disclose any particulars about her spirit guide, Brown would only admit to the existence of such a figure. But in subsequent conversations she told me that although she has seen him a number of times dressed as an Indian, more frequently she merely feels his fur against her skin as she walks through a doorway. Spirit voices without individual identity speak to Brown, but her Indian guide is distinct from all other spirits, for he is a welcome visitor. Brown's Indian is one of a group of five spirit guides common to followers of popular spiritualism, which assist communication between the human and the spirit worlds. Distinguished as "the protector," the Indian guide "guards the passageway" keeping evil spirits from harming the vulnerable believer.[11]

I have had voices speak to me. 'Course I was running at first. Then they come back three days later, so I might as well stand still and hear what they got to say. If I don't know, they show me. Only thing I ask of 'em is not to materialize. When they're around me I know they're there, but I don't want to see 'em. I don't ask 'em who they are either. But one I know I have is an Indian guide. Sometimes when I pass my door I brush up against the fur of his coat, and I turn around and go back. Just sometimes. I'm not crazy: I'm just telling you about it.

They're here, but I don't want to see nothing. But if I *do* see a vision it'll flash, and I don't forget it. I hear voices sometime and what they tell me. They don't lie to me. There's a lot of spirits around me, but I do have an Indian guide. He's strong; he's a warrior. I was born a clairvoyant and a medium. I don't want the medium part, period, but I do know when spirits is around. They are up here. I told the guards, "Whenever you see these girls cussing the officers and raising a lot of heck and they're complaining about noises and walking in the cottage, you better start searching that cottage. You're getting a warning right here. When the girls start complaining about hearing noises, just start walking and you'll find out what's going on." Since I told 'em that, you don't hear too much, so evidently they're doing it. [Brown]

Like Violet Star, Brown possesses an acute sensitivity to spirits; she can sense their presence when others cannot. A guard, though, must not simply be able to sense spirits, but she must also be able to read their warnings. Spirits in prison often signal trouble, and the vigilant guard understands their disturbances as signs of incipient disorder among the prisoners. Brown, on the one hand, sees these fiendish self-willed spirits as agents of chaos and, on the other hand, she understands spirits to be forces for order.

Clairvoyant, healer, jailer, and nurturer, Brown contemplates retirement as a continuation of her mothering role. She imagines "adopting" a couple of the inmates she has tended these last twenty-two years:

There aren't a lot of lifers in here, but there are some with ten to twenty-five years. I call that life, don't you? But it's not for murder either; it's for a little bit of everything. Life is too long for these women anyway. Fifteen years is a long time for a woman to try to make it. If the Lord bless me with any money, there's two lifers I want to ask the governor for. I don't know if he'll let me have them or not. I don't have no premonitions he won't let me have 'em. Opal has done a lot of time. She's eight months behind me, and I say I been here doing time right along with her. She come in eight months after I started working twenty-two years ago. And another lifer that don't have any people. Maybe by me working with 'em and knowing 'em the governor'd let me give 'em a home.

See, Opal's in her forties, and she needs a chance to make something of herself. Staying in prison, that woman has aged. She look like a woman seventy years old, and she's a young woman. Every time they turn her down [for parole], she age that much more. The Lord didn't tell us to take it upon ourself to punish people. We're supposed to forgive and to try to understand. Sometimes people get into stuff because they're pushed.

I help the girls, but they're not supposed to help each other. They're not supposed to give each other anything. They try, but they'll get a write-up, a lock-up if they loan their clothes or give their commissary away. They're some come in and feel sorry for the other and try to divide with her, but they're not supposed to. They're not supposed to be best friends. They're not supposed to get that close. [Brown]

In an institution that prohibits expressions of kindness, statements such as Brown's of concern for others are rare indeed. I am not implying that other guards do not share a concern for the women they oversee, but most feel that any expression of sympathy will make them look unprofessional to their superiors and vulnerable to prisoners. In order to maintain discipline, a guard is taught to treat all with the same degree of aloofness. Staff members generally believe that any expression of personal concern for an inmate will erode a guard's authority, leaving her susceptible to inmate manipulation.

Considered by most of the prison population as beyond their child-bearing years,[12] this penal officer, the two murderers, and the writer of bad checks discussed in this chapter have declared themselves authorities of the supernatural and supranormal, encouraging younger woman to confide in them and to seek their spiritual counsel. Unlike other women who may have witnessed a vision or experienced something they might call a psychic phenomenon (usually at the time of a family crisis) these women successfully integrate frequent uncanny experiences into their normal existence and have done so since childhood.

They make no secret of their powers, seeing them at once as both innate and inspired, both mother-given and God-given. Of the fourteen women I interviewed who considered themselves and whom others considered spiritually gifted, all traced their ability to sense spirits or to achieve visions to either a mother or grandmother; one (Violet Star) claimed to share her gift with her grandfather as well as her mother. The folk belief in a matrilineal line of foreknowledge distinguishes

these women from the visionaries of Judeo-Christian prophetic tradition in which one's relationship with God renders all family ties irrelevant. Implicit in Western notions of prophecy is the assumption that
one is the mouthpiece of God, speaking His words rather that one's
own.[13] Individuality dissolves in the moment of prophecy; the prophet
becomes the mere vehicle for the ventriloquizing God. These women
experience no such humbling effacement; God speaks to them not
through them, and their visions insure them a rich social identity.
More technically "seers" than prophets, they interpret spiritual and
psychic messages for those around them, claiming some power over the
rigid structure of their total institution.

Characterized by fierce pride and charismatic personalities, these
women stand out in an institution where officers hide their fear behind the guise of harsh indifference and prisoners learn quickly to
mistrust everyone. But these women win the tolerance of the staff and
the trust of prisoners who seek their spiritual nurturing.

7. Visions in the Context of Life Stories

To collect and classify vision narratives is to frame segments of recollective narration and set them apart as generic objects, formally and thematically similar. Vision narratives are fragments of life stories prisoners reconstruct in confinement for themselves, for other inmates, and for the outside interviewer. For the prisoner, talking about her past and her family helps pass the time or, more seriously and therapeutically, helps rationalize her crime. When the folklorist extracts the vision fragment from its larger narrative (the life story of victimization, the adventures and misadventures of a "picaro," or the story of divine election) she depersonalizes it by shifting attention from the whole to the part and from individual informant to the group of informants. Whereas such abstraction defines a body of similar accounts, it nevertheless fails to demonstrate the vital and compensatory role these narratives play in the lives of their tellers.

To illustrate the place of vision narratives within the lives of their tellers I have chosen selections from the life stories of Betty Jones and Eraina Roberts, two middle-aged black women: the former has spent her life in reform schools, in wards of mental hospitals, in prison, and on the street; the latter was, at the time of our meeting, in prison for the first time. Neglected and shunned by their families as children, both Jones and Roberts fantasize new roles for themselves. Jones casts herself as the tomboy fighter who between periods of reform school, jail, and brief returns home leads the nomadic life of the streets. She looked so much like a boy, Jones recalls, that truckers and dock workers shopping for sex in Baltimore's inner harbor area were willing to pay her a little more. Jones's "play" life as a boy on the streets offers an alternative to a chaotic family on the one hand and to hostile institutions on the other. Much of what follows covers the periods in her life when she was confined in "Crownsville," a place where rebellious youths were often locked in cells side by side with mentally disturbed patients.

Eraina Roberts chronicles a bizarre life story distinguished by its sporadic and intense moments of divine revelation. She compensates for a neglectful mother, an absent father, and mocking siblings by enacting versions of family with her invisible friend. But what begins as a child's imaginative play turns in adulthood to the sinister delusion that leads to Roberts's crime, the ritual purification of children she believes to be polluted. The themes of pollution and purification play an important part in these stories of incredible impoverishment. Bodily corruption is drawn out by soil, purged, cut out, and killed by harsh cleansers. The clean, ordered penal institution that disinfects all who enter would seem, on the face of it, to provide a haven from pollution, but according to Jones and Roberts it merely harbors its own impurities.

All the women in this book inhabit a world over which they exercise little control. In the preceding chapter I discussed four women whose visions afford them some sense of control over the all-powerful institution that surrounds them. Unlike those women, Jones and Roberts have attracted no group of followers or fused no prison family. Their visions, rather than insuring a sense of power, offer instead a release from a world out of their control.

Betty Jones

Betty Jones was born on May 21, 1936, the night that Joe Lewis defeated Max Schmelling, and she credits that fight with her nickname, "Bummer," a name that was given to her at birth and that sticks with her still:

> After that match Schmelling named Lewis "The Brown Bummer." And they called me "Bummer" from then on. Some of the kids called me "Brown Bummer"; some of 'em called me, "Hey, Bummo." Ever since I was a baby, always "Bummer." It was a long time till I knew my real name. [Jones]

After the much-publicized fight, Schmelling *actually* called Lewis "The Brown Bomber," not "The Brown Bummer." Not only is Jones's real name displaced by a nickname, but the nickname itself, "Bummer," is a substitute for "Bomber." The story of Jones's life is a catalogue of misfortunes, with her earliest memories those of loneliness and hunger. Sent to school with neither lunch nor money to buy it, Jones begins leaving school at recess time to scavenge or steal her lunch from the nearby market:

> I snatched food off the stands 'cause it was open stands. And they would throw a lot of spoiled food away if it would have a speck or somethin' on it like that. I would go in and take it, clean it off, and pick out the bad part. I'd eat that spoiled food all the time. I would stay out [of school] till it was three-fifteen and I would go home.
>
> My father would never buy me any clothes, and mine were so bad I started stealin' my mother's skirt or my sister's jacket. One time I messed up her jacket jumpin' a fence, and I tore her jacket. Got a beatin' for that. So then I started stealin' my brother's clothes. I'd throw them out the window or hide them in the bushes to change into when I left the house. I was about eight years old at the time. [Jones]

Criminal behavior in Jones's life story is a response to need; prostitution an economic fact of life:

> I think I was grown when I was five years old. I had sex with a man when I was nine. I did it to survive. The grocery store man across the street used to give me cookies. I used to sell bottles to him — milk bottles and soda bottles y'know, and sometimes when I used to have to go to the store to get milk for my mother he used to give me cookies and stuff. And he used to feel me, stuff like that.
>
> I know his name. I know his wife's name. I know his son's name; he later became a doctor. This grocery store man was a Jewish guy, and he used to play with me. Then it got more, and when he put his penis in my mouth I couldn't understand that. I used to get sick. But then, as I got hungrier and hungrier I realized I had to do something. He used to give me two dollars or food and stuff, and I told my mother I scrubbed steps and cleaned up 'cause I used to take the food home and help her. [Jones]

Jones is first jailed at the age of nine. Having been caught stealing, she is "turned in" to the truant officer by her mother in an effort to teach the wayward daughter a lesson. The young Jones spends the night in jail and is later given the choice by the juvenile judge of returning home or of entering the Maryland Training School for Girls. Jones elects to go to reform school. It is there that she grows even tougher, learns to steal in more clever ways, and experiences her first homosexual encounter, one involving an older girl assigned to help out in the infirmary where Jones is spending a week with a minor illness.

Reform school teaches Jones to fight back. Large for her age, she finds that she can even take on the older girls. Winning fights with them is the first success that Jones ever knows:

> I whipped that sixteen year-old! Yes, I whipped her! Back then you didn't go to the matrons and snitch on anybody. We'd go down in the laundry room in the basement. After that I was pretty proud of myself. Nobody could tell me nothin' then. [Jones]

Fighting becomes the one means of control available to Jones. Her aggression, which might be tolerated were she a boy, is viewed by the juvenile justice system as aberrant, and she is sent to a psychiatric hospital for evaluation. When she strikes one of the nuns there, authorities transfer the twelve-year-old Jones to the more secure "Crownsville," an institution which "treats," among others, the criminally insane. Her long description of the horrors of life in the psychiatric ward is embedded in a life story of the child vagabond who continually fights, both physically and imaginatively, those who would imprison her. And the more she fights imprisonment, the more brutal that imprisonment becomes.

Jones's description of the time she spends at Crownsville, especially the nearly two years in solitary confinement, detail a period in which the imaginary and the irrational appear much more substantial than any real world that might exist beyond the double doors of her spare cell. The chronology is a bit confusing, but the narrative, with its extreme episodic quality, describes a place in which reality could be much more horrifying than any monster of the imagination.

In a world in which bizarre distortion is commonplace, how does a young girl maintain her identity? Jones aggressively preserves some sense of herself by defending herself against the attacks of fellow inmates that might come even as she sleeps. She also assists the staff in cleaning up, thus periodically restoring some order to the polluted world around her. And throughout, she maintains a sense of God's presence. That is not to say that Jones constantly protects an ego aloof and intact throughout her time in Crownsville. At times she gives in to the institution by displaying crazy behavior in order to obtain drugs and by seeking shock treatments in a desperate effort to extinguish the memories that fuel her rage.

I was in the House of Good Shepherd [a mental hospital in suburban Baltimore] when I was twelve and a sister, Sister Margaret, tried to pinch me and put me in a corner, wanted me to stand on one leg, and I banged her upside her head. So they sent me to Crownsville, and I was there when my mother died. My sister came and got me, took me to my mother's funeral and then took me back. I stayed at Crownsville 'till I was fourteen.

I had to keep myself together 'cause you never know when one of those crazy people's gonna wake up. You slept right beside each other, and you never knew when one of 'em were gonna wake up and attack you. You had to fight to keep 'em off you. The one thing you had to do to them sick people out there was to prove to 'em that you wasn't afraid of 'em. And once they sensed that you wasn't afraid, they wouldn't bother you.

I used to bathe 'em. I used to feed the ones that couldn't feed theirselves, and I used to have to clean 'em. Some of 'em painted theirself up in feces and stuff like that. I cried many days washing feces off of 'em and washing walls down because I was the only one really capable of helpin' 'em 'cause I wasn't as sick as they was. I know that God was with me then, too.

You'd hear 'em scream and holler half the night. They kept 'em sedated practically all that time with some stuff called HMC. It was a pill; they put it in a cup and poured a certain amount of cc's of sterile water on it to dissolve it, then skin-popped it in 'em. It'd make 'em high, tired. When they first give me one, I liked it, so I used to raise hell just to get it. Get a free high! I think it was a morphine. I believe it was, because thorazine really hadn't came down; they were still using shock treatments.

Over the years, I've had twenty-three shock treatments. I asked for 'em 'cause I couldn't understand why I kept fightin' all the time. You didn't feel 'em. They put you on a table, put a salt bag between your spine, took a shoe heel, put it in a sterile towel, and you bite down on it. They put this rubber band around your head with these two little metal plates that they put gel stuff on. The doctor be standin' at the back of your head so you can't see him, and you don't know how many volts they give you. But when you wake up you have a terrible headache. You'd be in bed, tied down to keep you from wandering. I used to help

put 'em in bed after other girls had shock treatments, and I used to see
'em. It throws you into fits, makes you have fits like you're having
seizures. I never seen myself havin' 'em, but I've watched other girls have
'em, and their eyes be blood-red like on fire. And sometimes, only way
that I knew that I had had my treatment is if I feel around my head, feel
the gel, where it got hard at.

The treatments were supposed to force me to forget some of the
things that happened in the past, but I didn't forget no God-damned
thing! I ain't forgotten nothin' ever happened to me. [Jones]

Neither shock treatment, alcohol, nor heroin can exorcise the memories of years of neglect, an abusive father and a horrifying rape at the
age of eleven; they always return. After that two-year stay in Crownsville, Bummer, aged fourteen, her mother now dead, returns to the
streets of Baltimore, an environment freer and, ironically, less violent
than either home or institution. On the streets she can play like a
child, dress in boys' clothes and befriend the bums and winos. But
also on the streets she faces the problem of nightly shelter, returning
like her dog to the back porch to sleep.

I left Crownsville when I was fourteen and I wound up—for some
reason I always wind up—on Baltimore Street [major street in downtown
Baltimore]. Even before I was nine I used to go to the square across from
the people's courthouse. I used to play all day in that great big square. I
knew the winos, used to sleep on them benches and stuff. And I used to
feed the pigeons. I used to go up these big steps to the two big lions in
front of one of them big buildings. There were these two great big stone
lions there, and I used to get on their backs and ride 'em. I used to play
on 'em.

After my mother died, my sister, Martha, and her boyfriend lived in
my mother's house. Sometimes I used to go back there at night and
sneak in the back yard. We had a dog named Rudolph—he was half
German shepherd, half something—and I used to sneak on the porch
and sleep with Rudolph 'cause my sister's boyfriend didn't want me to
stay there in the house. But my mother raised all of us in that house and
my sister took care of everything in there, but her boyfriend paid the
rent. I used to sneak back there like if I couldn't find no cars open or
nothin' like that. And I got afraid of sleepin' in people's cars, in their
backseat 'cause you can scare 'em. Once this man caught me in his car
and coulda hurt me seriously. So that's when I started sneakin' back.
Don't care how far I was from there; I'd walk all the way 'cross town at

> three or four in the morning by myself to where my sister and her boy-
> friend lived. I knew she wasn't gonna let me in, so I used to sleep on the
> porch with the dog.
>
> Sometimes her boyfriend would be comin' in late. I'd hear him, and I
> would get down and get under the porch 'cause the porch was built up
> from the ground. Only thing about that was I was scared of rats; they
> had rats runnin' through their yard. [Jones]

In a fight with her sister's boyfriend Jones attempts to subdue her
rival and rescue her sister. Although she wins the fight and stabs the
boyfriend, while remaining herself unhurt, she fails to secure what she
really sought—his place inside the home. Squaring off with the man
for the defense of the female only wins her further jail time. It is
easier, as this story demonstrates, to fight one's way out of a family
than to fight one's way back in. It is also more culturally acceptable
for men to assume the roles of fighters, both attackers and defenders.

> But I got locked. I was a teenager when I got locked up by my sister.
> Her and her boyfriend got to fightin'. I was tryin' to help her, and I
> started to come at him with a can-opener. During that time you had
> can-openers that had a point on the end. And I just stabbed him in his
> shoulder, and both me and him got locked up. But he had a fine; she
> paid his fine and I went to jail. I was there about thirty days. Then I got
> out and wandered around. I wandered up on Monument and Caroline
> Street. That's where all the Arabs [pronounced "A-rabs"] hang out. I
> used to Arab[1] too, teamed up with an old man named Hotney Tot.
> [Jones]

Finally, this story presents little contrast between life at the institution and at home. Sleeping at home with rats under the porch or sleeping in feces-smeared Crownsville, one must always be poised for attackers. Life on the streets offers the only alternative, the only release.
When Jones dresses as a man and hangs out with groups of men she
experiences a calmness absent at other times. Only at home or in the
institution does she become violent.

On her second stay in Crownsville the staff does not enlist the help
of this tall and strong full-grown fighter in the care of fellow patients;
because she "busted out of" every room they put her in, they confine
her deeper into the institution in a cell called "the double doors." Behind "the double doors," subdued by drugs, Jones grows weaker and

weaker as corruption gradually replaces her rage. She describes a body being literally eaten away by her prison.

> Another time I was in Crownsville for two years and ten months. I was in solitary confinement. They put me in there for fightin', but I'd pick the lock and get out, so they put me in a special cell they called "the double doors." There was an outside door, then a little space to walk in and a real thick door with a grill in it with a big padlock on it.
> That's when they started putting thorazine in my food. They was slipping me 250 milligrams of thorazine three times a day, kept me knocked out all the time. But then Dr. Barker came, and he took me outta there. My muscles had decayed so I couldn't stand. I was just eat up with infection; I was so rotten. He had to cut all that infection out, and the nurses used to take a wooden chair, put it in front of me to hold me up. They had to take me off of the thorazine by using phenobarbital, let me down slowly. If they didn't I coulda died. And they had to pick me up and put me in the tub, bathe me, wash my hair, feed me. I didn't even know what was happenin'. The doctor took me outta that cell, but when he went on his vacation they put me back in there. And then he got transferred to another hospital. But it wasn't as bad because I'd got all the medicine outta me.

Ridding the body of corruption is an important theme in narratives by women in prison. Over and over they attest to the importance of daily showers to clean the prison filth from their bodies, to the regular and thorough disinfection of their rooms in order to preserve one small clean space to inhabit, and to the lack of adequate medical treatment that would prevent a minor infection from spreading. But their notion of prison as house of pestilence contrasts strikingly with the institutional view which locates corruption outside the prison and guards against pollution from entering inmates by mandating stringent cleansing procedures and quarantine. During the first stage of their orientation, naked prisoners must "disinfect" themselves before the scrutinizing eye of an officer:

> The thing I dreaded most was when they use this disinfectant on you for in case you had lice or crabs or something. They gave this stuff to you and you were supposed to put it on all parts of your body where hair grows. So I did, and it burned like fire. And then they told me after I got through, to stick my head down in it. I had long hair and I did that. It was real strong. I was raised on a farm, and it smelled like what you

run sheep through. It smelled like sheep dip and disinfectant you use on
hogs for hog lice. I always had pretty hair and took good care of it, and I
thought, "Oh, my God." [Anna May]

Such humiliating purification marks the prisoner's passage from the
foul outside world into the sterile institution. This harsh baptism, designed to protect one woman from another and the staff from all inmates, reinforces the cellular structure of the ideal prison: each inmate
separate and innocuous. But from a captive's point of view, antiseptic
institutions can breed their own pestilence, corrupting and weakening
the body as in Betty Jones's account.

The debilitating drugs and weeks of solitary confinement that paci-
fied Jones also leave her body polluted: the treatment becomes the
disease. Jones's fate lies utterly in the hands of her overseers. With the
help of a benevolent doctor and two motherly attendants who routinely clean the infected lesions on her body, Jones eventually heals.
As she recovers, her two kindly caretakers bring her food from home,
occasions Jones uses to fantasize herself transformed into the ideal
man of the streets — the dude. Among the activities she enacts as this
idealized version of herself are cleansing rituals:

I only had one sheet and a gown, and I'd tie the sheet at both ends of
the mattress and pull the mattress real tight and pretend that I was goin'
out to dinner. And sometimes I'd pretend I was in a car drivin', usin' the
mattress for a car. I always played that I was a dude. I'd pretend to take
my bath, take my shave, pretend I put on a watch and cologne. I just
went through the whole procedure, pretendin' I was goin' out and stuff
like that. That's kinda symbolic.

I used to roll my mattress up in the daytime and sit by the window
that was cut real low. From there I could look down in the bullpen. That
was a big courtyard where the patients downstairs were let out for recreation. I've seen some terrible things there, goin' on in that yard. There
was this guy they called, "Turkey," a grown man, but he just had the
mind of a child. He just looked and acted like a turkey. He was a black
dude from the "A" building who used to come over and play around in
the yard. There was a hole; he played in it. This is the truth, I swear!
There was a hole in the ground, and he used to put his penis in the
ground and have sex with the ground! I've seen some terrible things.

Particularly interesting in this narrative are the complicated relationships between inside and outside and between public and private.

Within the institution, within the cell called "the double doors" Jones, by night, plays the part of a fashionable young man in the outside world getting ready and going out to dinner. By day she looks out of her cell window at what appears to be "the outside" but is, in fact, another institutional scene: the man called "Turkey" copulating with the ground. When Jones looks "out" of her cell she merely looks "in" at the institution; when she gazes into her imagination she invents a scene exterior to the institution, an idealized vision of life on the streets.

In a place where inmates perform events so extraordinary and mythic as copulating with the ground, Jones stages her simple scene for only herself. Private acts can in institutions become public performance, and the common practices of washing and eating can take on the significance of private ceremony. Compared with the strange events taking place around her and, indeed, with the horrifying events of her past, Jones's transformation of her mattress into a car and a bathtub and her cell into a fancy restaurant seems peculiarly ordinary. By consciously dramatizing her fantasies in a theater of one, assuming the roles of director, actor, and audience, Jones creates a fiction of liberation. Imaginatively freed from the gender that restricted the lesbian Jones all her life, she plays the part of a man completely in control of his own life. This transformation of cell into stage coincides with Jones's healing, but one might argue that her play merely signifies her complete "adjustment" to imprisonment. The institutionalization has finally broken the fighter when she no longer attempts to break the doors that confine her but, instead, imagines them gone, magically transferring herself outside the walls of the institution.

At the same time that Jones engages in such compensatory play she also undergoes transporting dreams that resemble out-of-body experiences:

> After I came off the medicine I started havin' dreams. I used to have these dreams: every night I traveled to someplace else. I've been all over the world in dreams. I done been everywhere in the whole wide world! I been to different native ceremonies.

Unlike her conscious play in which she dramatizes events she knows to be fantastic, Jones insists that in these dreams she really does travel through both time and space. She can identify no specific purpose to these nocturnal journeys. She learns no previously undisclosed truth and brings back no message, although she believes these to be divinely directed journeys. They provide her with further evidence that God is with her during her confinement.

Jones passes through stages of release from play to dream to vision. After a few months of exotic nightly furloughs she experiences her two most vivid visions: first, an assault by the devil and, second, God's promise of freedom. By casting her struggle as cosmic drama (the eternal battle between the devil and God, between death and deliverance) Jones successfully replaces fight with flight as the means of her liberation.

> One night the devil was in the room after me. I went to get up off the mattress and go over and bang on the door, and he grabbed me, my gown, and pulled me back. As I jerked away from him I fell and hurt the back of my head. But I got to callin' on the Lord, and he went away.
>
> But while the devil was in my room I got a good look at him. He was the prettiest man I ever seen! He had a moustache, just a little, small moustache, a little, small piece of hair, not too long. And he had two horns that was real short. You could barely see them stickin' through his hair. He was dressed in black, black and white, a black suit like a denim suit. He was a good-lookin' man! But he was ready to kill me. Then I called the Lord.
>
> And another night I was layin' down and I was dozin' off. I was havin' a bad feelin' like I was scared about something; I was frightened about something. I don't know what it was. I was just scared to go to sleep. I was layin' down and I prayed and I prayed, and all of a sudden, my room was lit up brighter than I ever seen in my life — I never seen nothin' like that in my life! And it seemed like the sky just opened up, and I just heard these words. It was God talkin' to me. And he told me, don't worry, that somebody would come and help me. He said he would send someone to help me and take me outta that place.
>
> And right after that a white lady came. I didn't know her; I ain't never seen her before in my life. She took me and showed me a door that was unlocked, and I ran away.

This period in Jones's life is characteristic of the whole: living on the streets, followed by a period in custody, and then back out on the streets again to cope as best she can. It is during her periods in custody when visions appear to her, when she experiences the threat of menacing figures and the promise of divine deliverance. The result is a life history told in stark realism but punctuated by moments of enchantment.

Only in Jones's most recent stretch in prison does the fighter seem to have been beaten for good by the institution. In poor health and too tired to fight any more, she sits out her time along with the other "adjusted" inmates of the Maryland Correctional Institute for Women and recalls the days when, as a youth, she "stirred things up."

Eraina Roberts

Born in Madden, Mississippi, on September 1, 1938, Roberts is serving a ten-year sentence at the Indiana Women's Prison for reckless homicide, neglect, and criminal recklessness. Unlike the other women in this book, Roberts does not regard visions as discrete events in her life story; her life story, itself, is told as vision. From the moment of birth when she was illuminated with divine knowledge, educated by "the Invisible Man," through her crime, conviction, and imprisonment, God guides her life. Roberts insists that her life is divinely scripted and that she is incapable of any action, even any thought, that is not inspired by God.

I was a gifted child. The Father know'd me before I was got. I was not a infant in my mother's womb; I was like I am in my mother's womb. I come like I am from my mother's belly, and I ain't ashamed to tell that! When I was little I would tell my mother things that was gonna happen, and she would scold me. The Father would reveal these things in a vision to me.

And I was taught by the Invisible Man from the time I was six years old. I thought that he was the Invisible Man. When I was six years old I was in my room cutting out paper dolls, and this invisible man appeared to me and talked to me. He was a brown-skinned man with kinky-looking, wavy hair. I said, "Who is you?" And he said, "You would not understand." He would sit there talking to me and help me cut these paper dolls out. He said, "Put the man up there." And I put the man paper doll up there. "Put the woman up there." Then he cut a boy and a girl, and he said, "This is a family." This is the way he taught me. He was just real like I and you, but at that time he was just the Invisible Man. He would teach me things that even doctors, lawyers, counselors, administrators will not understand.

Misunderstood from birth, Roberts attracts no childhood friends, and siblings merely jeer at her weaknesses. A fragile, sickly child, Roberts spends much of her early childhood in bed isolated from the rest of her family, too weak to attend school, shown little care by her family. But through her visions and her play Roberts compensates for the lack of a nurturing parent and an education. Her "Invisible Man" constructs for her, in place of her abnormal family, an ideal, paper-doll family and communicates superior knowledge. Supernatural beings visit her in place of childhood friends. Through play Roberts exchanges the status as family outcast for the station of chosen child, thus defending herself against the neglect and ridicule of those around her.

> When I was a child, every time I got up I would fall, but then the Invisible Man would come into my room and lift me up strong. My bones was like gristle bone. My limbs couldn't hold me.
>
> Then when I was ten and a half years old I see some babies up in the south corner of the house. I screamed for my mother, and she told me, "Shut up!" They had red hair, and they was reddish looking. They had real red curly hair just like you would curl somebody's hair—big curls. And the first song they sung was [sings], "I fly away, oh, by and by. When morning comes, glory, glory, hallelujah!" So then I would call again, and she would scold me. These babies had wings on them; they was real! I'd get up and draw pictures of them and show my mother the pictures. "Stop," she say. My brothers and sisters say, "You dumb thing, don't even go to school, you don't even know nothing, don't even know how to read." Then I say, "I am a genius. I know what I am." Then they make fun of me.
>
> See, I never went to school; I was taught by the Invisible Man. He taught me to read. I heard a voice say, "A,A,A." Every letter he repeat three times. I learn my ABC's that way. Then after that I remember he started teaching me to write. It took me like two weeks, but see, my family, they didn't know that I could do those things. My mother would scold me. My brother and sister would make fun of me.

The child receives the divine tutelage of "the Invisible Man" in the confinement of her room. Misunderstood and even punished by her family, she lives the isolated life of a child of God whose fantasies of family critique reality.

Finally, when unable to cope with the fighting between her mother and her step-father, Roberts runs away to the swamps when she is nearly eleven. She claims that for two weeks she wandered through the swamps alone, kept from harm by God, until two Indians discovered her and for a time became her protectors.

> Burkey and Dempsey (some Indians — they call them Choctaws in the country but they really Indians) found me. They had built a little hut in the swamps so that when they go fishing they would stay there. I was hid in their hut when they got there. When he open the door, Burkey said, "What you doing in here?" I said, "I ran away from my mama 'cause I can't stand no fussing and fighting. I can't take it; I have to leave." He said, "I'm taking you back." I said, "I'm staying or I run away again." So then he said, "I'm not gonna leave you up there." So he carried me on back to the house and tell my mother, "I'm taking her home with me. I just stopped to get her clothes." My mother said, "You can't take my child away from me." He said, "She run away and you didn't know where she was at, did you? You don't care about her."

And so, for several months the girl lives with Burkey, Dempsey, and their infant son. But Roberts's adoption into this new-found family provides only temporary security. When Burkey and Dempsey's baby dies (a death for which Roberts cites no cause) her new family collapses and she finds herself once again in the intolerable situation back home.

But during this brief period at home between her life in the swamps and her marriage at eleven Roberts performs her first purification. With satisfaction, she tells how as a child under Christ's instruction she cures a neighbor of cancer:

> Then when I was ten and a half years old this man I thought was the Invisible Man, he came to me and he said he was Christ. He said, "I want you to go and heal this lady." I said, "I'm just a child." He said, "Don't say that you is a child," and then Him slap His hand on my mouth and put all His words in there. Then I went back to my room. I had sneaked out of my room to the barn because they keep me in my room all the time. So I crawled back into my room. Then at twelve that night I sneaked over to that white woman's house.
>
> I told this woman's husband, I said, "Jeffrey, a man by the name Jesus told me to come over here and to tell you to buy some vinegar and something with the letters, "LY." I don't remember all the letters." He said, "Lysol?" I said, "Uh huh, now you go and get it." He went and got it. So when he come back I said, "The man is here. He also tell you

to put the water on and let it boil. Him telling me what to tell you to do." So then after the water was boiled He said, "Take the pan, clean it." I had him washing a pan. Then He told me to ask for a white sheet. Then a white sheet went on me. I wrapped it around. I said, "I ain't no Lord; I'm a human being." The way it was wrapped, it was wrapped like what Christ had. I didn't understand because I wasn't old enough to understand. So then He said, "Put the water in the pan." I did it. Told me how many cap ful of Lysol to put in. I did it.

Miss Betty had a cancer, and a hole was in her stomach. It had eaten a hole in her stomach the size of a half dollar. And then Him said, "Dip the gauze in the water and squeeze it in there." I said, "I can't do that." And then Him said, "Do what I tell you do!" And then after that I felt free to do it. I stuff that gauze into the hole in her stomach. I stayed out all that night. My mama and them were looking for me, and when they find me my mama said she was gonna whup me. I said, "You're not getting me." She said, "You better not keep sassing." I said, "I ain't scared of you. Him standing over there saying you better not put your hand on me!" Then she got scared and she backed off. I said, "I can't leave; I have to stay here." Mama don't understand, but me know what I supposed to do. I stayed there three days, three nights, and it just started healing up. [Roberts]

Roberts sees the conflicts between her parents' authority and God's, knowing that obedience to a divine summons sometimes violates a parental command. At the age of ten and a half, dressed in Christ's garments, speaking the uninterpreted word of God, she performs the first holy act of her divine ministry. That act illustrates the single most important motif in Roberts's life story: ridding the body of corruption. Throughout her life Roberts performs cleansing rites in a desperate attempt to restore the body (her own and others') to its original purity. One can only speculate that at the root of such obsession rests a personal violation so frightening she tries constantly to wash it away.

In order to escape a turbulent home, Roberts marries at an age that seems even to her shamefully young. Happy to see her daughter taken care of in marriage, Roberts's mother lies about her daughter's age, swearing that she is fourteen rather than eleven "so it wouldn't look so disgraceful." The child, who has only managed to live a child's life in her fantasy is not ready to become a woman and a wife:

> When I was married I wouldn't have much to do with my husband. He
> tied my hands and he tied my feet, and that's the way he got both
> babies.

In marriage Roberts only exchanges one brutal family situation for
another. In an effort to rescue herself from the tyranny of an older,
violent husband, Roberts eventually leaves her two daughters with her
mother (along with $224 for their care) and hitchhikes from Missis-
sippi to Indianapolis where her brothers live and where she plans to
work until she saves enough money to return to Mississippi and bring
her two daughters back to Indianapolis with her.

In Mississippi, Roberts discovers that her husband has taken the
children to live with his family. Determined neither to abandon her
plans nor to confront her husband directly, Roberts "plays along." Playing along implies the outward show of a submissive will and the in-
ward conviction of rebellion. Her performance, a form of necessary
trickery, allows Roberts to rescue her children from their dangerous
father and to avoid injury herself:

> I got to the farm where my mother was staying with this white man, and
> my babies wasn't there. I didn't say nothing; I just got up and started
> walking. When I got to their father's house I treat everybody real nice. I
> played along because I knew that he either kill me (he would have 'cause
> he was drunk, stayed drunk seven days a week) or I have to steal my
> babies. So I have to steal them from him. When I brought them here
> Ruth was three years old and Marlene was two years old. I worked sixteen
> hour a day taking care of them. Then on Saturday is a rigid Sabbath
> day. That day I didn't work. I didn't do nothing. [Roberts]

Roberts works hard to raise her children and her grandchildren in
what she considers a "pure and Christian" home. But no matter how
hard she tries to purify her home, corruption always sets in. Even the
Altar of David, which she carefully reconstructs in her home, cannot keep out worldly corruption. Roberts's life story bends back and
forth between the mundane and the miraculous, between corruption
and purification.

Purification allows Roberts to stabilize, at least temporarily, an infected world in which the family is always on the verge of disintegra-
tion. On one occasion Roberts's fourteen-year-old daughter, distraught
over a romance with a married man, attempts suicide, but before the

paramedics take her to the hospital, Roberts insists on following God's instructions, a treatment that, in the end, is more powerful than human medicine. Roberts believes that had she not administered the purgative, her daughter would, indeed, have died.

> The Father tell me what do do. I told the man holding her, "You ain't gonna carry my daughter anywhere." I said, "Marlene [Roberts's other daughter], you go in there and get the skillet and get some lard, a cup of lard, and melt it. Before you put her in the ambulance, she's drinking this here grease." See, the Father taught me what to do when somebody drink the poison. Anytime anybody drink poison you melt a cup of grease, get it warm and give it to 'em and it saves 'em. The grease kill the poison.[Roberts]

And another time, Roberts observes God's instant healing of her burned foot. But between the affliction and the cure Lucifer appears to Roberts as a man in a black pin-striped suit to challenge her faith. If Jesus had loved her, Lucifer maintains, He would not have allowed her to burn her foot. As if as an immediately refutation of the devil, God heals Roberts's badly burned foot:

> See that foot right there? The whole foot was burned. My Father healed that foot. He led me to my garden every morning at 7:30 to work my garden. I take this foot out there in the garden all swolled up. It was green, and my brother was scared it was going to set in gangrene. So in August I went out one morning in the garden and a hole busted and the stuff came out—a cup and a half of it. He heal me!

There is nothing particularly unusual about Roberts's infected wound breaking and draining while she works out in the soil. In fact, a common folk practice for inflamation consists of applying a poultice made of manure or rich soil. What is unusual is the insistence that such home remedies as household astringents to cleanse wounds, lard to treat ingested poison, and soil to release infections are the unique prescriptions of God. Roberts has so internalized both folk methods and divine disclosure that they become inextricably connected. Nothing in her life can exist apart from God. Others may participate in tradition, but Roberts sets herself apart as one who stands outside of tradition. The notion that one's life consists of a collection of divinely inspired moments collapses history into periodic revelation.

The devil, in all his manifestations, can corrupt the world, and only

God and disciples like Roberts can cleanse it. The most striking example of contamination and cleansing in Roberts's life story is her crime itself, the ritual "purification" of six children: three grandchildren in her custody and three children living with their mother in Roberts's house. Believing the children "filthy" she fed them salt as a means of "wiping away the spirits of the devil." The most excessive doses she reserved for those children who, like their mother, had performed fellatio. On the first night in her house, Roberts reports "that woman fell out like a snake and crawled like a rare snake telling James [Roberts's brother], 'Let me suck your thing.'" Then a few days later her grandson reports on the children, "Grandma, they is sucking dingalings, too!" Roberts applies her "remedy." In an already malnurished condition, the young children ingest large quantities of salt. One dies; the others are hospitalized.

> I don't know why they want make a criminal outta me. I never stold nothing. I never took another man's wealth. This woman [the children's mother] lied. Everybody know salt kill nobody. Then she lied and said I was under the demon's power. I don't know about demons. In my house I got the real Altar of David. Christ said, "Build it three cubits by three cubits by five cubits apart." I got it in my house, you understand me? He said, "I will build the tabernacle of David." And it was built in 1970 in my house, but I never used that altar until 1976. They said I was under the demon's power, but I was under *God's* power. The Father told His disciples, "I give you authority to go out and kill and cast out demons and heal disease." He give them authority to do it. It's *His* power, *His* strength. Without Him they can't do nothing. He wake them. He rise them. He let them breathe!
>
> You know what kill folks? Satan. Adam didn't sin. Eve sin. The devil deceive her. When God tol' them not to eat of this forbidden tree, they ate. Satan was a man that was in that tree. He was a real man, I tell you. There was a fork in this tree, and here Satan sit right up in this fork. OK, Eve goes to the tree and sits down with her legs spread wide. Satan then comes around aswinging under the limb talking to her like a snake. Then he tell her, "You can eat." You know what she eat? It wasn't no eating. That mean they have sex together. Eve's first baby was a Satan baby. The second baby was her Adam baby. But by Adam letting her deceive him, that made Adam sin, too. Then God could not pick a body on earth for him to enter in. He *made* the body in Blessed Mary from clay stone. I made outta clay stone, too, you see. [Roberts]

According to Roberts's revisionist biblical history the original sin, sex with Satan, produced Eve's "Satan baby," Cain and marked all further generations. Therefore, God must construct from scratch (or from clay) a proper vessel, Mary, to give birth to Jesus. In such a way Roberts understands Mary's conception as well as Jesus's and, indeed, her own to be immaculate, ("I was filled with the Holy Ghost in my mother's belly; I come like I am."). By explaining her origin in this way Roberts frees herself of the corrupting mixture of sexual fluids that she believes engenders filth rather than life.

Sexual disease afflicts the woman who moves into Roberts's house with her three children, and the corruption she brings with her threatens to contaminate the entire household. When Roberts first sees this woman she is sleeping in Roberts's bed — large, dirty and diseased:

> She didn't bring no clothes. She had on old blue pants and an old gold sweatshirt. It was filthy. She has this rash, syphilis plague, up her arms.

Recognizing little difference between literal and figurative filth, Roberts employs desperate purification measures. In an effort to cleanse her home of the filth brought by this woman, Roberts attempts to treat the children and justifies herself as an authority on raising clean, healthy kids.

> These kids was so poor, let me tell you, they ate three plates of food and in fifteen minutes turn around and wanted some more. You know what I did? I just put on a big pot of rice 'cause I was working in my garden. I just put them on a big pot of rice, and I cooked that and I said, "Now I be back in here when this rice get done." That's the only way I could fill them up 'cause I hada give them six eggs already, and it wasn't enough. I said, "Well, I know how to fill them up." So when they ate, one hour later they were so hungry, they were just begging. I said, "You all ain't got to beg. I tell you what you got to do. I'm gonna set this food on this cabinet." My grandbabies, they go in and get what they want. I didn't care 'cause they were mine, and they knew how to keep clean. These other kids wasn't even eating clean. They slap their hands all over the wall. I told her, I said, "A bucket of water here. Wash after every time they put their hand in something." I told her, "You welcome to things till James can get here." James left a whole week. I didn't know where he was at. "When I get in touch with James he can take you all back."
>
> So the kids got to crying. They didn't want to go back with him.

They cried all that Thursday, all that Friday night of the first week they was there. My brother, Jake, say, "Stop them darn kids mouth 'cause I got to go to work Saturday morning." So I said, "William"—the boy's name Donnie, but for some reason I want to call these kids these names: Katherine and Daniel and William, but she's telling me their names was Shana and Sharrod and Donnie. For some reason I been wanting to call them kids their other name. And I know why I been wanting to, 'cause that's what the Father was giving me. He wanted me to call them by their natural, real names, not the names she said.

In the meantime, I said, "OK, I'm not gonna let you all go back to Kentucky. You don't want the kids; give them to me. I love children." That's why I got my grandbabies. That's why I help the neighbor with their kids. I go fishing or on a picnic, I gather up all the kids and carry them with me. I teach them the Bible in my yard. And at the trial they wouldn't even let the mailman testify the truth, that he seen me teaching them kids.

Roberts's home is a house of confusion in which strangers enter to stay and from which family members go elsewhere to live. In an effort to reimpose order Roberts resorts to ritual practices, none of which she spells out very clearly in her narrative. What should be clear, though, is the conflict between her insistence that her actions are holy and loving and the reality of horrifying child abuse, confirmed by arresting officers. But even such obvious contradiction becomes twisted in her account. When one of the arresting officers accuses her of murder she responds by calling him a murderer, claiming that at the moment God presents a vision of this officer beating to death a man he took into custody. And the other officer she fixes with a glance from her other-worldly eye:

Then the other tall white police—he was nice—he went left-hand side of my basement. He stood and was trembling. He was shaking 'cause he saw my eye. You ever seen a human being eye wobble all over, nothing but the white showing? You ever see somebody just go out on their knees, just drop down on their knees and hit the concrete floor? That's the way I was when he carried me in front of him. Then he took me to the little boy. Then he said, "Do you have a flashlight, Ma'am?" I said, "Oh, yes." Then I raise and found one and gave it to him. He took the flashlight and shot it on the picture of Christ, and then he shined the light back on me. Then he shined it back on that picture and back on me. That was the nice police.

I went forward, slowly walking. Then he said, "What's your name?" I said, "No name?" He said, "No name?" I said, "No name." But see the Father had knew that they'd want my name. But see, my name is Earline. I ain't no Eraina. See, James and Marie, his wife, started calling me Eraina. See, James talk about me so much this woman, she think she knew me. I said, "You don't know me, and I don't know you. I never seen your ugly face before James brought you here in my life. You sure do lie."

Not only does Roberts accuse one of the arresting officers of murder, but she also learns that her own brother, the one who defiled her house with this filthy woman, had committed murder as well. But Roberts tries to distinguish herself from these other murderers and from the mother who participated in the ritual with Roberts by maintaining that actions she may have committed are justified by God. Even if we follow Roberts's own twisted logic we cannot fail to see that, given a sign that the little boy still lived, she failed to revive him but remained silent. "God's way," finally, is the way that justifies the sacrifice of little children.

In all this time they never put the oxygen on that little boy. They never touched that baby. They never put they mouth to his mouth. See, the Father teach me to do this. All they done was point me as a murderer. The little boy was laying on the floor. I laid the little boy like that. I picked the little boy up, and laid the little boy in my arms, sitting there on the bed with him. Then I laid him back down on the floor.

While they had me jammed up against the furniture in my own house, the short police picked up James and then when they got there he says to James, "You killed your wife with a double-barrel shot gun, but we couldn't prove it." That was in 1968, and I was in Richmond, Virginia, with my husband. I didn't even know she had been dead. Been dead for years, and I didn't even know it.

In the meantime, that little boy turned. His eyes followed me, and the Father said to me, "He told you he wanted to be your brother, and I have tooken him in a trance. He is not dead." He wasn't dead. I never told them nothing. I didn't say nothing. But that little boy was not dead. I declare it to the Lord in Jesus' name! He was not dead; he was in a trance.

Okay, after they couldn't get nothing from me—see, I was unspeechly! Like a dummy in front of them. They couldn't get nothing from me, not *nothing*! Because if I woulda opened my mouth I'da got forty years. I mean forty years they woulda put me in here! Forty years for *God's way*. The faith is in me.

Roberts's faith that she can act in no way other than God's way renders her invulnerable and, as in the case when she returns to Mississippi, enables her to play along. It not only justifies her crime and protects her from any guilt, but it also isolates her from the rest of the prison population. She assumes a role that she considers more powerful than any other, the role of Christ. A life story that began with the instruction of Christ ends with a more complete identification between the visionary and the subject of her visions. Conviction and imprisonment merely confirm for Roberts her holy status, and the visions she sees become herself.

> So when they took me they were looking at my fleshly body. They were not looking at the soul that would come from above. He said, "I will take that light and enter you." The light entered me, blindfolded me in His glow. I didn't even know I was in jail up there for four days. He was singing songs through me, "Take me back. Take me back to prison while the pharaohs crucify, hung up on the cross. I die for all you." That's not me you heard singing; that's Him. Then He sung another song, "Give me two wings, all I want is two wings to fly up to heaven." All the songs come off my tongue but it's His words. And He talk Hebrew. I know the Hebrew language. I don't know white man English here. I wasn't taught by white man. I was taught by the Father. So they didn't understand what He was speaking, even in His own language. I'm telling you now. But when He spoke that's what he spoke, the Hebrew language. But it wasn't me that they were looking on. I am His twin. Look at my hands. My hands not made like any other. Look at my feet. My feet not like any other. [Roberts]

What no transcript can adequately represent are the changes in voice and the drama that accompany such an interview. At the point above when Roberts sings the verses from the songs that God has spoken to her her voice lowers as if she were actually speaking as another person. At one point in an interview not quoted here she actually spoke in tongues and tossed over a chair. The strong conviction that God has chosen her to do his work on earth is clearly a belief Roberts clung to before incarceration. From her prison cell, that belief directs the martyr's tale her life story has become.

Roberts insists on reconstructing herself in narrative as the suffering Christ, punished for a crime that she did not commit, denied by all. Narrating her life as one visionary moment after another, Roberts interprets her every action as blessed. And with every action divinely inspired, she is incapable of evil. Although such a belief, confirmed by visions, assures Roberts of her divine status, it does not protect her from temporal punishment. According to Roberts "man's rule" and "Christ's rule" often conflict, and the individual must violate one in order to keep the other. In such a way she rationalizes as virtuous those actions others term vile. Although Roberts's defense fails in the courtroom (the claim that one committed criminal acts according to God's instructions seems an awful lot like "the devil made me do it"), such a defense transforms imprisonment into blessed suffering.

> But since I been here [in prison] they don't recognize my Sabbath. On their Sunday all they make you do is just get up and clean your room. But my Sabbath day they don't recognize. That's just their rules. They not going by Christ's rules. See, they thought Christ was strange, too; that's why they crucified him. See, Christ wasn't a murderer. He didn't kill no one. Those that crucified him held him at fault for what *they* had done. But the murderer was hanging on the left side of the Father and the thief were hanging on the other. The white man was the murderer, and the black man was the thief; he done the stealing and that's why the black people have so many plagues on them.
>
> They done me the same way as they done my Father. They convicted me for something I didn't do. See, all these words in this Bible is for us this day: "Heaven and earth will pass away, but His word will never pass away." So we all got to walk by His rule. That's all it is here is man's rules. You never hear them say one time about God rules or God laws. God is the judge. Ain't no man on earth is judge. God is the judge. God said, "Judge ye not, and ye shall not be judged."
>
> Let me tell you one thing. I suffered misery. I was just like the Father. He said, "The father is not to be put to death for the children. The children is not to be put to death for the father. Every man must be put to death for his own sins." This what was coming out of me in court. They didn't like it. I said, "You took'n Moses' law and throwed them aside and put the white man's law up to hide your face behind." And what I'm convicted for, I'm convicted through slander. I'm not convicted for no crimes. They convicted me because they were prejudice 'cause

they were looking for a white man to come down. They were looking for a white man to come out with these words, not a black woman.

Victimized by parents, by her husband, and by the legal system, Roberts describes her imprisonment as one more episode in a tale of persecution. In prison the shrill insistence on her divinity wins her no followers, only deeper isolation in a world where she still finds disorder and corruption to condemn. When she first enters prison, "the Father" instructs her to "Hold thy peace," and to perform as she had in other hostile situations, in other words, "to play along." But within a short time God lifts her silence and Roberts soon becomes the prison snitch, reporting any drugs and other contraband to prison authorities. It is not long, though, before even officers, generally eager to discover hidden dope or a pot of hooch, stop listening to her reports. Shunned by all, Roberts's final consolation is the biblical-style narrative in which she plays multiple roles: prophet, savior, and disciple:

> They lead me like a lamb to the slaughter. They got me now laid in this prison holding me afault. But I know my purpose here: to bear the namesake of Christ. My purpose is to lead these people. You sinners turn to God! This is my purpose. I done tol' 'em. They can't say that I didn't tell 'em. But when I gone they gonna realize they had a prophet among 'em.

When officers fail to heed her warnings and inmates scoff at her admonitions, Roberts recasts the ultimate martyr's story as her own in a desperate attempt to make a legend of herself: "when I gone they gonna realize they had a prophet among 'em." Ironically, the only legendary status Eraina Roberts ever achieves surfaces in the factually loose accounts of "The Salt Lady" still circulating in central Indiana. The protagonist of these stories is, as you might imagine, more demonic than divine.

What is divinity to Roberts is delusion to others. Throughout her life story the doubters and nonbelievers refuse to share her characterization of herself as chosen one, interpreting instead her outrageous claims as clear signs of insanity. Even early in her life story she defends against the charge of madness:

Then as I kept growing they finally started taking me to doctors. There were head shrinkers. These head shrinkers ask me about the "magic power." I said, "Ain't no such thing as a magic power; it's a mystery." I said, "When I was baptised in the water didn't no one lead me in the water. I walked in the water myself. The preacher was standing in the water up to his neck with the two deacons, and my mother said, "Get my child. Don't you let her drown; she can't swim." And the preacher said to my mother, "He got her, the Lord got her." Then when I got to him he didn't take me and dip me. I went under the water and up out of the water. I shouted, "I see that heaven. I see that heaven. I see that heaven door open." And of the things I saw, there were only three things I can tell: that was the sun with a orange base around it, some pink flowers that smelled like honey, and a big old sunflower that you bust the seeds and eat the nuts out of. That's all I could tell; that's His paradise."

The "head shrinkers" ask Roberts to identify her "magic power," and she responds with an account of her baptism, one that contradicts both doctors and mother and one that describes her extraordinary experiences in the context of traditional Christianity. The fact that religious ecstasy resembles madness is not a novel notion, nor is the fact that believers and psychiatrists often refer to the same experience in radically different ways. Ironically, the story the patient narrates to prove her sanity only serves as further evidence of insanity to the psychiatrist.

In his book *A Social History of Madness*, Roy Porter takes up the question of the relationship between religious ecstasy and madness. In a historical account (from Erasmus through the Reformation and the Puritan revolution to contemporary evangelical Christianity) Porter discusses the Christian concept of "good" madness, religious ecstasy that transports the ecstatic out of her senses and puts her in touch with a transcendental power, from which perspective she may hear heavenly voices, receive visions or become the voice of prophecy.

Roberts certainly makes these claims for herself. She considers herself the instrument of God, one of the spiritually gifted who can cure, see into the future, and sense when things are wrong at the prison. The only problem is that no one listens to her. In prison as in childhood Roberts has no friend but her invisible friend. Suspicious rather than caring with fellow inmates, she inspires no confidences, just the indifference of those who view her as crazy and the avoidance of those who regard her as evil. With more brutality than affection she applies her judgment of other inmates. In the past Roberts has set fires to smoke out the devil she believed to be inhabiting a room with an inmate. With such a guardian, one needs no enemy. Few things frighten a locked prisoner more than a fire. In fact, a fire set by an inmate ignited a prison-wide riot the year before I began my fieldwork at the Indiana Women's Prison.

Even before her crime and imprisonment, Roberts was living an allegorical existence. Her stories have an Old Testamant, ritualistic quality. Like Jones, she inhabits a chaotic world, a world splintered and fractured, full of suicidal daughters, scabrous strangers, and suppurating wounds. In response to this chaos, Roberts employs an extreme means of "keeping house" through ritualistic notions of purification. The pollution that plagues women and children must be cleansed away. Her efforts to keep her house in order, to clean things up, take on manic proportions, and the instruments of cleanliness become instruments of murder. Roberts's narrative is a tale of home remedy gone haywire.

Portraying herself as the righteous woman in an unrighteous world, Roberts makes use of folk behavior in an environment that is inhospitable to it. Lard works to counteract the poison taken by the suicidal daughter, but not the suicidal impulses themselves. Salt is generally accepted as a substance that will rid the body of germs, and Roberts's motive is to cleanse the children of social infection, but the disinfecting of children turns into murder. The impression her narrative gives that there is too much chaos to control, too much pollution to be rid of.

Roberts's impulse to speak as the real voice of God manifests itself as a multiplication of voices, another symptom of her inability to maintain control. Self-division becomes a desperate way to defend herself against pollution. She is "Eraina," "Earline," "No Name," and even Christ and speaks at times in the deep low voice of Christ or in the babble of tongues, but that defense is an unstable one. Having been sent to prison, an absolutely clean well-ordered place, she finds more pollution: drugs. Her story confirms the impossibility of purification. Her failure is that she cannot keep the world pure.

The real tragedy, according to Roberts, is not death but the subjection of rites of purification defined by "Moses' law" to an alien law, "white man's law," that does not work; drugs come into the prison. The woman who before prison lived as domestic priest, keeping the home a clean and holy place in which she built the Altar of David, becomes in prison the lamb led to the slaughter, the martyr.

Three years after she came to the Women's Prison the Indiana Court of Appeals overturned Eraina Roberts's conviction. The prosecution, according to the Court of Appeals, had failed to prove her sanity at the time of the crime. Twenty months later the Indiana Supreme Court reinstated her conviction on the grounds that the Court of Appeals had usurped the jury's right to weigh evidence and decide whom to believe.

As evidence of her sanity, Supreme Court Jusctice Alfred J. Pivarnik stated that Roberts "led a fairly normal life, kept her home clean, was able to care for herself. . . ."[2]

Afterword

Three hundred and sixty women were serving time at the Maryland Correctional Institution for Women when I began my fieldwork. Within four and a half years that number doubled; as a result, the institution became even more restrictive. A new building was erected to replace a dilapidated structure, but planners had so grossly underestimated future increases in prison population that a building designed to accommodate one prisoner per cell began double-bunking the day it opened.[1]

Faced with tight budgets and unexpected increases in prisoners, the Maryland prison, like other prisons across the country began spending limited resources on increased fortifications rather than on inmate programs. In 1986, as I concluded my interviews with inmates, staff members anticipated the construction of a second perimeter fence. I was amazed to learn that in times of such overcrowding and tight budgets the prison was erecting a border fence identical to the first. When I questioned prison officials, they explained that this prison was being brought up to Department of Corrections standards. New security standards applied without regard to gender. In the past, women's prisons had required less fortification, presumably because female inmates are less likely to attempt escape than male prisoners.

In their fight for equal treatment women prisoners have failed to win the education and job-training programs they sought; what they got was more barbed wire and more locked doors. The tightening of security in Maryland follows a trend in this country to rehabilitate women's prisons in the image of men's. No longer are women's institutions permitted more lax security systems than men's. The classification system, designed with a male prison population in mind, ideally distinguishes violent from nonviolent offenders with the intent of varying the security accordingly. In practice, though, female minimum security prisoners rarely have the opportunity to serve their time in a minimum or medium security facility. Most states maintain only a single institution for women, and all (minimum, medium, and maximum security inmates) reside in a maximum security prison. The abandonment of any rhetoric of rehabilitation and the new zeal for security on the part of state departments of corrections was just beginning to be felt at the Maryland Correctional Institution for Women when I concluded the bulk of my fieldwork in 1986.

Three years later I returned to discuss my conclusions with three key informants (Violet Star, Wilma Bond, and Luscious), to seek their corroboration, and to solicit their criticism. Too many scholars, it had seemed to me, merely appropriate a community's lore while failing to subject their own conclusions, for better or worse, to the scrutiny of the community. I was showing my respect, I felt, by returning to the community's elders, acknowledging their secrets, and disclosing my interpretation for their blessing or their curse. It all seemed so ethnically sound.

As a venture to gather the reflective comments of informants my return trip (totaling two days) was a marvelous failure. More interested in delivering narrative accounts than in interpreting them, Wilma Bond and Luscious politely dismissed my comments as irrelevant. And despite a cordial letter to Violet Star requesting an interview, she refused to meet with me. The witchcraft and Satanism that Star had so adamantly proselytized three years earlier had given way to a new fervor for Buddhism. In that three years a lame-duck governor, on the eve of his departure, commuted Star's sentence from death to life in prison, and the Satanism with its shocking emphasis on the individual will, which had served the death row inmate, gave way to a religion of resignation.

Although Violet Star had changed in the three years of my absence, Wilma Bond was still the well-dressed, cheerful prisoner, lending a touch of grace to an otherwise oppressive scene, truly the "lily on the dustbin."[2] She kindly listened to my classification of visions, my notion of families in the prison, etc., and answered my requests for comments with verbatim reiterations of the vision narratives she'd already told me. I had never experienced such exact retellings of personal narratives before: every detail recounted precisely as it had been three years earlier.

I looked forward with most pleasure to my meeting with Luscious. I eagerly waited for an officer to escort her from the solitary confine-

ment wing in the new building. But when she arrived the officer refused to unshackle her hands, tightly cuffed behind her back. Luscious
protested. I protested — until the new assistant warden was called. She
explained that she was required by the State Department of Corrections regulations to keep this woman handcuffed during our interview, but that she would permit Luscious's hands to be secured in
front rather than behind her.

Luscious, the forger, the prisoner with a reputation for cursing "the
androids" (the officers), the woman I had spent hours and hours with,
was no threat to me, to herself, or to the institution; she was merely
being punished, and so, in a more subtle and certainly less severe way,
was I. The comfortable illusion that during my interviews prisoners
were in some way taking a break from the prison to recall their pasts
and to reflect on their present conditions was shattered by the heavy
steel cuffs that held her hands neatly in place on her lap. I realized
that I had aggrandized my role as collector into one of liberator who,
as an outsider, could demand a few hours every day in a quiet room
to listen to prisoners and to rescue their stories. The presumption that
the interview in some way transcended its context was my form of vision, one that sustained me during four years of periodic fieldwork.
But the reality of this lively black woman seven inches shorter than
I, dressed in segregation "blues," the metal between her hands rubb-
ing with each inhibited gesture, dissolved that illusion. My tape machine
recorded the details of new visions, but I hardly heard a word, fixed
as I was on the steel that married her wrists. The awful brilliance of
those silver handcuffs blazed as garishly as the visionary Miss Silver
whom Luscious had recounted from her youth.

About to return to her cell, Luscious told me that she, too, would
someday write a book about this place, one she'd call *The Steel Lady*
after the institution. Every woman in the prison, claimed Luscious,
had a piece of that Lady's steel in her: in some it was a coil about to
spring, in others a cold hard empty place.

Appendix 1

Criminological Debate on the Subject of Women in Prison

Two questions dominated the early studies of women in prison: Why do women commit fewer crimes than men? What kind of women are criminals? (And, by implication, are they made or born?) In answer to the first question, writers maintained either that women were morally superior to men and could control their violent impulses to a degree greater than men or simply that women lacked opportunities for crimes (Datesman and Scarpitti). Writing in 1950, Pollak challenged the assumption that women do, in fact, commit fewer crimes than men. He claimed that the crimes of women remain undetected because they take place within the home. But because female crime, according to Pollak, is hidden from societal scrutiny, no empirical data could either support or refute his contention. Pollak's argument was one based on conviction rather than evidence, and it failed to consider the fact that if the domestic crimes of women are hidden from societal surveillance, then the domestic crimes of men are equally obscure. The evidence to refute Pollak's thesis has appeared in the last twenty years. The seventies and eighties have seen the penetration of the legal system into the home, and what criminologists have found are that preponderantly more crimes against children and spouses are committed by men than by women (Saunders 182).

Not only did Pollak charge women with the commission of a whole body of hidden crime, but he charged them with the crime committed by men as well: "The lack of social equality between the sexes has led to a cultural distribution of roles which forces women in many cases into the part of the instigator rather than the performer of an overt act." (3) Pollak sentences all women to the role of Lady Macbeth: though no performers of "overt" acts, they engender crime.

To discover what kind of women were criminals Lombrosco concentrated his famous study on the physical characteristics of criminal women (their cranial dimensions, bodily hair, posture, and physiognomy) and contrasted them with the characteristics of white, middle-class noncriminal women. While the work of Lombrosco sounds foolishly outdated and racist today, recent studies in search of the chromosonal explanation of female delinquency (Cowie, Cowie, and Slater) have similarly sought to locate the mark of criminality on women's bodies.

Others in recent years have asked us to recognize a new "breed" of female felon: tougher, more aggressive, harder to control. Among female offenders they note increases in the last twenty years in what have been traditionally regarded as "masculine" crimes: murder, aggravated assault, armed robbery, burglary, auto theft, vandalism, and arson (Datesman and Scarpitti). Freda Adler blames women's liberation for the new, harder female offender but bases her argument on such weak evidence as the following: "Newspapers in many countries are increasingly informing the public about a changing breed of feminine offender" (Adler 1980, 153). The myth of the Amazonian criminal, the feminist turned monster, is convincingly refuted in the works of Smart and Weis.

What criminologists have offered us is not a portrait of the criminal female but two faces: the face of the sick child in need or nurturing and the face of the cold, calculating woman, less likely to experience pain than men (Lombroso) and incapable of a higher masculine morality (Thomas). In response to this schizophrenic characterization of the criminal woman, Hutter and Williams call for a definition of the female deviant, the woman who acts beyond the bounds of normal society. But Morris and Gelsthorpe question whether it is, indeed, possible to identify a criminal personality—male or female.

Crime is easy to define; criminals, whether male or female, are not. One of my informants told about the first time she committed a "criminal" act. Sent to school at the age of five with no lunch money, she left school at lunchtime, ran over to the nearby market, and stole her lunch. Another, fascinated by a high-class thief she watched weekly on a television series, dressed as this character (complete with penciled mustache) and committed her first robbery. It is clear that when we listen to the stories of women rather than analyze statistics about them, generalizations are much harder to make.

I don't mean to suggest that we ignore the statisticians. On the contrary, it is important to keep in mind when considering any study of women in prison that although 16 percent of all crime is committed by women (Datesman and Scarpitti 19) only 4 percent of the total prison population is female (Raftner 177). (Three-quarters of the convictions handed out to women are for non-violent petty crimes such as petty larceny, drug offenses, immorality, drunkenness [Tjaden and Godeke].) Because women are less likely to commit violent crime and because they are less likely to be repeat offenders, some female criminals never make their way to state prison, serving their sentences of a year or less in county jails. Of the women actually convicted of violent crime, 72 percent have had no prior prison commitments (Kruttschnitt 124).

Since Pollak's study in 1950 alleging the preferential treatment of women by the legal system, there has been a tendency on the part of criminologists to view the courts as sentimental and patronizing toward women. After all, women are more likely to be given pre-trial release, less likely to be convicted, and if convicted, more likely to avoid incarceration. But what Tjaden and Godeke show in their more recent study is that when previous records of men and women are accounted for, the apparent disparity in their treatment by the courts vanishes.

Once incarcerated, women often experience more restriction and fewer incentives in prison than men. With fewer opportunities for education, job training, recreation, visitation, and pre-release programs (Tjaden and Godeke), women are only just beginning to bring these differences to the attention of the courts. In March 1986, prisoners at the Indiana Women's Prison charged the state with discriminatory treatment and won their case.[1] Not only did the district court in this case find that the education and job-training programs for men were superior to those for women, but it also acknowledged that the state severely restricted the communication of women prisoners. Phone call priviledges of women were more limited than those of their male counterparts. All touching among women was prohibited. Women were forced to abide by an unwritten rule preventing them from talking to other inmates in the halls.

Appendix 2

Narratives

The following narratives illustrate in further detail the range of supernatural and supranormal experiences related by women in these prisons.

Grandmother in Danger

I've had things that I dreamed that halfway come true. I had this one dream about my grandmother. I was cryin' and everything. She was being robbed, and I couldn't get to her to help her. I went through this whole big change in this dream, and when I woke up the first thing I did was tell my mother, "Grandma got robbed." And she said, "Girl, what are you talkin' about?" I'm sayin', "I have to call. I have to call." She only lived around the corner, and I called her on the phone and my aunt answered the phone and said that a couple next door had just been robbed. So it was next door, and it wasn't her. [Miller]

A Warning

It was another time I had this dream—I didn't live too far from D.C. jail, and everytime somebody escapes they look in our neighborhood at first, but they never find 'em there. But I had this one dream that somebody had escaped from jail and they were in our house. And I kept hearing these noises and I was telling myself to wake up and call the police, but I thought that I was woke.

About three o'clock in the mornin' I heard my mother and them up, and I got up, looked, and the police were out front of our house. They had just caught a guy that has escaped out in front of the house. Come to find out, the guy musta been hidin' on our porch because the next day after it was daylight and everything, they found a gun in the bushes in the front yard. [Miller]

Grandfather's Death

When my grandfather died I just kept feelin' that they was keepin' somethin' from me when he was sick. I kept sayin', "I know that he's gonna die, and they're not gonna tell me on the day that he does die." I had to keep gettin' permission to use the phone to see if he was okay. And once I come up here in the office (Miss Graham called me) and I said, "See Miss Graham they're keepin' somethin' from me. One thing I made them promise was to let me know the same day that he die. I kept sayin' "They're not gonna let me know; I know they're not gonna."

They did the day after, but not the same day. He died on Sunday, and they let me know on Monday. My family had hoped he was gonna live, but somethin' kept tellin' me that he wasn't gonna live. On that Sunday I kept tellin' people, "I know that he died. I know he did."

And when the officer told me that he died, the first thing I said was, "He didn't die today; he died yesterday." [Miller]

Mother's Death

One time there was a lady that came down here to do some work for the social worker department: Kathy McKim. So anyway, she had a front-end group, a group therapy session where you discuss your views and where your goals are at and what you want to do. So anyway, Kathy was in there, and I grabbed her hand. I don't know why I did it, but I grabbed her hand and I said, "Kathy, they're going to kill my mom." And she says, "What are you talking about?" And I says, "I don't know; I'll see you later." So she's running down the hall after me and she says, "Come here, Luscious. Miss Martin come back here now!" So I never discussed it with her anymore. I never said anything about it.

And then my mom died September the 30th, and I was sort of prepared. It's just a weird thing. It's just like something talks to me; I can't explain it. It's not a voice; it's not anything like that. It's just a knowing feeling that this is going to happen. [Luscious]

Vision through Cell Walls

It's overwhelmingly eerie sometimes. It's so keen! The other night I was talking to Carla [inmate in the next cell, separated by a concrete wall], and I told her everything she was doing. She says, "You're rich, Luscious."

"Don't say that. You're gonna ruin it! Don't."

"What am I doing now, Luscious?" she says.

"You went to the window."

"You heard me walk."

I says, "Take your shoes off." So she took her shoes off.

"What am I doing now?"

I says, "You're standing by your sink and you're holding your toothbrush, and it's red."

She says, "I wanna get outa here!"

It's uncanny. [Luscious]

Out-of-Body Experience

I had an experience where I stepped out of this life into—Wait a minute, I can't explain these things. I'm not as forward 'cause I'm afraid of it, but I'll try to explain it so you can understand. I was laying on the bed, and this hand came through the air, and there was a partition like a thin curtain. This knowing thing inside me said, "Take the hand," and I took the hand that came through the air. It took me to another time.

It wasn't a dream. I was wide awake. These experiences very rarely ever occur when I'm sleeping. But as I left I looked back through the air, through the curtain, and I saw my body just stretched out on the bunk wide awake and breathing. I looked at the man who gave me his hand, and I said, "Who are you?" I was in another different, totally different, place. It was like the only thing that was separating the two different lives was this curtain of air, this partition like a spider web (not a spider web—it was air), and that was the only thing that separated the person I had become from the person I was. I could see me laying on the bed and I could see me here.

Then the hand took me through another partition, and we were walking right straight through. That's when I saw who the hand belong to. It was this black guy, but he had on this white wig and he had on knee-high, silk stockings and this black suit. I says, "Well, who are you?" He says, "I'm your great-great-great-grandfather." I says, "I'm going back." He says, "No, I want to show you—" So I followed him and he showed me all kinds of things: a blacksmith shop, a jewelry maker, a weaver. And the weaver, who was my great-great-great-grandmother, taught me a stitch. I mean I actually came back from that life or whatever it was, and I could stitch just as well as she was doing it.

Everybody's saying, "Luscious, where'd you get that stitch from?" And I says, "From my great-great-great-grandmother." The stitch looks like two rams' heads and has an eight-point star around it, and then around that is a circle. I crocheted it after this experience. Don't ask me how I did it. I don't know, but I crocheted it. I would have made another one, but they confiscated the crochet needles and yarn.

When that happened I stayed away for a long-short time; I can't explain the time. But I didn't want to say anything to anybody 'cause they would have thought that I was really nuts. But it turned out, the gang, though, they accept it more than I do. [Luscious]

Out-of-Body Experience II
Sometimes when I leave the body and I'm traveling I feel released, and I'm traveling towards this light. The body's still alive and the spirit will come back to it. But I believe if you wanted to, you could probably stay away. But I've never really really wanted to, but it could be done. [Star]

The Disturbing Prophet
This one particular girl, Grace Bush (she said that I could mention it), she was sitting looking at the soaps and I began to prophesy, relate things that happened to her and that would come to pass. She said, "Luscious, wait a minute, and she turned the TV off. This other girl in the rec room felt it herself. Somebody else in the room can feel the emitting of this power. This other girl said, "Oh, Luscious, shut up!" She wasn't angry at me; it's just that she felt it when I was talking to Grace.

"Grace, I have to tell you, get it all out." This other girl yelled, "turn the TV back on." She was scared. I said, "Calm down, I mean you no harm; just calm down."

"What are you doing Luscious? I'm afraid."

"Don't be afraid," I said. I know because it scares me sometimes. [Luscious]

Déja Vu

I have foreseen me being in the courtroon and the consequence of that before I ever got there. I was sleeping, but it was so real. And when it did happen I was standing there in the courtroom knowing I had been there before. It's real weird.

It's something that's so real that you can just reach out and touch it. And then when it happens, you say, "Oh, I envisioned that a long time ago." [Lee]

Prison Ghost

When I was here before, I coulda swore when I looked out that window one night that I saw somebody walking by that fence. My room faces the back and I saw this thing in white walkin' past that fence. And I know I'm not crazy. I blinked, but the image was still there. For a long time I couldn't go asleep at night 'cause I found myself every night trying to see if I could see it again. I never saw it again, but I was concerned that I was gonna see it again. I couldn't explain it. I wouldn't tell anybody about it because they'd think I was crazy. [Lee]

Suffocating Shapes

When I was younger I never did drugs. To me, I woulda blamed it on drugs had I done 'em before then. I don't know if it was because of fever or what, but I don't think I was sick. And it happened quite often. It was like huge pillows, but they were like as big as this room, just keep comin', just keep comin'. And I could see 'em. And it was scary. I'd feel pressed but I wouldn't feel dead, you know. I don't know how to describe it. They were just big awkward shapes, but they were just huge. And one of 'em coulda covered me. But they would just keep comin'.

Burke: How did it end? Did you do anything to stop it?

Stone: No, it just stopped. I got older. I got sick. Now, I don't get colds. I'll get a fever, but I don't get the sniffles or any of that. And it happened to me and I just kept pushing it outta my mind.

A friend of mine, Randy, he's been meditating since I was real young, and him and I talked about it. We used to play games, mind control. We'd stare at each other, just crazy things and he'd say move that box over there. And I'd stare for hours. He'd teach me mind control, and with this mind control I'd just try to push this bad dream out. [Stone]

Dreams That Come True
The only disturbing dreams I ever had was right after my husband died. I had a dream of coming to—it looked to me in the dream like a mental hospital 'cause I thought I was cracking up after he died. But I dreamed I came to a place with lots of women that was an institution, but I thought it was a mental place from what it looked like. Of course, this prison is as close as I want to get to a mental hospital. Sometimes this place seems more like a mental ward than a prison. And, tell you the truth, there are women here who should be in a hospital. That was the only disturbing dream I ever had when I dreamed that I would be taken away from my family and put in an institution—which happened.

There have been times in my life that I have had dreams about certain situations that have come true later. I dreamed that there was going to be a death in my home and there was, only I thought it was gonna be me. I dreamed that something was gonna happen to my father. Later on, I found out he had cancer.

Mostly little silly things. I always knew, even as a very young person, even when I was twelve, thirteen that I was gonna fall deeply in love with somebody someday that was gonna cause an absolute disaster. And I knew it from my dreams because my dreams weren't bad dreams, but they were sad dreams. They were very very sad. The person I love was gonna disappoint me greatly, and he did. [York]

Hypersensitivity
I've woke up out of a half sleep and sensed a presence in the room. I guess 'cause I'm a light sleeper, I can always tell when there's somebody in the room with me. I am sensitive to things that go on around me. I am sensitive to a feeling or a room. I'm hypersensitive, which means that I can pick up things other people would pass by. I have walked into places, into houses and surroundings that's kind of given me a déja vu, and I've had chills go up my spine, like "what am I doing here," like I've been there before. I've definitely had those experiences. [York]

Seeing the Past

I have memories. I don't know whether they are things that were told to me as a child that I picked up on — it just seems like I have a memory beyond my own memory. Like I have a knowledge of past events in history that is not conceivable from my lifetime. It just seems impossible that a person of my age living in the 1980s could remember this event and that event in the clarity and the detail that I do. But I do have knowledge of them. And that's strange, because when people talk about some little strange incident, some off-the-wall incident out of the past, I know what they're talking about and I can add to it. I say, "Wait a minute; I know that". That's odd, but I've dealt with that in my life, and I've come to accept it as being part of what I am and my personality. [York]

Ghost at the Top of the Stairs

When I was about twelve or thirteen years [old], I still claim to this day I seen a ghost. It was in the forties, during the war, and my mom was working the midnight shift at the Chrysler plant, and she was upstairs in bed. Well, this particular time, our kitchen lights were in the process of being fixed. Us kids always came in and out of the kitchen through that entrance. We couldn't turn it off and on except by twisting these here little wires. And then in the hallway that led upstairs to the bedrooms wherever you turned it off at, it had to be turned on at the same place. Well, Mom would always turn it off at the bottom of the stairs so us kids could use it to turn on and see to come up the stairs, and she would always go up in the dark. Why, back then Mom had appendicitis attacks all of the time, and she would always black out a lot. But she would never give up and go to the hospital till they burst on her and she had to go.

This one time we were outside playing. It was a duplex house, and there was a door that adjoined from our apartment into theirs. Well, the girl that lived next door there, she was our babysitter, and she was outside with us. I had went inside the house. I was just tired, and I was sitting there in the kitchen drinking milk. I decided that I was just gonna go to bed, so I go to the hall and I flip on this light switch and no light would come on. And I'm scared to go up in the dark. I started to go up through anyhow, and I look and I see somebody sitting at the head of the stairs and about five steps down from the very top of the very top step. I can still see it. It was a woman, and she was sitting with her legs together and her back straight, looking down at me. She was just looking down at me. I don't know how to describe the color — it was misty like. It was a drab looking gray, off-white, but she appeared to be all the same color. She had long hair, and it was all the same color. I could not make out her features although I could see that there were eyes, nose and mouth. She never moved. She never said anything.

Because my mother was having these attacks of appendicitis and because I wondered whether it could be her, I called. I says, "Mom, Mom, Mom is that you?" My first impression was that it was her and that she was sick and trying to get downstairs. I didn't get any answer, but I kept straining my eyes to see. Well, because of the long hair and the color and everything, I realized that it wasn't Mother. I don't know how to explain how I felt, but I guess it was fright and wonder. I don't know. But anyhow, I left, I turned around, just kind of backed away from the doorway, and after I'd taken a few steps backwards, I turned around and ran. When I got outside, I started screaming. I said, "Why, there's somebody on our stairs." Of course everybody came running in. By that time, my mother had woke up and my stepfather had woke up, and Bonnie, our babysitter, their mother and everybody was over there. And they said it was probably just the moonlight shining in through the window. They had me stand there in that same place with the lights off again, and I didn't see it. [Murphy]

Ball of Fire

I have an interesting aunt. There's been several strange things that have happened to her. I can remember my great aunt, Johanna. As a matter of fact, I was even with her at the time we witnessed one particular thing. I don't know what it was, but she was rather old at this time, and I was just a small child. She was a very religious woman. We were out in the garden, and I was helping her pick green beans. All at once, she just raised up, and she says, "Oh, Lana what ever in the world is that?" I remember she just threw her hands up. She was gathering beans, and they all went every which way. It scared me. I was just standing there real dumbfounded and she was, "Oh, praise the Lord!" and going like this.

I don't know what it was. It was a big ball of fire, and it circled all the way around. It was traveling up, and it would come down, but it never did come close to the ground. [Murphy]

Premonition of Freedom
There's been about ten people that's had the same experience, the same one I did. The white man [a fellow witch and friend] I was telling you about said they were all praying, and on the third day they saw me walking down a wooded lane. Some of the psychics in England have seen the same scene, and I've seen it, too, since I've been here.

That lane is in North Carolina near my trailer, but they didn't know that. [Star]

Predicting the Ultimate Disaster
I knew something, something was gonna happen of great magnitude, and I even told Reverend Dorsey about it. It was just before that nuclear thing happened in Russia, you know, when there was that explosion?

Burke: Chernobyl?

Bond: Yeah, before that happened I told him, "Something is gonna happen; it's gonna be in the air." I knew it was gonna happen, but I didn't know when. I said, "It's gonna be in the air and it's gonna be something that will destroy." So, within the next week, this nuclear thing exploded.

I can see this world coming to a close by 1990. Something terrible is gonna happen. I can see it; it's just like something going on in my head. I keep telling my family this. I keep telling my husband. I keep telling my daughter. I keep telling my sisters, all of them, that something is gonna happen. I can see it in the picture. I see it coming, and I been praying, asking God to reveal what it is. And if God reveals it, I will tell as many people as I can. I know something's gonna happen. [Bond]

The Whispering Voice
The day that I knew that my life has turned around, I remember that day. There's special moments in your life you'll never forget. One day, I was sittin' in my room—the first year I was here—I was so confused and so mixed up. I took my chair and put it to the window. I was depressed; I was a manic depressive person. I never saw a psychiatrist or nothin'. I never took a pill or nothin' to go through the things that

I went through. I never went on medication of any kind. But, I was hurtin' and I wrote all kinds of poems just to write out how I was feelin'.

And I took my chair to the window and sat over, straddled the chair and looked out the window. And right outside my window, I never noticed it, but it was a tree. It was like in the winter time. (Remember I told you I came in January?) And it was a tree—real, real empty of everything. The grass was ugly, dewy lookin' and burnt out like. And seemed like a whisper came to me and said, "See that tree right there Ruth Jackson? You see yourself in that tree. And all through your life you were stripped just like this tree. But it's up to you to come around and next summer, fully blossom and let people pick the flowers offa you." And that stayed with me, and I never stopped goin'. I don't know what it was—a insight, inspiration. Something came to me as I was lookin' out my window, and it changed my whole outlook on life. I started out with my G.E.D. then my B.S. degree and never stopped. [Jackson]

Frankenstein

In all the stealin' I've done it's never been excitin' and fun. It was part of survival for me. And I guess, a lot of it I did for attention. A lot of times I used to do things and then go and turn myself into the police station for attention. I suspect I just broke the law a lot just for attention 'cause I never had anybody to care for me except my mother, and I watched her lose her mind over my father. I couldn't understand that. I was ten or eleven when my mother lost her mind; she had a nervous breakdown, but I didn't know what was happenin'. My oldest sister knew and got her booked at Johns Hopkins. When that happened I ran away; I ran away from home and ran in the street, stayed in doorways, sneakin' around in places. See, people at that time had white marble steps and vestibules and cellars. You could crawl up under the steps and drop down into the cellar. Except this one time, I jumped down in this cellar, and there was this man standin' down there. He had on all black, and he was tryin' to catch me.

He was one of them Hopkins experiments I know. See, those Hopkins students had a certain amount of bodies that they had to experiment on and do autopsies on. I know; I used to sneak underground and see. They just didn't keep them bodies hung up in that freezer like that for nothin'; they used to be experimentin' on people back in them days. We used to call them "student doctors." A lot of people was missin' back in them days. They don't know where they are to this day. I know what happened to 'em. Ain't nobody told me; I just felt it. Like I felt my way through life. I learned by watchin', listenin' and feelin'. [Jones]

Getting Busted
See, I had a dream that me and this person got caught [for homosexuality], and I shoulda went with that dream 'cause the next day we got busted in the bathroom for physical contact. After that I said, "If I ever dream anything like that again, I'm gonna trust it." [Wilson]

Glossary

adjustment: a punishment; literally, an adjustment in one's status. A woman may receive an adjustment for having food in her room, talking to a fellow inmate when she is not supposed to, passing a note, being "disrespectful" to an officer, etc.

androids: guards

bama girls: unsophisticated, backward, rural women whose "bama dresses" reveal their origin.

black witchcraft: a form of witchcraft in which Satan is honored as the chief deity. Those who practice black witchcraft may call forth demons to execute good or evil in the world.

contraband: any item found in a woman's cell which is either not on the approved list or exceeds the allowed numbers. One book more than the legal number of seven, for example.

cottage: a prison building that houses female prisoners. In the nineteenth century when separate prisons were built for women new terminology described these new institutions. Prison yards were called "campuses." Cells were referred to as "rooms," and the buildings which housed these "rooms" were called "cottages." This language is still in use in many women's prisons.

The Cut: the larger, male prison near the Maryland Correctional Institution for Women officially known as the House of Correction. Many women believe that "The Cut" received its name from the violence of its inmates. A staff member, though, told me that this prison was built at the site of an old railroad cut.

fem: the feminine partner in a lesbian couple, usually regarded as heterosexual.

fish: a synonym for "bitch," this frequently heard expression shares no meaning with the same term as used in male prisons. According to Cardoza-Freeman, men use the term "fish" to apply to "suckers," those unsuccessful criminals unfortunate enough to be caught (57–58). The term "fish," according to my informants, is a generic, though derogatory, term applied to women because of their genital odor.

front-end group: a psychotherapy group.

House that Martha Built: another name for the Maryland Correctional Institution for Women. Martha Rose, at eighty-eight the oldest inmate in the prison, was once imprisoned in the nearby male prison, the House of Correction, and along with many others petitioned the state to establish a separate facility for women.

in population: a term describing the majority of the women housed in prison, those who are neither in quarantine nor in solitary confinement.

kite: a note passed from one inmate to another. Many women are disciplined for "passing" or "flying" a kite.

mess hall mishaps: kitchen staff.

my heart: a term of affection applied to one's child or grandchild: "he's my heart."

on lock: in solitary confinement. Generally, a prisoner is confined to her cell for twenty-three hours and is allowed one hour to socialize with other prisoners.

on seg or *on segregation:* in solitary confinement.

The Plantation: the prison buildings and surrounding grounds.

play: to practice homosexuality. The question "Do you play?" is often a form of solicitation directed towards new admittees by lesbian inmates.

play mother: an older woman who "adopts" and looks out for a younger inmate.

play father: a "stud" who functions as a surrogate father for a younger inmate. Together this young woman, her play father, and her play mother constitute the "play family."

preference people: lesbians.

quarantine: a time (two to six weeks) and a place (a specific floor or wing of the prison where new admittees are housed in single cells). During their stay on quarantine they are given a battery of health, psychological, and educational tests.

rec: unstructured time when women are allowed to socialize.

stud: the "masculine" partner in a lesbian couple, to be contrasted to her "feminine" bisexual partner.

ticket: the formal, written accusation by an officer charging an inmate with violation of a prison rule.

The White House: the oldest building at the Maryland Correctional Institution for Women, a brick building with a small white dome on top.

white witchcraft: a form of witchcraft that employs magic for healing or other positive ends.

write-up: synonym for "ticket"

Notes

Preface

1. For a full discussion of toasts, see Roger Abrahams, *Deep Down in the Jungle* . . . : *Negro Narrative Folklore from the Streets of Philadelphia* (Chicago: Aldine, 1970); Bruce Jackson, "Circus and Street: Psychosocial Aspects of the Black Toast," *Journal of American Folklore* 85 (1972): 123–39, and *"Get Your Ass in the Water and Swim Like Me": Narrative Poetry from Black Oral Tradition* (Cambridge: Harvard University Press, 1974).

2. For discussion of the application of the principles of performance to the private exchange between interviewer and informant, see Richard Bauman, *Story, Performance, and Event* (Cambridge: Cambridge University Press, 1986); Dan Ben-Amos and Kenneth Goldstein, eds., *Folklore: Performance and Communication* (The Hague: Mouton, 1975); Dell Hymes, "Breakthrough into Performance," in *Folklore: Performance and Communication,* 11–74; and Daniel J. Crowley, *I Could Talk Old-Story Good: Creativity in Bahamian Folklore* (Berkeley: University of California Press, 1966).

3. See, for example, the work of William Clements, Sandra K. Stahl, Jeff Todd Titon, Juha Pentikainen, John Robinson, and Robert A. Georges.

1. From Home to Prison

1. These reminiscences are collected in two publications: Carol Burke, ed., *Plain Talk* (West Lafayette, Ind.: Purdue University Press, 1983), and Carol Burke and Martin Light, eds., *Back in Those Days: Reminiscences and Stories of Indiana,* special issue of *Indiana Writes* 2, no. 4 (1978).

2. Since even a simple personal disclosure can sometimes be used as a subtle weapon within prison, I have substituted pseudonyms for the names of my informants. Each quotation is from a tape-recorded interview in the author's possession.

2. Women in Prison

1. See Erving Goffman, *Asylums* (New York: Doubleday, 1961), for a more complete discussion of the multiple roles played by individuals living in total institutions.

2. See Margaret Brady and Elizabeth Petroff on the authority visions bestow on women.
3. While the term "memorate" most precisely describes the majority of these personal narratives, it is a term familiar largely to folklorists.

3. Signs

1. According to Gurney et al., telepathic messages could be sent one mind to another, from an "agent" (a person undergoing some crisis) to the "percipient" who understood this message as a visual, auditory, tactile, or inner knowing.
2. It is interesting to note that the contemporary "experience-based" research of David Hufford shares this empirical preoccupation. See *The Terror That Comes in the Night: An Experience-Centered Study of Supernatural Assault* (Philadelphia: University of Pennsylvania Press, 1982).
3. For a perfect illustration of this, see Bruce Jackson's essay, "The Perfect Informant," *Journal of American Folklore* 103 (1990):400–16, about a man who constructs a heroic past for himself by telling personal stories about the war in which he never fought.

4. Return of the Dead

1. A Greek Orthodox woman told me of the belief in the return of the dead 40 days after death. She said that her father appeared to her on the 40th day, evidence, she interpreted, of his desire to assure her that he was well and on his way to heaven.
2. In this respect my findings differ from those of Patricia Rickels, who found the "cauchemar," or spirit who rode its victims at night, to be unknown to the victim. ("Some Accounts of Witch Riding," *Readings in American Folklore*, Jan Harold Brunvand, ed. [New York: Norton, 1979], 53–63).
3. For a discussion of such attacks see Montague *The Vampire in Europe* (New Hyde Parke, N.Y.: University Books, 1962), 134–35.
4. Important scholarly work remains to be done comparing the subjects of women's visions with the subjects of male visions. The image of the hand was certainly more predominant among my female narrators than among Hufford's subjects. The image of the hand (namely God's hand) provides a powerful visionary subject for St. Teresa.
5. In a song that Luscious wrote, she plaintively sings from the point of view of a woman treated indifferently by her lover. Unable to have the lover or to shake the longing for him, she sings, "You ride me like a demon." A copy of the lyrics are in the author's possession.

5. Gods and Demons

1. See also Jones's account of her struggle with the devil who entered her cell, ch. 7.
2. Women obtain pen pals through the mutual exchange of inmate newsletters between the two institutions and through mutual friends. They typically correspond about their lives prior to prison, their lives within prison, and their beliefs. Sometimes these prisoners even carry on courtships through the mail, exchanging passionate love letters.
3. The narratives of episodes in these women's lives often stand as ironic comment on their tales of passivity. At Moore's trial, the prosecution pieced together a story of a prostitute who beat her live-in boyfriend with a baseball bat and strangled him with an extension cord. A jury of six men and six women found her guilty of first-degree murder.

6. Gifted Women

1. Elaine J. Lawless's pentecostal women in Missouri also note the spiritual powers they possessed as young girls, *Handmaidens of the Lord: Pentecostal Women Preachers and Traditional Religion* (Philadelphia: University of Pennsylvania Press, 1988). That the motif of the special child is a traditional feature in women's spiritual life histories is an interesting hypothesis to examine in a much more comprehensive way than either Lawless or I undertake.
2. June Macklin's research corroborates the belief in the natural inheritance of psychic powers. In fact, all the spiritualist mediums that Macklin interviewed claimed to have relatives with spiritual gifts. ("A Connecticut Yankee in Summer Land," *Case Studies in Spirit Possession,* Vincent Crapanzano and Vivian Garrison, eds. [New York: Wiley, 1977], 68).
3. Imitative (of family and prison) rather than subversive, such a social organization prospers in women's prisons but not in men's. Male prisoners organize themselves into powerful social subgroups based on force (or the fear of force) rather than imitation.

    The construction of homosexual relations also illustrates this difference between male and female prisons. In the absence of women, male prisoners force other inmates to become "ladies." They "dominate and subjugate them" according to John Coggeshall in his provocative essay, "'Ladies' Behind Bars," *Anthropology Today* 4, no. 4 (1988):6–8.

    Women, on the other hand, voluntarily elect to play the role of "studs." They wear what many nonstuds refer to as "little boy clothes," imitate masculine hairstyles, practice a male walk, lower their voices, and fashion sock codpieces.
4. For another account of the fatigue that follows visionary experience see Genevieve Foster and David Hufford, *The World Was Flooded with Light* (Pittsburgh: University of Pittsburgh Press, 1985), 43.
5. Unfortunately Jackson's successful year did not end in early parole.

6. The prophet is not simply the blind instrument of God. She is instructed and corrected by the divine: "When a god comes to reside in a prophet or shaman, divinity is not simply present; it also instructs, admonishes, and directs the faithful" (Clarke Garrett, *Spirit Possession and Popular Religion* [Baltimore: Johns Hopkins University Press, 1987], 195).

7. Curiously, the only people without the prominent "prison stare" are the ministers who come once or twice a week to conduct religious services, the prison chaplain who works full-time at the prison, and an occasional teacher or counselor.

8. Letter (name withheld by request), Long Beach, Calif., Summer 1977. Quoted in Margot Adler, *Drawing Down the Moon* (Boston: Beacon, 1986), 134.

9. Despite the young woman's lack of interest in a sentence reduction, her lawyer persisted and finally won a reduction from death to life. Star won the same commutation the next year.

10. The concentration of individual spiritual energy to achieve collaborative goals is inherent in the notion of a coven. On particularly important occasions or to achieve particularly difficult results, several covens or individual witches separated by great distances will join their collective energies. (See ch. 4 for an illustration of such an event organized by Violet Star.)

     One of the most interesting legends that circulates among witches credits several covens throughout England with achieving the downfall of Hitler. At precisely the same time these groups performed the same ritual.

11. Lena Waters, a member of Spiritualist Camp Chesterfield in Chesterfield, Indiana, a "Clairvoyant" and "Healer" (according to her business card) told me of five spirit guides: master teacher, doctor, chemist, Indian guide, and joy guide. Each has a special function: helping the believer acquire deeper philosophical truths, maintaining the body's proper chemical balance, focusing thoughts, escorting the visionary back to earth so that she will not remain in the spirit world, and warning her about temporal dangers (Interview, Camp Chesterfield, Indiana, Aug. 18, 1988).

     Shirley Srogi, a medium and fellow member of Camp Chesterfield, reiterated Waters's classification. I have quoted Srogi here (Interview, Camp Chesterfield, Indiana, Aug. 18, 1988).

12. Cross-culturally the priestess is generally a woman near the end of her physical fertility or beyond it, one who can devote her energy to spiritual matters (Judith Hock-Smith and Anita Spring, *Women in Ritual and Symbolic Roles* [New York: Plenum Press, 1978]).

13. See Wittreich for a more complete discussion of prophecy.

7. Visions in the Context of Life Stories

1. The term "Arab" (pronounced "A-rab") refers to a man who, even to this day, sells produce from a horse or mule drawn cart on the streets of Baltimore.

2. *Indianapolis Star,* Oct. 21, 1982. P. 39, C 2.

Afterword

1. The name given to this new building, "192" (named for the number of prisoners it was designed to hold), ironically reminds prisoners and staff of the inadequacy of the state in accommodating an increasing population.

    Additional officers were hired to supervise this burgeoning population, but the administrative staff remained the same. The number of Classifications counselors—those in charge of keeping track of an inmate's time, preparing documents for parole boards, and responding to concerns of inmates and their families—actually decreased, leaving each counselor with a caseload in excess of 140 inmates.

2. The phrase comes from the title of Austrailian Nancy Keesling's book on women's slang, *Lily on the Dustbin* (Melbourne: Penguine, 1982).

Appendix 1

1. The case of Carolyn N. Pinkston, Carol Ann Wilds, Mary Sink, Denise Mc-Conomy, Patricia Leslie, Plantiffs versus Robert D. Orr, Governor of the State of Indiana, Gordon H. Faulkner, Commissioner of Indiana Department of Corrections, Clyde Shuler, Deputy Commissioner for Operations of Indiana Department of Corrections, Clarence Trigg, Superintendent of Indiana Women's Prison, Defendants, was decided in favor of the plaintiffs on March 12, 1986 (Case No. IP 81-1283-C).

Bibliography

Abrahams, Roger. *Deep Down in the Jungle . . . : Negro Narrative Folklore from the Streets of Philadelphia.* Chicago: Aldine, 1970.

Alder, Freda. "The Interaction between Women's Emancipation and Female Criminality: A Cross-cultural Perspective." *Women, Crime, and Justice.* Ed. Susan K. Datesman and Frank R. Scarpitti. New York: Oxford, 1980. 150–166.

———. *Sisters in Crime.* New York: McGraw-Hill, 1975.

Adler, Margot. *Drawing Down the Moon.* Boston: Beacon, 1986.

Bauman, Richard. *Story, Performance, and Event.* Cambridge: Cambridge University Press, 1986.

Ben-Amos, Dan, and Kenneth Goldstein, eds. *Folklore: Performance and Communication.* The Hague: Mouton, 1975.

Blagg, Helen, and Charlotte Wilson. *Women and Prisons.* Fabian Women's Group Series, No. 3. London: The Fabian Society, March, 1912.

Brady, Margaret. "Transformations of Power: Mormon Women's Visionary Narratives." *Journal of American Folklore* 100 (1987): 461–68.

Brunvand, Jan Harold. *The Study of American Folklore.* New York: Norton, 1986.

Bullard, Thomas. "UFO Abduction Reports: The Supernatural Kidnap Narrative Returns in Technological Guise." *Journal of American Folklore* 102 (1989): 147–70.

Burke, Carol, ed. *Plain Talk.* West Lafayette, Ind.: Purdue University Press, 1983.

Burke, Carol, and Martin Light, eds. *Back in Those Days: Reminiscences and Stories of Indiana.* Special issue of *Indiana Writes* 2, no. 4 (1978).

Cardoza-Freeman, Inez. *The Joint.* Springfield, Ill.: Thomas, 1984.

Carlen, Pat. *Women's Imprisonment.* London: Routledge and Kegan Paul, 1983.

———, ed. *Criminal Women: Some Autobiographical Accounts.* New York: Basil Blackwell, 1985.

Celmina, Helene. *Women in Soviet Prisons.* New York: Paragon, 1985.

Chestnut, Charles W. *The Conjure Woman.* 1899. Ann Arbor: University of Michigan Press, 1969.

Clements, William. "Personal Narrative, the Interview Context, and the Question of Tradition." *Western Folklore* 39 (1980): 106–12.

Coggeshall, John. "'Ladies' Behind Bars." *Anthropology Today* 4, no. 4 (1988): 6–8.

Cowie, John, Valerie Cowie, and Eliot Slater. *Deliquency in Girls.* London: Heinemann, 1968.

Crosland, Newton. *Apparitions.* London: Effingham, Wilson, Bosworth, and Harrison, 1856.

Crowley, Daniel J. *I Could Talk Old-Story Good: Creativity in Bahamian Folklore*. Berkeley: University of California Press, 1966.

Danielson, Larry. "Paranormal Memorates in the American Vernacular." *The Occult in America: New Historical Perspectives*. Ed. Howard Kerr and Charles L. Crow. Urbana: University of Illinois Press, 1986. 196–217.

Datesman, Susan K., and Frank R. Scarpitti. "Unequal Protection for Males and Females in the Juvenile Court." *Women, Crime, and Justice*. Ed. Susan K. Datesman and Frank R. Scarpitti. New York: Oxford, 1980. 300–19.

de Boismont, A. Vrierre. *Hallucinations: The Rational History*. Philadelphia: Lindsay and Blakiston, 1853.

Dégh, Linda. "The 'Belief Legend' in Modern Society: Form, Function, and Relationship to Other Genres." *American Folk Legend*. Ed. Wayland Hand. Berkeley: University of California Press, 1971. 55–68.

———. *Folktales and Society: Storytelling in a Hungarian Peasant Community*. Trans. Emily M. Schossberger. Bloomington: Indiana University Press, 1969.

——— *People in the Tobacco Belt: Four Lives*. Ottawa: Museum of Man, 1975.

——— "UFO's and How Folklorists Should Look at Them." *Fabula* 18 (1977): 243–48.

Dégh, Linda, and Andrew Vazsonyi. "The Memorate and the Protomemorate." *Journal of American Folklore* 87 (1974): 225–39.

Devlin, Judith. *The Superstitious Mind: French Peasants and the Supernatural in the Nineteenth Century*. New Haven: Yale University Press, 1987.

Dobash, Russell P., R. Emerson Dobash, and Sue Gutteridge. *The Imprisonment of Women*. Oxford: Basil Blackwell, 1974.

Dorson, Richard. "The Legend of the Missing Pajamas and Other Sad Sagas." *Journal of the Folklore Institute* 14 (1977): 115–24.

Edwards, Susan. *Woman on Trial: A Study of the Female Suspect, Defendant, and Offender in the Criminal Law and Criminal Justice System*. Manchester, Eng.: Manchester University Press, 1984.

Evans, Christopher. *Landscapes of the Night: How and Why We Dream*. New York: Viking, 1983.

Farrer, Claire. "Women and Folklore." Introduction. *Journal of American Folklore* 88 (1975). vii–xvii.

Finucane, Ronald C. *Appearances of the Dead: A Cultural History of Ghosts*. London: Junction Books, 1982.

Foster, Genevieve, and David Hufford. *The World Was Flooded with Light*. Pittsburgh: University of Pittsburgh Press, 1985.

Freedman, Estelle B. *Their Sisters' Keepers: Women's Prison Reform in America, 1830–1930*. Ann Arbor: University of Michigan Press, 1981.

Garrett, Clarke. *Spirit Possession and Popular Religion*. Baltimore: Johns Hopkins University Press, 1987.

Gattey, Charles Neilson. *They Saw Tomorrow: Seers and Sorcerers from Delphi Till Today*. London: Granada, 1980.

Gelfand, Elissa. *Imagination in Confinement:Women's Writings from French Prisons*. Ithaca, N.Y.: Cornell University Press, 1983.

Georges, Robert A., "Do Narratives Really Digress? A Reconsideration of 'Audience Asides' in Narrating." *Western Folklore* 40 (1981): 245–52.

———. "Feedback and Response in Storytelling." *Western Folklore* 38 (1979): 104–10.

———. "Toward a Resolution of the Text/Context Controversy." Topics and Comments. *Western Folklore* 39 (1980): 34.

Goodman, Jeffrey. *We Are the Earthquake Generation: Where and When the Catastrophes Will Start.* New York: Berkley, 1979.

Goffman, Erving. *Asylums.* New York: Doubleday, 1961.

Greeley, Andrew. "The Sociology of the Paranormal: A Reconnaissance." *Sage Research Papers in Social Sciences* 3, 23 (1975).

Green, Celia, and Charles McCreery. *Apparitions.* London: Hamish Hamilton, 1975.

Gudas, Fabian. *Extrasensory Perception.* New York: Scribners, 1961.

Guibord, Alberta S. B. "Physical States of Criminal Women." *Journal of the American Institute of Criminal Law and Criminology* 8 (1917–18): 82–95.

Gurney, Edward, Frederic Myers, and Frank Podmore. *Phantasms of the Living.* 1886. Rpt. with an intro by Leonard R. Ashley. Gainesville, Fla.: Scholars' Facsimiles and Reprints, 1970.

Haft, Marilyn G. "Women in Prison: Discriminatory Practices and Some Legal Solutions." *Women, Crime, and Justice.* Ed. Susan K. Datesman and Frank R. Scarpitti. New York: Oxford, 1980. 320–54.

Hall, Angus, and Francis King. *Mysteries of Prediction.* London: Aldus Books, 1978.

Heidensohn, Frances M. *Women and Crime: This Life of the Female Offender.* New York: New York University Press, 1985.

———. "Women in the Penal System." *Women and Crime.* Ed. Morris and Gelsthorpe. Cambridge: Cambridge Institute of Criminology, 1981. 24–36.

Henry, Joan. *Women in Prison.* 1952. London: White Lion, 1973.

Hibbert, Samuel. *Sketches of the Philosophy of Apparitions.* 2d. ed. Edinburgh: Oliver and Boyd, 1825.

Hock-Smith, Judith, and Anita Spring. *Women in Ritual and Symbolic Roles.* New York: Plenum Press, 1978.

Honko, Lauri. "Memorates and the Study of Folk Beliefs." *Journal of the Folklore Institute* 1 (1964): 5–19.

Hufford, David. "Commentary." *The World Was Flooded with Light.* Genevieve W. Foster. Pittsburgh: University of Pittsburgh Press, 1985.

———. *The Terror that Comes in the Night: An Experience-Centered Study of Supranatural Assault Traditions.* Philadelphia: University of Pennsylvania Press, 1982.

Hutter, Bridget, and Gillian Williams, eds. *Controlling Women: The Normal and the Deviant.* London: Croom Helm, in Association with the Oxford University Women's Studies Committee, 1980.

Hymes, Dell. "Breakthrough into Performance." *Folklore Performance and Communication.* Ed. Dan Ben Amos and Kenneth S. Goldstein. The Hague: Mouton, 1975. 11–74.

Jackson, Bruce. "Circus and Street: Psychosocial Aspects of the Black Toast." *Journal of American Folklore* 85 (1972): 123–39.

———. *"Get Your Ass in the Water and Swim Like Me": Narrative Poetry from Black Oral Tradition.* Cambridge: Harvard University Press, 1974.

———. *In the Life: Versions of the Criminal Experience.* New York: Holt, Rinehart, and Winston, 1972.

———. *Killing Time: Life in the Arkansas Penitentiary.* Ithaca, N.Y.: Cornell University Press, 1977.

———. "The Perfect Informant." *Journal of American Folklore* 103 (1990): 400–16.

Jaffe, Aniela. *Apparitions: An Archtypal Approach to Death Dreams and Ghosts.* Irving, Tex.: Spring Publications, 1979.

———. *Apparitions and Precognition: A Study from the Point of View of C.G. Jung's Analytical Psychology.* New Hyde Park, N.Y.: University Books, 1963.

James, William. Review of *Phantasms of the Living* by Gurney et al. *Essays in Psychical Research.* Cambridge: Harvard University Press, 1986: 24–32.

Jones, Ernest. *On the Nightmare.* London: Hogarth Press, 1949.

Jung, C.G. *The Collected Works.* Vol 8. New York: Pantheon for Bollingen Foundation, 1960.

Kalcik, Susan. "... like Ann's Gynecologist or the Time I Was Almost Raped: Personal Narratives in Women's Rap Groups." *Journal of American Folklore* 88 (1975): 3–11.

Keesling, Nancy. *Lily on the Dustbin.* Melbourne: Penguine, 1982.

Kemp, Marjorie. *The Book of Marjorie Kemp.* Ed. Sanford Brown Meech. London: Oxford University Press, 1940.

Kiessling, Nicolas. *The Incubus in English Literature: Provenance and Progeny.* Pullman: Washington State University Press, 1977.

Klein, Dorie, "The Etiology of Female Crime: A Review of the Literature." *Women, Crime, and Justice.* Ed. Susan K. Datesman and Frank R. Scarpitti. New York: Oxford, 1980. 70–105.

Kruttschnitt, Candace. "Prison Codes, Inmate Solidarity, and Women: A Reexamination." *Comparing Female and Male Offenders.* Beverly Hills: Sage Publications, 1981. 123–42.

Lambek, Michael. *Human Spirits: A Cultural Account of Trance in Mayotte.* Cambridge: Cambridge University Press, 1981.

Lawless, Elaine J. *Handmaidens of the Lord: Pentecostal Women Preachers and Traditional Religion.* Philadelphia: University of Pennsylvania Press, 1988.

Lewis, I. M. *Ecstatic Religion: An Anthropological Study of Spirit Possession and Shaminism.* Middlesex, Eng.: Penguin Books, 1971.

Lincoln, Jackson Steward. *The Dream in Primitive Cultures.* New York: Johnson Reprint Corporation, 1970.

Lombroso, Cesare, and William Ferraro. *The Female Offender.* 1993. London: Peter Owen, 1959.

Luhrman, T.M. *Persuasions of the Witch's Craft: Ritual Magic in England.* Cambridge: Harvard University Press, 1989.

Macklin, June. "A Connecticut Yankee in Summer Land." *Case Studies in Spirit Possession.* Eds. Vincent Crapanzano and Vivian Garrison. New York: Wiley, 1977. 41–86.

Markievicz, Countess Constance. *Prison Letters of Countess Markievicz.* London: Longmans, Green, 1934.

Mattoon, Mary Ann. *Applied Dream Analysis: A Jungian Approach.* Washington, DC: V. H. Winston, 1978.

Mauskoph, Seymour H., and Michael R. McVaugh. *The Elusive Science: Origins of Experimental Psychical Research.* Baltimore: Johns Hopkins University Press, 1980.

McCreery, Charles. *Psychical Phenomena and the Physical World.* London: Hamish Hamilton, 1973.

"MCIW in Brief." Brochure. Jessup, Maryland: Maryland Correctional Institution for Women, 1986.

Meek, George, ed. *Healers and the Healing Process: A Report on Ten Years of Research by Fourteen World Famous Investigators.* Wheaton, Ill.: Theosophical Publishing House, 1977.

Melville, John. *Crystal Gazing and Clairvoyance.* Wellingborough, Eng.: Aquarian, 1979.

Mitchell, Janet Lee. *Out of Body Experiences: A Handbook.* London: McFarland, 1981.

Morris, Allison, and Loraine Gelsthorpe. "False Clues and Female Crime." *Women and Crime: Papers Presented to the Cropwood Round-Table Conference,* December 1980. Ed. Morris and Gelsthorpe. Cambridge, Eng.: Cambridge Institute of Criminology, 1981. 18–23.

Newall, Venetia. "West Indian Ghosts." *The Folklore of Ghosts.* Ed. Davidson and Russell. Cambridge, Eng.: D.S. Brewer for the Folklore Society, 1981. 73–93.

Noyes, John Humphrey. *History of American Socialisms.* New York: Dover, 1966.

O'Nell, Carl. *Dreams, Culture and the Individual.* San Francisco: Chandler and Sharp, 1976.

Peckham, Audrey. *A Woman in Custody.* London: Fontana, 1985.

Pentikainen, Juha. *Oral Repertoire and World View: An Anthropological Study of Marina Takalo's Life History.* Helsinki: Folklore Fellows Communications #219, 1978.

Petroff, Elizabeth, ed. *Medieval Women's Visionary Literature.* New York: Oxford University Press, 1986.

Pollak, Otto. *The Criminality of Women.* New York: A. S. Barnes, 1950.

Porter, Roy. *A Social History of Madness.* Ed. Mark Polizzotti. New York: Weidenfeld, 1988.

Raftner, Nicole Hahn. *Partial Justice: Women in State Prisons 1800–1935.* Boston: Northeastern University Press, 1985.

Ratcliff, Arthur. *A History of Dreams: A Brief Account of the Evolution of Dream Theories.* Boston: Small, Maynard and Co., 1923.

Reynolds, Reginald, and A.G. Stock, eds. *Prison Anthology.* London: Jarrolds, 1938.

Rhine, Joseph B. "Extra-sensory Perception: A Review." *Scientific Monthly* 51 (1940): 450–59.

Rickels, Patricia. "Some Accounts of Witch Riding," *Readings in American Folklore.* Ed. Jan Harold Brunvand. New York: Norton, 1979. 53–63. Reprinted from *Louisiana Folklore Miscellany* 2, no. 1 (August 1961).

Robinson, John. "Personal Narratives Reconsidered." *Journal of American Folklore* 94 (1981): 58–85.

Rockwell, Joan. "The Ghosts of Evald Tang Kristensen." *The Folklore of Ghosts.* Ed. Davidson and Russell. Cambridge, Eng.: D.S. Brewer for the Folklore Society, 1981. 43–72.

Rogers, L. W. *Dream and Premonitions.* Chicago: Theo Book Co.. 1923.

Roycewicz, Peter. "The 'Men in Black' Experience and Tradition: Analogues with the Traditional Devil Hypothesis." *Journal of American Folklore* 100 (1987):148–60.

Russell, W. M. S. "Greek and Roman Ghosts." *The Folklore of Ghosts.* Ed. Davidson and Russell. Cambridge, Eng.: D. S. Brewer for the Folklore Society, 1981. 193–213.

Saunders, Daniel. "Other 'Truths' about Domestic Violence: A Reply to McNeely and Robinson-Simpson." *Social Work* 33 (1988): 179–83.

Schneider, Mary Beth. "Female Inmates' Treatment Judged Unfair." *The Indianapolis Star,* 13 Mar. 1986, A1,10.

Smart, Carol. "The New Female Criminal: Reality or Myth." *British Journal of Criminology* 19 (1979): 50–59.

———. *Women, Crime and Criminology.* London: Routledge and Kegan Paul, 1977.

Smith, A. D. *Women in Prison.* London: Stevens, 1962.

Spaulding, Edith. "The Results of Mental and Physical Examinations of 400 Women Offenders with Practical Reference to their Treatment During Commitment." *Journal of the American Institute of Criminal Law and Criminology* 5 (1914–15): 704–17.

Stahl, Sandra K. "The Oral Personal Narrative in its Generic Context." *Fabula* 18 (1977): 18–39.

———. "The Personal Narrative as Folklore." *Journal of the Folklore Institute* 14 (1977): 9–30.

Starhawk. "Consciousness, Politics, and Magic." *The Politics of Women's Spirituality.* Ed. Charlene Spretnak. New York: Doubleday, 1982. 132–43.

Summers, Montague. *The Vampire in Europe.* New Hyde Park, N.Y.: University Books, 1962.

Thomas, W. I. *Sex and Society.* Boston: Little, Brown, 1907.

Titon, Jeff Todd. "The Life Story." *Journal of American Folklore* 93 (1980): 276–92.

Tjaden, Claus D., and Patricia Godeke. "Differential Treatment of the Female Felon: Myth or Reality." *Comparing Female and Male Offenders.* Beverly Hills: Sage Publications, 1981. 73–88.

Valiente, Doreen. *An ABC of Witchcraft.* Custer, Wash.: Phoenix Publishing, 1988.

Van Dijk, Teun A. "Action, Action Description, and Narrative." *New Literary History* 6 (1975): 273–94.

Vaughan, Alan. *The Edge of Tomorrow: How to Forsee and Fulfill Your Future.* New York: Coward, McCann, and Geoghegan, 1981.

Weed, Joseph J. *How to Predict the Future: the Complete Guide to Oracle and Prophecy Methods.* Wellingborough, Eng.: Thomas, 1978.

Weis, J. "Liberation and Crime: The Invention of the New Female Criminal." *Crime and Social Justice* 6 (1976): 17–27.

Wittreich, Joseph. A., Jr. *Visionary Poetics: Milton's Tradition and His Legacy.* San Marino, Calif.: Huntington Library, 1979.

Index

Adam and Eve, 147–48
Adler, Freda, 162
Adler, Margot, 113n, 114
apparitions, 26–27, 30, 47; as agents of social control, 63

Brady, Margaret, 25n, 27
Brunvand, Jan, 29, 60
Bullard, Thomas, 29

Cardoza-Freeman, Inez, 177
clairsentience, 30
clairvoyance, 30, 33–34, 36–37, 117, 120, 167
class, 16
Coggeshall, John, 95n
Cowie, John, 162
Cowie, Valerie, 162
cures, 82–87, 126, 143–44, 146–47

Danielson, Larry, 29
Datesman, Susan, 161, 162, 163
deathseer, 104
Dégh, Linda, 29
demons, 25, 28, 32–33, 61, 147
Dobash, R. Emerson, 19, 108
Dobash, Russell, 19, 108
domestic violence, 14–15
Dorson, Richard, 4
dreams, 28, 39–41, 43–44, 71, 139–40, 170; interpreters of, 100–3; and visions, 33, 50

English Prophets, 105
ethnicity, 16–17
Evans, Christopher, 30

exorcism, 73
extrasensory perception, 25, 42

Foster, Genevieve, 99n
French Prophets, 105

Garrett, Clarke, 105, 108n
Glesthorpe, Loraine, 162
Godeke, Patricia, 163
Green, Celia, 26–27
Gudas, Fabian, 29
Gurney, Edward, 29–30
Guttridge, Sue, 19, 108

hallucinations, 25
Hibbert, Samuel, 27
Hock-Smith, Judith, 128n
homosexuality, 39, 77–80
Honko, Lauri, 29
Hufford, David, 20, 30n, 54–56, 60n, 61–63, 99n
Hutter, Bridget, 162

incubus, 61–62

Jackson, Bruce, 30n
Jaffe, Aniela, 104
James, William, 30
Jones, Ernest, 58, 62

Keesling, Nancy, 158n
Kruttschnitt, Candace, 163

LaVey, Anton, 114, 116
Lawless, Elaine, 93n
life stories, 4–5, 8, 29, 87, 153; as

life stories (*continued*)
  accounts of divine elections, 130; as
  gothic narratives, 8–9; as picaresque
  narratives, 5–7, 130
Lombrosco, Cesare, 161–62
Luhrman, T. M., 114

McCreery, Charles, 26–27
Macklin, June, 93n, 104–5
McVaugh, Michael, 30
Mauskoph, Seymour, 30
memorate, 26n, 29
menstruation, 62
Montanists, 105
Morris, Allison, 162
Myers, Frederick, 29–30

nightmare, 61–62

out-of-body experiences, 77, 139,
  166–67

Pentikainen, Juha, 27–28
Petroff, Elizabeth, 25n, 27
Podmore, Frank, 29–30
Pollak, Otto, 161, 163
Porter, Roy, 154
prayer, 74–76
premonitions, 38, 42, 44, 46, 52,
  103–4, 123, 141, 166, 169, 170, 173,
  175; of coming to prison, 25,
  41–43, 119
prison: adjustment to, 60; classification
  of inmates, 157–58; communication
  in, 21, 23, 34, 43, 108, 163; families,
  11, 23–24, 95; friendships, 23; male,
  23–24; mothers, 17, 121; orientation,
  23; overcrowding, 157; plays, 95–96;
  private spaces within, 74; rehabilitation, 120; rules, 23, 34, 152; solitary
  confinement, 14, 23, 43–44, 65,
  95–96, 120, 133, 137–39
prophecy, 105–6, 108, 129
prostitution, 6–7

psychic powers, 17, 29, 34, 44, 50, 66–67,
  99, 110–11; and heredity, 93, 116
purification, 131, 137, 144–48, 155–56;
  by anointing with holy oil, 74; by
  prayer, 73

Quakers, 105, 108

Raftner, Nicole, 163
raps, 19
Ratcliff, Arthur, 126
Rhine, Joseph, 30
Rhine, Louise, 30
Rickels, Patricia, 56n
Rockwell, Joan, 56
Rogers, L. W., 56
Rojcewicz, Peter, 29

Saint Teresa, 60n
Satanism, 113–18, 158
Saunders, Daniel, 161
Scarpitti, Frank, 161, 162, 163
second sight, 25
Shakers, 105
Slater, Eliot, 162
Smart, Carol, 162
Society for Psychical Research, 29–30
spirits, 27, 28, 29, 50–52, 57, 63–67,
  122–29; communication with,
  59–60; return to settle a score, 94;
  spirit guides, 10
spiritualism, 126
Spring, Anita, 128n
superstitions, 46

Thomas, W. I., 162
Tjaden, Claus, 163

Valiente, Doreen, 114

Weis, J., 162
Williams, Gillian, 162
witchcraft, 59–60, 63, 71, 73, 93,
  112–14, 116–18, 158
Wittreich, Joseph, 129n